OTHER BOOKS BY SYLVIA ROTHCHILD

Voices from the Holocaust
Sunshine and Salt
Keys to a Magic Door: A Life of I. L. Peretz

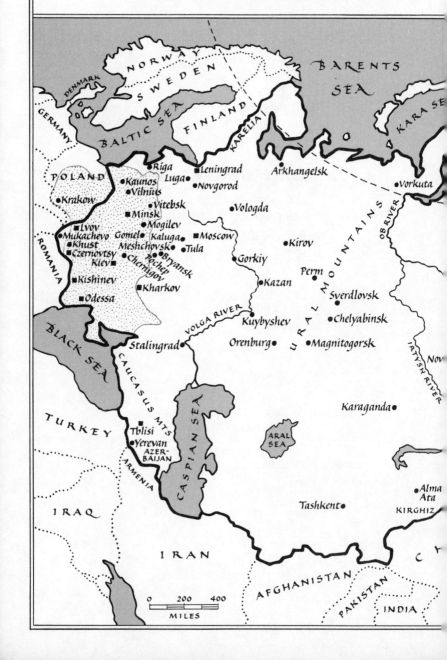

CENTERS OF
Soviet Jewish Population
BEFORE AND AFTER 1917

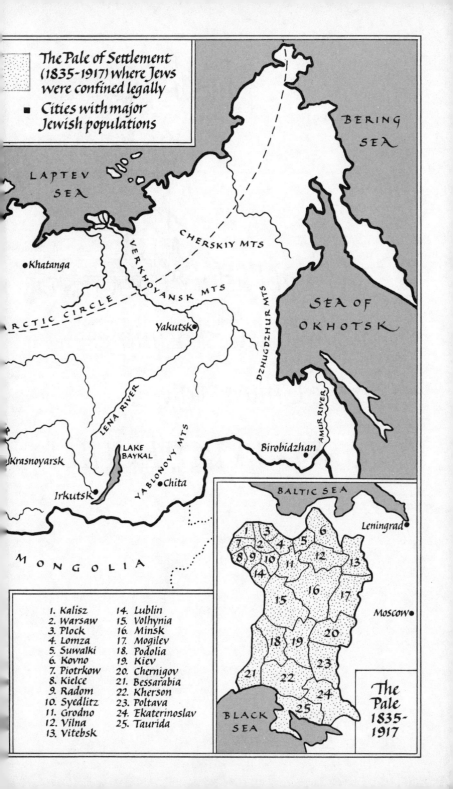

The Pale of Settlement
(1835-1917) where Jews
were confined legally

■ Cities with major
Jewish populations

LAPTEV SEA

BERING SEA

●Khatanga

CHERSKIY MTS

VERKHOYANSK MTS

SEA OF OKHOTSK

ARCTIC CIRCLE

Yakutsk●

DZHUGDZHUR MTS

LENA RIVER

AMUR RIVER

Krasnoyarsk●

LAKE BAYKAL

Birobidzhan●

Irkutsk●

YABLONOVY MTS

●Chita

MONGOLIA

BALTIC SEA

Leningrad●

Moscow●

1. Kalisz	14. Lublin
2. Warsaw	15. Volhynia
3. Plock	16. Minsk
4. Lomza	17. Mogilev
5. Suwalki	18. Podolia
6. Kovno	19. Kiev
7. Piotrkow	20. Chernigov
8. Kielce	21. Bessarabia
9. Radom	22. Kherson
10. Syedlitz	23. Poltava
11. Grodno	24. Ekaterinoslav
12. Vilna	25. Taurida
13. Vitebsk	

BLACK SEA

The Pale 1835-1917

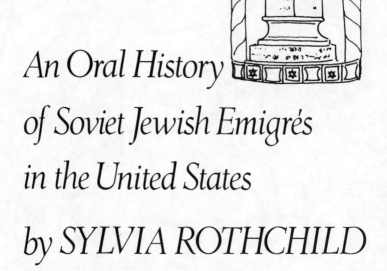

*An Oral History
of Soviet Jewish Emigrés
in the United States
by* SYLVIA ROTHCHILD

A SPECIAL LEGACY

SIMON AND SCHUSTER · NEW YORK

Published by Simon and Schuster
A Division of Simon & Schuster, Inc.
Simon & Schuster Building
Rockefeller Center
1230 Avenue of the Americas
New York, New York 10020
SIMON AND SCHUSTER and colophon
are registered trademarks of Simon & Schuster, Inc.
Designed by Edith Fowler
Manufactured in the United States of America

10   9   8   7   6   5   4   3   2   1

Library of Congress Cataloging in Publication Data
Rothchild, Sylvia, date.
    A special legacy.

    Includes index.
    1. Jews—Soviet Union—Social conditions.   2. Jews,
Russian—United States.   3. Soviet Union—Ethnic relations.
4. Oral history.   I. Title.
DS135.R92R67   1985   947'.004924   85-2090
ISBN: 0-671-47325-5

Acknowledgments

I wish to thank the William E. Wiener Oral History Library at the American Jewish Committee for the opportunity to participate in its project of recording the memoirs of Soviet émigrés and for the privilege of using its collection of 176 oral histories in the preparation of *A Special Legacy*.

The interviewing project was made possible by a grant to the library from the National Endowment for the Humanities. Their generous support provided for the training of thirty-one bilingual interviewers and the recording and translation of conversations with Soviet émigrés in twenty-five American cities.

I am grateful to Professor Zvi Gitelman of the University of Michigan and Professor William Taubman of Amherst College for their contributions as coadvisers for the interviewing project. Professor Gitelman's report to the National Endowment for the Humanities provided a helpful introduction to the material. I thank the interviewers, translators and transcribers who made the material accessible. My deepest gratitude is to the men and women who were willing to describe their lives as Soviet citizens, émigrés and newcomers to America.

Though *A Special Legacy* is based primarily on their stories, I acknowledge the influence of Monik Einzeger, the director of the American Joint Distribution Committee, who introduced me to my first Soviet émigrés in Vienna in 1972. I thank Milton E. Krents, director, and Irma Kopp Krents, senior con-

sultant, of the Wiener Oral History Library at the American
Jewish Committee, for their support and encouragement.

My sister, Miriam Goldkrantz, and my husband, Seymour
Rothchild, were very helpful as first readers of the unedited
manuscript. My greatest debt is to John Herman, my editor at
Simon and Schuster. His suggestions and sensitive criticism
were invaluable in bringing the manuscript to its present form.

SYLVIA ROTHCHILD

A Special Legacy is dedicated to the men and women whose stories it tells, and to their friends and relatives in the Soviet Union who have an unrecorded share in the history it reveals.

Contents

Introduction	13
Jewish Issues	27
The Legacies	58
The Actual Life	113
Parents and Children	135
Getting an Education	155
Professional Life	173
From Citizen to Emigré	242
America	291
A Note to the Reader	325
Index	327

Introduction

 I MET MY FIRST Russian émigrés at Schonau, a seedy hunting lodge in the outskirts of Vienna. It had once been a vacation place for Austrian aristocrats. There were rumors that Mozart had composed some music on the premises. The grounds were now scruffy, however, fenced in with barbed wire and guarded by dogs and nervous Austrian police carrying guns. It was 1972, a year of threats and letter bombs. The guards worried about Arab attacks and were surly toward visitors and the stream of Russian Jews who came to stay overnight and then went on to Israel, making room for another contingent of émigrés.

Schonau was leased and run by the Jewish Agency, staffed with Israelis chosen for compassion, flexibility and stamina. There were Russian interpreters among them, but Hebrew was the language of the place. The Austrian help spoke German. When I came to spend the day, I added English and Yiddish to the languages available. Some young émigrés could speak some English. Many of the people over forty understood some Yiddish.

In 1972, more than 96 percent of the émigrés went to Israel and very few came to the United States. The Israelis and the American representatives from the Joint Distribution Committee who were involved in the effort to resettle émigrés tried hard to humanize the ordeal of emigration. They saw them-selves as agents of the Jewish people, reaching out to long-lost relatives. The decision to leave the Soviet Union was perceived as an act of faith in the Jewish people as well as an act of re-jection of a country that was giving its citizens a very hard time.

The stop at Schonau was too short and too pressured to offer the émigrés the reassurance they needed. The Israelis were overwhelmed by the immigration papers that had to be filled out; the luggage to check for bombs; the arrangements for flights to Israel; places for immigrants to live where they could study Hebrew and acclimate themselves to a new cul-ture, new life, new language.

Some of the arrivals were immediately grateful for the ef-forts of strangers who had taken it upon themselves to feed, house and support people they knew nothing about. Others were too disoriented from the ordeal of leaving the Soviet Union to appreciate what was going on. They saw yet another line of officials with forms to fill out, asking personal questions, telling them of new restrictions and hardships that awaited them. Many were mourning the people they had left behind, and most of the older émigrés were terrified of going to a country they knew nothing about where their lives would be changed forever.

The director of the Jewish Agency watched what he called "a people on the move." They came from all walks of life, sharing only the "fifth point" on their identity cards that marked them as Jews. They were among the first to leave the Soviet Union since the 1920s. Their departure was seen as an unexpected "liberation." There had been no possibility of leav-ing until 1966. That was the year in which Premier Alexei Kosygin indicated that the U.S.S.R. would not obstruct efforts of citizens who wanted to be reunited with relatives abroad. At first people were reluctant to respond, afraid it was a trap in which they might be caught and punished.

At Schonau one could meet ballet dancers, conductors of symphony orchestras, university professors, engineers from Odessa, Georgian farmers, factory managers from Kiev and

Kharkov, bookkeepers, doctors, students in blue jeans and sandals who looked like their American counterparts, pensioners and young musicians with aggressive mothers eager to show them off. There were parents who had decided to leave to save their children the harassment and frustration they themselves had experienced. There were young people who had risked challenging the Soviet authorities because they didn't understand the dangers, and dissidents who had left the Soviet Union unwillingly, faced with the choice of jail, mental hospital or emigration.

Jews from Moscow, Leningrad, Riga and Kiev often looked so much like the Israelis and the occasional American visitors who came to witness the exodus that Schonau could have passed as the site of a family reunion. The Israelis and Americans were likely to have had grandparents from the parts of Europe now incorporated into the Union of Soviet Socialist Republics. The people I spoke to in Yiddish greeted me as "a Czernowitzer," recognizing the regional pronunciations I had learned from my grandfather.

It was a far-flung family that met at Schonau, with exotic branches which included the Georgians who looked more like Gypsies or Turks than New York or Moscow Jews. One swarthy, wrinkled grandmother tried hard to communicate with me though we had no language in common. She showed me a jug of borscht she had carried from Tbilisi and the flat loaves of pita she baked for her family. I declined what I thought was an offer of a taste; but she rolled up her sleeve, plunged her arm to the bottom of the jug and pulled out a ruby ring she had hidden among the grated beets. She had fared better than the worldly city people who were stripped even of their wedding rings at Chop, the last border for customs inspection and the last place of Soviet harassment.

I heard my first stories about the ordeal of emigration from émigrés still shaking from the experience. Many said they had not been sure they would make it to freedom until they had crossed the border. Schonau, with its barbed wire, armed guards and dogs, was not reassuring.

There were émigrés who had waited only a few months for

permission to leave and others who had waited several years as *"refusniks,"* deprived of work and school and threatened with imprisonment. The stories they told made it clear that the process of leaving had been designed to discourage emigration. Ten different documents had to be submitted to the emigration department, beginning with the *"visov,"* the invitation from relatives in Israel. I was often overwhelmed at Schonau by the men and women who handed me little pieces of paper with names and addresses, pleading that I help the people they had left behind who needed invitations so that they could apply.

The rules kept changing. In 1972 the U.S.S.R. instituted an education tax on people seeking to emigrate. The tax, which was as high as 35,000 rubles for the most educated (when the average salary was about 2,000 rubles a year), was dropped in 1973. For that year, however, families were thrown into a panic. Unable to pay for all their children, parents sometimes had to choose among them. I remember a weeping father I tried to comfort who said, "What kind of father am I? I chose between my sons. And how will they punish the one I left behind?"

Schonau was officially closed in the fall of 1973. Those who worked or visited there were not likely to forget the emotional atmosphere of the place. My strongest memory is of two little Georgian girls who attached themselves to me one day. They clung to my legs and covered my arms with kisses. They spoke only Georgian and were determined to find some way to communicate with me. The bright-eyed seven-year-old finally got an idea that pleased her. She pulled me into a room that had been set aside for religious services, found a prayer book, opened it and began reading out the Hebrew letters. She couldn't pronounce whole words, but had learned the alphabet. She handed me the prayer book with a flourish to see if I could read, to see if I was Jewish too. When I passed her test, she jumped up and down and squealed like any exuberant seven-year-old anywhere. The ancient letters linked us together. It seemed all the connection necessary in that anxious and emotional time.

Two years later, back in the United States, I sought out the Soviet émigrés who had settled in Boston, Massachusetts. The numbers of people choosing to come to the United States rather than Israel had begun to increase. By 1979, 65,000 Soviet Jews were making their home in American cities. Boston was especially attractive to academics and professionally trained men and women. I found it easy to meet them at the Hebrew College, where they took English lessons. I was both a journalist interested in writing about them and a neighbor who had spent time at Schonau and was concerned about them as newcomers in my city.

I knew that they had left the Soviet Union with very little information about the West. Beyond the hope that they would find work in their professions, they had no plans. "My purpose in leaving I knew. My purpose in coming I know not" was a refrain I heard again and again. The American Jews who were welcoming and supporting them were also unclear about their "purpose." They were openly disappointed when Soviet Jews with invitations to Israel chose to come to the United States. They called them "dropouts." They also assumed that Soviet Jews who had experienced persecution were seeking religious freedom in America.

Soviet émigrés came to the United States with many fears and fantasies about life in freedom. American Jews, concerned about Jewish survival and still feeling remorse for the millions of Jews they had been unable to save from the Holocaust, were sincere in their efforts to "save Soviet Jewry." Committees of citizens organized rallies and protests. There were empty chairs with the names of "prisoners of conscience" on the platforms of temples on the High Holidays to remind the congregations of the people who were not there.

The emotional involvement with the plight of dissidents, *refusniks* and "prisoners of conscience" was no preparation for the arrival of the majority of Soviet émigrés, who knew very little about Jewish traditions, kept no Sabbaths or holidays and were sometimes not even aware of the existence of Jewish

communal life in America. Many Soviet Jewish émigrés had
not experienced Jewishness as a source of spiritual nourishment and thought it only a defect, a misfortune to escape if
possible. The "J," the fifth point on their internal passports,
referred to their "nationality," not to religion, which was forbidden to Jews as well as to Christians. American Jews were
not prepared to meet Soviet Jewish émigrés who were assimilated Russians, though not completely integrated into Soviet
life. They could not understand the nostalgia for Russian culture and were dismayed to find some Soviet Jews who had
converted to the Russian Orthodox Church and scholars who
considered themselves more Buddhists than Jews.

Some émigrés spoke of their Jewishness as "an inheritance
of an ancient culture" about which they knew very little. Some
spoke of it as a sign of "specialness," of difference. "To be
Jewish is to be a rebel," said some of the young people. In
America they were invited to religious services and Jewish
community activities. The children were offered scholarships
in Jewish schools. Some were able to take advantage of the
opportunities offered to them. Many émigrés, however, found
Jewish activities and affiliations too strange and too threatening to share. Some took a year or longer to shed the fears and
prejudices that made it impossible for them to participate, even
as observers.

Pessimists, watching the struggles, deplored the destruction
of Jewish life and community in the Soviet Union and wondered whether Soviet Jews were beyond help. Optimists, however, saw the issue differently. They remembered that twenty
years before, the situation had indeed seemed hopeless. The
only reports had been of dwindling groups of old men and
women stubbornly clinging to forbidden religious practices.
The children and grandchildren of observant Jews had been
raised and indoctrinated in Soviet kindergartens to become devoted members of the Young Pioneers and Komsomol. Jewish
schools and institutions had been dismantled sixty years before. There had been no circumcisions, no Hebrew study, no
confirmations at thirteen and no Jewish marriages. There were

no Jewish books or periodicals to read, and the Bible was forbidden both as a religious text and as a work of "Zionist propaganda." The only official information available about Israel
was that it was "an artificial state, aggressive . . . violent . . .
destined to be destroyed." There was no reason to hope that
positive Jewish attitudes could survive in such a climate.

In 1965, Elie Wiesel was in Moscow in time to witness the
Simchat Torah celebrations. He was astonished to find crowds
of young people dancing and singing in front of the synagogue
on Arkhipova Street, as he reported, "openly celebrating their
faith in the people of Israel." If the years of silence and isolation had left a legacy of despair, that singing and dancing
brought on an explosion of unreasonable hopefulness. Wiesel
began to write not only about what he observed but also
about his dreams of what could happen. He was a fabulous
dreamer, and amazingly, his visions of demonstrations in Red
Square, of Jewish seminars and Hebrew study did come true.
There were no hopes for emigration in 1965, but the battles
for civil rights and the end of discrimination against religious
and ethnic groups had begun. When the "Save Soviet Jewry"
campaign began in America in the sixties, it also focused on
obtaining for Jews the same legal rights accorded all other Soviet citizens.

If young people could resist the indoctrination to which
they had been subjected, everything seemed possible. One
émigré, describing her school days, said, "I was raised in love
and devotion, respect for Stalin and the Soviet regime. These
were sacred things to us. We religiously believed in the purity
and justice of the Communist Party." But such young people
had set themselves against the authorities through protests and
demonstrations their parents would never have risked.

At Schonau I had met two young women who had danced
on Arkhipova Street. They and their bewildered parents were
on their way to Israel because they had been expelled from
their university for "Zionist activities." When I asked what
they meant by "Zionist activity," they seemed surprised at my
ignorance. In two-part harmony, they offered me a sample of

their incendiary songs: "David Melech Yisrael" (David, King of Israel) and "Am Yisrael Chai" (The Jewish People Lives). They didn't know the meaning of the words, but that didn't seem to matter to them or to the police who picked them up for "hooliganism." They were the Soviet children of the sixties, gentler and less strident than the American variety but still asserting their identity and enjoying the excitement of being part of a demonstration that was not organized by the authorities.

An older émigré, a fifty-year-old actress, described the demonstration from another perspective. Like most Muscovites, she knew nothing about Jewish holidays, and she had lived in Moscow all her life without knowing where the synagogue was. "It was only in the last two years before I left that I became curious." A friend, also an actress, invited her to come with her to the synagogue. "It was full," she said. "We couldn't get in. The streets were packed with young people. They were afraid of nothing. Without any fear they were singing Jewish songs, dancing Israeli dances, wishing one another a speedy liberation. This, I thought, is the spirit of freedom. I'd never seen anything like it before."

What lay behind the spirit of freedom was a mystery. When it was possible to emigrate, Jews were the first to apply. The decision most often came from fear of what they called the "zoological anti-Semitism"—the irrational behavior of the government which they could not hope to change or escape. They felt it as some ominous cloud that hung over their heads for life, whether it affected them directly or as witnesses to the humiliation of friends and colleagues.

Soviet Jews shared the hardships experienced by all Soviet citizens, but also had their own history to transcend. Older people knew that there were hundreds of anti-Jewish laws under the Tsar and that millions of Jews had fled to America before the Revolution to escape pogroms. There were men and women who remembered the hopes and promises of the Revolution, the pogroms of 1924 after the Revolution, the Stalin purges between 1935 and 1938, the Nazi purges between

1941 and 1945, the murders of Jewish intellectuals and doctors in 1948 and 1953. This information was not found in history books, but it was passed from parents to children. Young people might have known only the stridently anti-Semitic books published with government sanction in the early sixties, or their own problems in getting into universities and finding jobs. Some were sensitized by the vilification of Jews that began after the 1967 War in Israel or the restrictions that mushroomed after the first Jews applied for exit visas.

Soviet education was reputed to have created a country of men and women devoted to the state, a disciplined army of workers, farmers and educators who believed in communism for themselves and the rest of the world. Emigrés, however, would tell of individuals who did not fit the mold. In spite of censorship and restrictions, there were people with private opinions and independent thoughts. They didn't believe what they were told and read between the lines of the censored information available to them. They longed for freedom without knowing what it was. They clung to loyalties that were forbidden. We knew nothing about them in America, and they knew even less about us.

The censored official information we receive from the Soviet Union tells us what its rulers want us to know, not what actually happens. The past as well as the present is distorted and falsified to fit the political needs of the moment. Jewish history has been systematically deleted from textbooks and scholarly works. The ordinary life of all ordinary people is obscured by the official myth that life in the Soviet Union is the best and the safest in the world.

A journalist from Moscow now living in New York is convinced that Americans know more about what happens on the moon than about what happens in the Soviet Union. He had watched American tourists in Moscow and Leningrad carefully insulated from the actual life of the country. Even the journalists who tried to write objective reports were limited by the fact that seeing was not the same as feeling. Soviet citizens were products of a life that Americans couldn't imagine. Even the most beautiful cities in Russia revealed nothing of the psychology of the people who lived behind the charming facades.

The oral histories of recent Soviet émigrés were collected by the William E. Wiener Oral History Library of the American Jewish Committee in the hope that the experiences of a wide variety of living witnesses of Soviet life would bring us closer to an understanding of their society. The Soviet Jewish experiences are particularly valuable because they offer historical information that has been missing from Soviet and Jewish history.

The interviews were conducted with 176 émigrés in twenty-five American cities within five years after their arrival. The memoirists were mostly men and women with professional education who came with diplomas and certificates in art, music, engineering and medicine. The majority were between thirty and forty-nine years of age, but the study also included some accomplished men and women in their sixties and seventies and some students in their twenties. Some had experienced exile, imprisonment and the anguish of many refusals. Others had been able to leave with a minimum of harassment. Some had left eagerly and others with great reluctance, to avoid incarceration. Some were interviewed while still in the throes of euphoria about having made it to freedom. Many told their stories while struggling with the physical and mental disorientation caused by the radical change of culture.

Most of the interviews were done in Russian. The questions were open-ended, chosen to encourage the expression of feelings as well as for the gathering of facts. In my interviews of English-speaking Russians, I sensed the irony of collecting oral history from men and women who had been cautious all their lives about revealing their private feelings. Though there is no Russian synonym for the word "private" as it is used in English, Soviet citizens were accustomed to reticence. Many had been careful not to share their thoughts with their own children, who might repeat some indiscretion at school. Neighbors, colleagues, even relatives might be potential informers. Independent thoughts, heretical opinions and even jokes could be shared only with the most trusted friends. They had lived in "bugged" apartments, worked in offices and laboratories where every word had to be watched. In America, they were offered tape recorders; invited to share their opinions, memories, hopes and disappointments, without—if they could believe in such a possibility—fear of punishment.

In spite of uneasiness about the dangers of taping, the interviewers and the émigrés agreed that oral history was a necessary antidote to the official information available. Some things we could learn only by listening to people one at a time. Older people were grateful for the opportunity to leave something for the historical record, whether it would serve scholars or simply be there for their grandchildren to read. A college student from Moscow had read much propaganda about the West in the Soviet press, especially about how bad life was in America. In America he found only bad things to read about the country he had left, even though he missed some aspects of his life there. He blamed American confusion about the Soviet Union on the tendency to focus on isolated bits of information taken out of context. The interviews revealed the misunderstandings and prejudices created by insufficient or untrue information and the human need to come to conclusions before the evidence is in.

The collection of 176 oral-history interviews offers an extraordinary body of evidence, anecdotes, personal and general history, in the words of eyewitnesses. This book is both an introduction to an articulate group of Soviet émigrés who came to the United States between 1973 and 1980 and an overview of the issues they discussed with the interviewers from the Wiener Oral History Library. Their real names are not used, but their personalities and styles are revealed in their stories and observations.

These interviews include the memories of men and women old enough to remember the Revolution and young enough to have experienced the drug culture of the sixties. The majority of the interviews are with émigrés born between 1930 and 1950.

There are children of *shtetl* Jews among them, and second- and third-generation urbanized professionals. The grandchildren of rabbis and revolutionaries, of poor artisans and wealthy businessmen—all had received the same indoctrination. The recollections of World War II include those of children of partisans who fought in the forests and many whose parents or grandparents were murdered at Babi Yar.

Some speak of their personal suffering, bitter about the misguided or malevolent leaders, the "wicked fathers" who drove them from their "beloved Motherland." Others speak as if they had been born orphans, alienated and in exile from childhood, punished for crimes they had not committed. They describe emotional hunger and homelessness as if it had nothing to do with them personally, saying, "This is the kind of country it is . . . stupid, corrupt, irrational. I always hated it and thank God I'm out of it." There are gentle, poetic types among the memoirists and aggressive, belligerent personalities who had too much ambition and initiative for the constraints of Soviet life. Confirmed atheists who cannot imagine intelligent people who would care about religion and truly religious Jews who were desperate for a place where they could practice Judaism without mockery or harassment offer some clues to the place of faith, even in the Soviet Union.

While describing the pressures that led them to emigrate, they show how people respond to political situations, how they accept and resist indoctrination, how they deny what they cannot bear to believe. Personal and political life are intertwined. Poignant descriptions of family life, the struggles for education and work are included, along with dramatic stories of arrest and rehabilitation. They touch upon all the areas with sizable Jewish populations and describe the vestiges of Jewishness that kept identity alive in spite of the efforts to destroy Jewish life.

The following pages offer a collection of testimonies about what émigrés speak of as "the actual life" in the Soviet Union, their dreams and fantasies of America and their experiences with American Jews who welcomed them as family and found them to be strangers. The memoirists speak as people between worlds. They live and work among Americans and want their children to be good Americans. They fight nostalgia for the loss of language and culture—but not one wishes to return to "the prison" from which they came.

Jewish Issues

 THERE IS NO RECORD of a time when Jews, as a group, lived in comfort and security in Russia. Between 1772 and 1795, Russia inherited the largest population of Jewry in the world when it shared in the partition of the old Polish republic. Catherine II at first welcomed Jewish merchants and traders in the hope that they would stimulate the economy. The period of welcome and tolerance, however, was short-lived. This was one of the many shifts between acceptance and repression that have characterized Russian rule. The Pale of Settlement was delineated by Catherine II. It was an area from the Baltic Sea to the Black Sea that included the provinces of Grodno, Vilna, Volynia, Podolia, Minsk and Ekaterinoslav, the Bessarabian and Belostok oblast, and the Kiev province, excluding the city of Kiev. Jews could also live in the urban areas of the Kherson, Kogilev and Vitebsk provinces, in the Chernigov and Poltava provinces, in Courland and Riga and in the villages within fifty versts of the western frontier. Close to five million Jews lived in this area, making their living as craftsmen, small traders, innkeepers and bakers, butchers and vintners.

A small number of Jews were permitted to travel to Moscow or St. Petersburg as First Guild Merchants. Most Jews never left the Pale, where they lived in crowded ghettos. They were a literate, urban people with limited economic opportunities in a preindustrial society, and were often employed as agents and intermediaries between the peasants and the town dwellers. For the most part, they were religious. They ran their own communities, paid heavy taxes to the tsar and hoped to be ignored by their autocratic rulers, the landed gentry who used them as scapegoats, and by the peasants, who were easily incited to violence against them.

During the reign of Nicholas I (1825–1855), six hundred anti-Jewish laws were passed. Jews were driven out of villages where they'd lived for generations. Yiddish and Hebrew books were censored, the government interfered in the curricula of Jewish schools and many Jews were conscripted into the Russian army.

During centuries of Jewish life in Poland there had been no conscription of Jews. Jews were considered too weak and religious to make good soldiers. Nicholas I, however, had faith in the power of army discipline. Jewish subjects, like others, were expected to supply their quota of recruits. Jews lived under the same legal system as others, but under laws that exhibited a definite anti-Jewish bias. Though the law promised religious freedom to all, Jewish soldiers were subjected to pressure to convert. Prayer books were taken from them. They were forbidden to speak Yiddish and were billeted only in Christian homes. Memoirs of that time tell of the beatings and torture used to convince young Jewish soldiers of the wisdom of baptism. It was thought that half of the conscripts were converted during the time of service, which lasted for twenty-five years.

Though the draft age for Russian soldiers was twenty to thirty-five (though unmarried boys of seventeen could be offered as replacements for married members of their family), Jewish children could be conscripted at the age of eight or nine. Officially they were to be taken between the ages of twelve and twenty-five, but there were eyewitness reports of battalions of frightened children who died like flies of fever and exhaustion.

The effect of conscription on the Jewish communities, which provided the quota of eight recruits per thousand, was as threatening to Jewish communal life as the loss of the recruits. The communal leaders who needed to fill the quota invariably took the children of the poor and powerless, the rebels and the nonobservant. The *khappers* (snatchers) kidnapped children, searched out fugitives and might nab a fellow Jew found traveling without a passport. The search for recruits provoked hatred between classes and provinces; it encouraged criminality, bribery, distrust and open hatred between Jews. Rabbis were often *de facto* agents of the government, silent about the evils themselves, concerned with protecting themselves and their families.

When Alexander II came to the throne in 1858, the age of conscription was made the same for Jews as for Christians. The schools and universities were opened to Jews, and some found their way into the professions and into the newly educated intelligentsia. Alexander II liberated more than twenty million people who were classified as serfs and bound to hereditary labor on their landlords' estates. His reforms led some Jews to believe that Jewish restrictions would disappear if Jews gave up their customs and superstitions.

Alexander II's liberal reign did not last long. He was assassinated by revolutionary terrorists in 1881. A wave of pogroms swept through more than two hundred cities with large Jewish populations. Jewish men, women and children were killed by mobs of peasants. Their homes and shops were looted and destroyed. In May 1882, Alexander III enacted new laws that narrowed the Pale of Settlement. Jews lost the right to own mortgages and leases. Old claims were cancelled without compensation, and new educational restrictions left thousands of students stranded in the middle of an education that could not be completed. Civil and economic restrictions and a fresh wave of pogroms set whole communities to flight.

By the end of the century there would be a million Russian Jews looking for freedom and safety in the United States. Another million followed in the wake of new massacres, World

War I and the outbreak of the Revolution. Among those who remained, Zionists, encouraged by the Balfour Declaration, urged Jews to create their own state in Palestine. Bundists advocated socialism and the promotion in Russia of secular Jewish culture.

In 1905 Lenin was already fighting Zionism, both as a form of nationalism and because he believed it diverted Jewish workers from the struggle for communism. In his writings on the Jewish question he envisioned only a choice between assimilation and separation. He opposed Judaism as he opposed all religions, which he considered "forms of spiritual oppression."

Zionists meanwhile warned that the struggle for communism diverted Jews from the awareness that there would be no place for Jews or Judaism in a communist country. The Jewish Socialist Bund tried to gain concessions from Lenin. They had played an important role in spreading Marxist ideas in Poland, Lithuania and White Russia. Their constituents were Yiddish-speaking unassimilated Jews who lived within the Pale and whose lives were bound up in Jewish observances. Lenin fought the Bundists' demands for the autonomy of their party. His message to the Jews was that they would have to give up all vestiges of Jewishness and merge with the rest of the population.

Older traditional Jews interpreted this as just another version of what had been offered by Nicholas I. Many young people, trapped in the restrictions of the Pale, rebelling against parents, rabbis and the poverty and inequality they saw around them, were willing to give up Jewishness for the Revolution, for the promise of citizenship and unity with humanity at large. It seemed the only way to escape their ignominious status as subjects of the Tsar. Until 1905 there were no citizens in Russia. There were only subjects, who had no inalienable rights, only privileges granted or withdrawn at the emperor's discretion. Jews were among the subjects on whom special restrictions were added to those they shared with the rest of the population. They were educated enough to know that the Jews of France had been enfranchised in 1791 and that equal rights for Jews had been acquired by the Jews of central and western Europe by the 1870s. It was only in Russia that conscription came without citizenship and civil rights.

It was the rare Jewish family that was not divided by these issues. The older generation, for the most part, would not give up their faith and observances. The young "moved with the times." Some became Bolsheviks; some held with the Bundists who refused to take orders from Lenin; still others adhered to Zionism. "We left the religious spirit in which we were raised," said Frieda K., who lived through those tumultuous days. "All the young people strove to become part of the new way. It was what we thought was progress."

The downfall of tsarism seemed proof of a new dawn and encouraged Jews to hope for equality and freedom. The Pale of Settlement was abolished. Literate and educated Jews flocked to the capital cities, where there were opportunities for education and work. Merchants traveled freely without restriction. Most important, however, was the fact that Lenin was surrounded by Jews, offering evidence that there were unlimited opportunities for those who separated themselves from Zionism and Jewish traditions. Trotsky, Kamenev, Zinoviev and Radek were all Jews as well as leading revolutionaries. Later, under the Litvinov regime, the Soviet Foreign Office was called "the synagogue" because the majority of the Soviet ambassadors were of Jewish ancestry. Jews, for a brief time, felt themselves equal to other citizens. For the first time in Russian history they played a role in government, and they were also visible in the Cheka, a precursor of the KGB.

The process of assimilation was accelerated in schools where classes were conducted in Yiddish. Such secular Jewish schools eased the children of religious Jews into a new time and a new ideology. Frieda K., who studied in such a school and planned to teach the next Yiddish-speaking generation, found by the time she graduated that Yiddish was being denounced. Repudiated as a leftover from the "medieval, ghetto phase" of Jewish history, it was considered unacceptable in the Soviet Union.

Older émigrés, reminiscing about the years just after the

Revolution, spoke of "forgetting we were Jews." They willingly gave up Jewish ties and traditions to reach "higher levels in life." They were not threatened by the closing of synagogues because churches were closed as well. Jewish schools were shut down because of a lack of students. The future required fluency in Russian and the repression of Jewish gestures and accents. They were certainly not nostalgic for the moribund villages in which they had been born.

Lena B., born in Mogilev, Byelorussia, in 1898, came to Kiev just after the Revolution and reflects the mood of her generation. "Why should I have been interested in Jewish history?" she asks. "Nobody cared about it when I was young." She had nothing but contempt for pious Jews who wore side curls and black coats. She was aware of anti-Semitism wherever she turned but did not take it personally. " 'Here, *Zhidovka!*' they'd say at the store and the market, but what was there to say? Why should I quarrel with a stupid market woman?" Though she had grown up in an Orthodox family and had memories of Passover, Sabbath and holiday celebrations, she felt detached from it all. It was only "the hardship of life" that she recalled. She remembered only the bitter struggle to survive.

Sophie M., a lawyer born in the Kaluga province in 1898, was the daughter of a country doctor. She grew up in an assimilated family, with parents who supported the Revolution. She knew nothing about traditional Jewish life, but retained vestiges of obligation and responsibility that seemed eccentric in her school. Pained by the terrible conditions of Turkish war prisoners, she put up a collection box for alms, which earned her a severe scolding from her teacher. She compulsively sent food packages to Siberia when her friends were sent away. Some older patterns remained long after Jewishness itself was forgotten.

Frieda K., born in Moldavia in 1914, had memories of *shtetl* life but claimed that her "spirit was free." She accepted the lessons she learned at school and yet without openly rebelling against her parents. She said, "I knew that the communist spirit was against religion and that science had proved all religion to be fanaticism, but I still fasted on Yom Kippur because of my relationship with my parents. It was an act of obedience and respect." She took pride in her Jewishness and also felt "one with humanity." She had memories of a time when it had been a crime to use the word *Zhid* and it was possible to call a policeman and have the culprit punished. When she looked back on the ordeals she had lived through, she separated the "international" purges that afflicted people from all the groups from the specifically Jewish persecutions. The former seemed easier to bear because she was "a citizen, equal to the others."

The brief time of faith in the Revolution was remembered as a high point in the émigrés' lives. "We thought we were on the way to a new life," said Minna M. "We had dresses made of burlap and torn shoes, but we were overwhelmed with happiness. Everybody was equal. No more richer and poorer. Everything was just and beautiful. And then came the thirties and the killing of the intelligentsia."

The memoirs of older émigrés reveal the faith and the disappointment that followed. Jews did not last long in the Party leadership. Their careers in the diplomatic service and the higher echelons of the army were short, and they were eventually excluded from many spheres of academic and public life. During the purges they, along with millions of other victims, were imprisoned, tortured and shot for crimes they had not committed. Some took comfort from the fact that those who were persecuted as enemies of the state came from all walks of life, all religions and nationalities. Others were well aware that the arrests of doctors, "cosmopolitans" and Zionists affected only Jews.

Eighty years after Lenin argued against Jewish separateness, Soviet Jews carry internal passports on which the fifth point notes their nationality with a "J." They remain an anomalous minority in a country based on territorial units. The fifteen Soviet Socialist Republics were determined by the nationality of the majority of the inhabitants. Close to three million Jews live in the major cities of the Soviet Union without any status as a collective entity. They speak Russian but are not Russians. They speak Georgian but are not Georgians. They live under the same legal system as other citizens, but official policies and unofficial vestiges of prejudice set them apart. In spite of all the efforts to suppress Jewish history and to discourage Jewish study and communal life, there are still Soviet citizens who think of themselves as Jews.

Individuals may remain Jews even without affiliation or association. Though they have no representatives to speak for them or to defend them, no archives or historical societies to keep their records, no Jewish memorials or commemorations to encourage feelings of dignity and self-worth, Jewish accomplishments and struggles are preserved in stories and anecdotes passed on within families as a special legacy, and shared in small circles of trusted friends.

The stories of Soviet Jewish émigrés show that families remained close and protective long after traditional Jewish observances were abandoned. Grandmothers influenced the grandchildren they cared for. Two and often three generations shared one or two rooms. The older people had memories of life before the Revolution, of World War II, of arrests and purges, of evacuations. When they did not speak of their experiences, their anxieties and behavior spoke for them. History books were censored and rewritten to fit changes in ideology and policy, but the family stories remained as an enduring record and a standard against which altered history could be measured. They also affected the endless identity crisis in which Soviet Jews found themselves, the lifelong struggle for equilibrium, for solid ground on which to stand.

Many émigrés spoke of their Jewishness as "a matter of blood," out of their control. They felt it as something "mysterious . . . unfathomable," a wellspring of feelings that inundated them from time to time. Those who experienced "inexplicable" Jewish loyalty in spite of the fact that they were not religious, knew no Yiddish and had no Jewish education were in contrast to others who claimed no vestiges of "Jewish mentality," no connections to pious grandparents and even immunity to the overt anti-Semitism that awakened Jewish awareness in so many Soviet Jews.

"I just don't have a sense of being Jewish. The mere fact that an anti-Semite calls me a Jew doesn't make me a Jew," said a fifty-year-old philosopher and art critic. "Inside myself I felt Russian, not Jewish in any way," said a forty-year-old museum worker who wanted only "to be like everyone else, to have a Russian face and a Russian name" and not to feel like an alien in the city of Leningrad in which she was born.

A psychologist, slightly older, also from Leningrad, tried to acquire intellectually what she couldn't feel emotionally. She read Jewish history, studied the Jewish holidays and even managed to acquire a rare copy of the Bible. "I made an effort," she said, "but it didn't enter my flesh and blood. It's not my nature, my essence, to be Jewish." She was too thoroughly assimilated into Russian culture, too deeply immersed in the language, literature and world outlook to change. She chose, however, to explain to her four-year-old son that he was a Jew so that he would not have to face the fact suddenly in the street. She encouraged him to be "a fierce fighter," so that he could defend himself. She said, "I consciously gave him this compensation."

An English teacher from Moscow found another solution. She was convinced that she was a Western person who had accidentally been born in the wrong country. "I don't belong to Jews or Russians or Americans. I belong to whatever contains some intellectuality and goodness. People who create art are my chosen relatives."

More typical, however, were émigrés who did not believe they could choose their relatives. "My parents are Jews, so I am a Jew," said a thirty-five-year-old editor and teacher from Moscow. "I would never say I'm Russian if someone asked who I am." He accepted himself as a Jew, claimed to have "Jewish feelings and mutual understanding with other Jews." His language, however, was Russian. He could speak no Yiddish but was fluent in Georgian and swore in Azerbaijanian. His identity, however, was private and unchangeable, even though he said he was not religious.

A forty-five-year-old physician from Moscow had no ambivalence about his identity. "Both my grandfathers were religious Jews," he said. "They went to synagogue and celebrated holidays. By the time I was sixteen I knew I belonged to religious people in the same way that I knew that I wanted to be a doctor and fight cancer and tuberculosis. I never felt myself to be Russian."

An engineer from Moscow in the same generation said simply, "I am the son of my parents. I have no choice. The stamp is on my face. I could become a Muslim or a Christian, but the way I look and my identity card will still say 'Jew.' "

Every Russian has a name and a patronymic, the father's name plus a standard suffix. Writers, musicians and public figures who are Jewish often have Russian pseudonyms, but their fathers' names give their identity away. Some Jews in the Soviet Union, as in a pattern also seen in other countries, have changed their names to their Russian equivalents. Slava Isaakova became Sofia Alexandrovna. Moishe became Moise which became Michael, and Baruch became Boris. But the changes are obvious; no one is deceived.

Emigrés suggested that the very effort to hide became a constant reminder of what was to be hidden. A forty-five-year-old physician had taken his mother's Russian name at the age of sixteen and was sure that he had risen higher in his profession because he was not so easily recognized as a Jew. He was, however, the son of a famous doctor, and his father's connections were also of help to him, even though they exposed him as a Jew. He concluded from his experiences that it is impossible to be half a Jew in Russia. He said, "If you have a quarter or an eighth of Jewish blood you are considered Jewish. It's just as it is in America with blacks. If they have a drop of black blood, they are black."

An engineer from Odessa in the same generation offered another variation on the problems of hiding Jewish identity. He had a typical Russian name and face in spite of having two Jewish parents. When he was issued his internal passport at the age of sixteen, the clerk neglected to ask his nationality and his fifth point was stamped "Russian." He didn't correct the error. "I had no Jewish upbringing," he said. "I knew nothing about Jewish religion and didn't understand a word of Yiddish." His name, face and identity card spared him any experience of anti-Semitism. He insisted, however, that he felt Jewish. His problem was that he couldn't bear to see other Jews mistreated. It upset him to hear expressions of anti-Semitism that he could not challenge. He married an officially Jewish woman who felt such things even more strongly.

Many émigrés spoke of their conscious efforts to avoid thinking about Jewish problems that were both painful and impossible to resolve. "I preferred to ignore this side of my life," said Semyon R., an editor and translator from Odessa. "I didn't approach it as a political issue, didn't examine it in sociological terms and made no effort to protest or defend myself."

It was not unusual for Soviet Jews to try to live as "marranos"—to be, as they said, "Jewish only in my soul." Many tried, like Semyon R., "to ignore the facts, even though I knew them from childhood." Sooner or later, however, the strain became too difficult and the pressures too personal to deny. The problem began with the assumption that assimilation, or what was called "Russification," required that all Jewish ties and loyalties be repudiated and discarded. Jewish traditions and history were to be forgotten, and all evidences of Jewishness in name or face were to be understood as defects. Jews who were trying to reach "higher levels of life" were expected to be at least outwardly anti-Semitic.

The memoirs of Jewish émigrés show that it was harder to uproot and destroy vestiges of Jewish tradition than had been expected. This was in part because official anti-Semitism increased Jewish consciousness. The determined efforts to turn individualistic urban educated Jews into undifferentiated Russian workers awakened resistance rather than compliance. Jewish parents were prone to devote their lives to helping their children excel as students. Parents who had been able to acquire higher education during brief periods of tolerance and those who had been unable to slip through before the gates closed were equally determined to see their sons and daughters accepted in university or institute. Meanwhile, the quotas that regulated acceptance of those who had the "J" as their fifth point kept Jewish consciousness alive.

Jewish feelings were described as a source of pride or shame, superiority or inferiority, and often as a confused mixture of all of these. Ilya K., a forty-year-old Moscow engineer who chose between the options open to him said, "You can either be proud or spend your life crying. I decided it's better to feel proud and let others worry about how difficult and dangerous it is to be a Jew. I know Jews who changed their names, who hide the fact that they are Jews and would never help another Jew get a job. Not me! I celebrated the main Jewish holidays. I went to synagogue twice a year in spite of the KGB who came with their tape recorders and in spite of the large poster that said, 'God save our government, the foundation of peace in the world.' I knew the feeling of unity with my people." He made it clear that he preferred to be among the persecuted rather than the persecutors. He insisted that he chose pride rather than shame because it suited his personality.

Eugenia S., a high school teacher of German, who grew up in an assimilated Moscow family, claimed that her strong national feelings waxed and waned in response to official anti-Semitism. She said, "We know only that our parents are Jewish and we are proud of our people's history. But it is all very vague because we don't know the history. We don't know the law or the customs. We do know, however, who the famous writers are. We know which musicians and painters are Jewish. The first thing we ask about a famous person is whether he is Jewish and one of us, sharing our misfortunes. We take pride in belonging to a talented and persecuted people."

An Odessa violinist ten years older than Eugenia S. confirmed the fact that it was a kind of hobby to collect the names of famous Jews who hide their identity. She taught her children that the best scholars and musicians were Jews. She said, "I told them that Jews were the most interesting people and that their customs and laws were based on common sense, good hygiene and scientific understanding." She saw this as Jewish education in the city of Odessa, where it was impossible to study Jewish history, culture or religion.

The preoccupation with Jewish superiority was often adopted by Russian and Ukrainian women who married Jewish men and took on Jewish attitudes. Lia K. told of an aunt by marriage, "a pure Ukrainian peasant girl who acquired a Jewish face and mannerisms living in a Jewish family." When her Jewish husband was hanged for participating with the partisans during World War II, she sat on the ground and tore her clothes according to Jewish custom. She would not permit her daughter to marry a "goy," and when called "*Zhid*," she would say, "So I am, and better than you."

There were also stories of intellectuals, "pure Russians who called themselves honorary Jews to show they were special, different and rebellious and in opposition to the government."

In spite of more than sixty years of official hostility and repression of Jewish life, it is possible to find Soviet Jews in all the generations who have authentic connections to traditional Jewish life and who do not speak of it as a vague abstraction or a metaphor for rebellion and individuality.

An English teacher born in Riga in 1949 said, "I knew what it was to be Jewish. My parents spoke Yiddish. I had only Jewish friends and felt different from the others. In my crowd of kids we sang Yiddish songs, ate Jewish food. Our parents fasted on Yom Kippur. When the road to the synagogue was blocked with a truck full of hay on Simchat Torah, we just climbed over it. Once a year we went to the site of a former concentration camp to plant flowers. Jews had put up a few monuments, and it was our meeting place."

In recent years the memorial meetings were disturbed by Russian soldiers. The area was used for military maneuvers, and the concentration-camp site was surrounded by signs that said that the road was closed for repairs. In 1973 Jews left their cars behind the barriers and went to their annual memorial meeting on foot. They found police waiting for them. "They provoked a fight," she said, "so they could use their clubs on the kids and the old people. One of the policemen screamed that he'd be glad to finish up what Hitler started, and then the police vans arrived, just out of the blue sky. They did everything they could to stop us, but it just made us more determined."

Polina N., a forty-five-year-old professor of physics at the University of Chelyabinsk, remembering her childhood, said, "There were *matzot* at Passover and *hamantashen* at Purim. We spoke Yiddish." While the majority of the Jews around her were trying to forget or conceal their Jewish background, she openly spoke Yiddish to protest against the official attitudes toward Jews. She said, "My mother and aunt would say 'Shh' when I spoke Yiddish in public, and I would say, 'Why shh?' Russian is my native language. I spoke Yiddish to let people know that I'm a Jew and proud of it, and whatever they wanted to think of that didn't matter to me because I was not interested in their opinion. If they were narrow-minded and ignorant, that was their problem. I'm a Jew. That's all there is to it."

Moysei F. was born in Khust in 1947. It was a city of thirty thousand people with six hundred Jewish families. It had been Czech until 1946. There was a beautiful synagogue in the center of the town, and there had been a yeshiva there before World War II. His parents had lived in Khust when they could still travel to Prague and Budapest, but by the time he was born the border was closed and the people of Khust were considered Russian citizens. Many of its Jews had died in Auschwitz or had gone to Israel. The rabbis were no longer there; there was only a ritual slaughterer who acted as rabbi. Moysei remembered when the city officials decided to use the synagogue building for a gymnasium and the Jewish women held a sit-in in the synagogue for days and would not let the renovators in. After a time the city officials gave up. It was during the Khrushchev era, so they weren't forced as they would have been by Stalin.

It was impossible for him to have a Bar Mitzvah in Khust. He said, "We were afraid the neighbors would inform and

I'd lose my chance to go to college or my father might be fired from his job." The family went to a nearby town where they were not known. A few friends and relatives came along to hear him say the blessings and the prayers he had learned before they jailed his teacher. He couldn't read from the Torah and did not get to see a Bible until he came to the United States. The rabbi, however, had written out the portion he was to read. He had been told Bible stories by his father and uncle, but no books were available. Jewish life was continued without books. He said, "My mother lit her candles. We had *chale* and *kiddush* and made all the blessings. I never ate *chametz* on Pesach. We fasted on Yom Kippur, had fun on Purim and went to *shul* on Shavuot."

Similar experiences were described by Leyb L., a twenty-five-year-old student from Mukachevo, another town of about thirty thousand people in the Carpathian Mountains. He had grown up in a close, protective Jewish community of the kind that was no longer possible in the larger towns and cities. He said, "We helped one another in every way we could. If something happened to a Jew, his family was cared for by the community. It was a good feeling to be part of a *minyan* on Rosh Hashanah and Yom Kippur. We were part of something. We had an identity and support." Leyb L. thought that under harsh Soviet conditions it was impossible *not* to be a Jew. He said, "The persecution pushes you to live in a tight community."

Leyb had also had a secret Bar Mitzvah, in the house of a friend. His father was in prison at the time, but his uncle taught him what to say. He had gone to synagogue, passing the KGB spies shouting their slogans and taking the names of the young people. Later, at school, the names were called out for chastisement and ridicule. He said, "I would always try to sneak in without being seen, but one of the kids would usually catch me and report. Then I had to stand before sixty or seventy kids and hear all the mean stuff being said about me, my parents and Jews in general. It was very hard to go through that at the age of fourteen and fifteen. But there was nothing you could do. You were helpless. You just had to swallow your pride and go on living."

Many parents went to synagogue but discouraged their children from coming, to save them from harassment. Mikhael M., an engineer from Odessa, learned early in life that educated Jews separated themselves from organized Jewish society to avoid rejection by universities and institutes. The upwardly mobile tried to mix with the general population. He believed that the people who openly participated in religious services were "mostly uneducated people who had no hope of improving their lives." He knew that every month some people, not of his "cultural circle," appeared at his door and his father gave them some money to support the synagogue. This came to an end in 1948 when the synagogue in the center of Odessa was closed. It was a fine building built before the Revolution, and it was reopened as a museum of natural history. A skeleton of an elephant was in the place where the rabbi used to stand, and around it were exhibitions of different species of animals. "The worshipers wept when they saw it," said Mikhael. He was thirteen at the time and old enough to know that his parents did not want him to go to the museum, which was felt to be a symbol of Jewish humiliation. After that time services were held in a disreputable neighborhood in the outskirts of the city.

The expectation that Jewish identity and loyalty could be destroyed by edict is not borne out by the stories of Jewish émigrés. Nor is the assumption that forced assimilation and persecution will eradicate Jewish national consciousness. Stories of family life show the power of grandparents and early-childhood experiences in a Jewish environment.

Mikhael M., born in Odessa in 1935, had a grandfather who taught him the Hebrew alphabet when he was seven. When his family was evacuated to Tashkent during World War II he had his first encounter with observant Jews. Forty years later, he could remember going up to a boy of his own age to ask him why he wore a large cap on his head. When he was told he was forbidden to go around with his head uncovered,

Mikhael pulled the cap off to tease him. He said, "He covered his head with his palms and begged me to give it back. Something stricken in his eyes and his voice got to me and made me feel guilty and ashamed." Mikhael's father later told him about Jews who followed the laws and commandments strictly and gave his son permission to go hatless except when speaking the name of God. Mikhael's formal Jewish education was halted abruptly when the bearded and black-coated teacher who was preparing him for Bar Mitzvah disappeared in the purge of rabbis and teachers in 1948. Thirty-five years later in America, he felt he was paying off some debt to his lost teacher when he had his son study Hebrew. He also felt bound to cover his head at services even in Reform congregations where the rabbi wore no skullcap.

There were many émigrés with memories of determined grandmothers who kept the faith, maintained dietary laws and secretly owned Hebrew prayer books. Felix B., a forty-year-old conductor of the Children's Theater in Moscow, said, "My grandmother was a typical person of her generation, always afraid of a knock on the door. But it was something to see her transformed on Friday night and Saturday. She'd fix her hair and put on a special dress. She'd share the kosher chicken we got for her, and then we'd sing the songs she taught us and listen to her stories." This particular grandmother was the widow of a rabbi, one of six rabbis shot by the Red Army in Kharkov in 1931. Maintaining a synagogue was considered anti-Soviet activity at the time. This painful family history made every Sabbath an act of resistance, a kind of memorial service.

Felix B. promised his grandmother he would say *kaddish* for her when she died. A rabbi wrote the words for him in Russian letters, since he could not read Hebrew, and he went to the synagogue in Moscow on the anniversary of her death to light a candle and say the proper words. "I went with some fear," he said. "It was dangerous for a young person to go into a synagogue."

It was also dangerous for a mature individual to be seen entering a synagogue. Promises made to dying parents and grand-parents, however, were hard to break. A professor of biochemistry at the University of Kiev told of the elaborate plans he made every year to attend meetings or conferences in Moscow at the time of his father's *yahrzeit*. Unknown outside his native city, he could slip into the synagogue and say the traditional blessings in the proper way.

Though Yuri B., a fifty-year-old economist from Moscow, was sure that there were no authentic, observant Jews after the turn of the century, the stories his contemporaries tell show that traditions were maintained in secret within families long after public worship was forbidden. Zinaida T., an art historian from Moscow, attributed her Jewish awareness to her grand-mother. The grandmother was a doctor, a woman who was emancipated from the time of the Revolution, but who had mysteriously retained what her granddaughter called "the old Jewish mentality." She taught Zinaida to speak Yiddish. She ordered matzah for Passover and cooked in the traditional Jewish style, evoking memories of holidays that could not be celebrated openly. One family came together on every Jewish holiday, but "to mask for the neighbors we pretended that each one was someone's birthday." The efforts to subvert the prohibitions against Jewish assembly and worship created feelings of independence and assertiveness and kept the sense of identity alive.

Soviet Jews who had no positive Jewish experiences, however, spoke of their Jewish identity as an unmitigated misfortune. "The worst thing that can happen to a child is to be born Jewish," said Albert D., a forty-year-old engineer and journalist from Odessa. "It would be better to be an Eskimo or African savage." Emigrés spoke bitterly of their resentment against a society that made Jews work so much harder than Russians for acceptance. "My Jewish identity comes from my last name, from the ridicule of students and from the anti-Jewish sentiments that are so deeply ingrained in the Russian people," said another journalist from Odessa. In the little villages, grand-mothers put their grandchildren to bed with "Go to sleep or the *Zhid* will come!" It was, however, not only the "simple" people but the city people who, without thinking, said, "He is a Jew, but a nice man." Alla G., the only Jewish girl in her class in Magnitogorsk, found that even a teacher's praise could cause her grief. She was eleven when her teacher, who was a Tatar, said, "Alla is not Russian—she is Jewish; but her test is perfect." Eighteen years later she still remembered her embarrassment. "It was awful," she said. "Suddenly everybody is asking me what is Jewish and who is Jewish and are Jews people from another planet."

When Alla asked her mother why there was so much excitement about her Jewishness, her mother told her about Jewish history and pogroms. She heard for the first time about her religious grandparents who had died in Babi Yar and learned that she must not lie about being Jewish but also not speak of it out loud. "I knew that I must keep it to myself because no one will want to hear about it in the city of Magnitogorsk and the rest of Russia as well."

When schoolteachers tried to make it easier for Jewish students, their good intentions were remembered as part of the problem. Irma Z., at the age of forty, remembered that she was the only Jew in her class when she was nine. The teacher came up to her desk so she could whisper her nationality without the others hearing, but she didn't understand and shouted, "Jewish," just as the others had shouted, "Russian." "Everyone laughed," she said, "in a way that made me understand that it was shameful to be a Jew."

In spite of all the promises of equality if Soviet Jews would separate themselves from their history, religion and traditions, émigré stories reveal a deeply rooted, irrational anti-Semitism encouraged by official policy. Jews learned as children that to be visible was to be vulnerable. Those who could hide behind Russian names and faces hid as long as possible. Those who could not tried to compensate for their "defect" by working harder, paying larger bribes, cultivating all the possible connections so that they might not be caught for life in the lowest levels of society, where anti-Semitism was likely to be the strongest. It was generally believed that safety and civility would be found in the academic institutions and in the places where educated people recognized Jews as peers rather than threatening pariahs. Soviet Jews cherished their Russian friends who were free of the anti-Semitism they spoke of as a national sickness. They were remembered as the exceptional people, the rare friends who made life possible.

Children of parents who did not identify themselves as Jewish within the family were almost invariably taught a different lesson by their playmates. The experience, though not life-threatening, was never forgotten. "I was five," said a forty-year-old engineer from Odessa, "when this older boy threw me on the pavement, sat on my chest and took me by the ears and beat my head on the pavement, spitting and crying, 'Jew, Jew, Jew.' I couldn't understand what I had done to deserve this, but I knew from then on that I was different and a Jew and because of that would have my face spat at and my head beaten."

Efim S., growing up in Moscow, began by identifying with his enemies. "I hurled my first anti-Semitic slurs when I was five," he said, "and was as good an anti-Semite as any kid on the block." In 1961 his family lived in the house next to the Israeli Embassy. The Israeli boys brandished their toy water guns, and he and his friends skirmished with them and called them "kike kids." "I, with my Jewish accent, yelled, 'You damn Jews get out of our yard.' My mother saw this and said nothing. She waited for me to go to school. I came home the first day asking, 'How come they call me a Jew?' And she said, 'Because you are.' "

Efim S. was his class scapegoat. "There I was, this chubby kid with puffy cheeks and fat legs," he recalled. "I was a poor writer but the best reader in the class. I had a good memory and could recite long verses by heart. The teacher liked me, but I was fat, learned and Jewish. What more could the kids ask for?"

The childhood assaults were even more troublesome during World War II. Kira G. did not know she was Jewish until the kids in her yard greeted her with "Now you will be killed because you are a Jew." She was eight years old at the time. Yelena K., from Leningrad, had a similar experience in the small town in the Urals to which her school had been evacuated. She was in the fifth grade, and when she gave her nationality, the boy sitting next to her said, "Now I will kill you." Fear of him kept her from going to school until her boredom at home became greater than the fear. She went to school thinking, If he kills me, he kills me.

Some émigrés described overwhelming terror during the time of the Doctors' Plot and the postwar fear that Stalin would carry out his plan to deport and possibly exterminate all the Jews in the Soviet Union. Others remembered the everyday efforts to avoid confrontation and insult. A husband described his wife's daily efforts to apply her makeup so that it would diminish the Jewish curve of her nose. Anastasia N., a psychologist from Leningrad, remembered watching children pushing to get ahead in a line, "thinking, If I were Russian I could push like the others, but since I am a Jewess I must be careful lest someone accuse me of pushing. I never dared to push. I realized my inferiority."

Anna D., a physician born in Moscow in 1918, remembered a time when Jewishness was not a problem for her and her friends. "Before World War II our parents would ask, 'Whom did you meet? Was he Jewish or Russian?' And we couldn't answer because we paid no attention and didn't know among our friends who was Jewish and who wasn't. The subject never came up and we were absolutely indifferent to it. At that time Russian intellectuals were disturbed by the anti-Semitism of nonintellectuals. We Jews were used to it and ignored it." Like many in her generation, she believed that anti-Semitism had been brought by the Germans and that the bad feelings began during the war when Jews were being killed not as communists or as partisans, but only as Jews.

Konstantin S., the son of a military man, a lieutenant colonel who was a member of the Communist Party and served in Stalin's guard, had heard from his father that anti-Semitism began in 1943 when the Byelorussian leader Mazerov decreed that Jews should not be allowed to take part in partisan combat. Other reports from the Ukraine suggested that Ukrainians believed that they had lost their freedom because of the Revolution and blamed the Jewish Bolsheviks for their troubles.

Some of the younger émigrés, who had no memories of the years when Jews were under attack as "cosmopolitans" or as murderous doctors, thought that Jewish problems had begun in 1967. Still others blamed the State of Israel and the early émigrés for the decision to keep Jews out of the institutions of higher education. Older émigrés, however, remembered the impact of Stalin's toast, "To the great Russian people," in 1944—the first public notice that Jews would not be counted as Russians.

In an address to a delegation from the French Socialist Party in May 1956, Nikita Khrushchev explained and defended the Soviet attitude toward Jews. "At the outset of the Revolution we had many Jews in the leadership of the Party and the State," he said. "They were educated, maybe more revolutionary than the average Russian. In due course, we have created our new cadres. Should the Jews want to occupy the foremost positions in our republic now, it would naturally be taken amiss by the indigenous inhabitants . . . who do not consider themselves less intelligent or less capable than the Jews."

That kind of logic prevailed. It was accepted as natural that Jews in important positions would create jealousy and hostility. Jews meanwhile felt themselves to be second-class citizens. Though some had lived in Moscow or Leningrad for three generations, the "J" on their passports separated them from the "indigenous" population. Moishe S., a fifty-five-year-old painter from Odessa, looking for an image that described his feelings as a Jew in the Soviet Union, said, "To understand the problems of an average Jew in Russia you have to imagine a rabbit surrounded by wolves, trying somehow to live with them in the same forest."

All the efforts to maintain perspective and all the discussions about Russian xenophobia and "the natural anti-Semitism of Ukrainians" were of no help in mitigating the pain of personal confrontations with anti-Semites. Galina K., an English teacher from Leningrad, remembered that there was no escape from the problem because the people with whom they shared their apartment were anti-Semitic and never concealed their feelings. She said, "I was always on the alert for a harsh word, always scared. My parents were the same. They thought that if I behaved perfectly and was excellent in school, that would save me." When she became a teacher she begged her father not to go to synagogue because it might threaten her job.

Everyone who graduated from high school in Odessa in the fifties had a story to tell about gold medals. Jewish parents urged their children to study hard and try for the gold medal that made it possible to enter a university without taking entrance exams. So many succeeded in their studies that it was forbidden to give Jews gold medals. Those who earned one got a silver medal. Those who earned a silver medal got nothing. All students were offered the same opportunity to prepare and take exams, but the results of the tests could not be seen. The quotas for Jews were unwritten but maintained. Those who were accepted explained that "Jews are a minority. If they accept ten Russians and one Jew, it is as if they took ten Jews." Those who were rejected were less philosophical.

Rejections of other kinds were also remembered. Rosa G. was born in 1925 in Kiev and grew up during the brief period when Jews thought the days of exclusion were over forever. At the end of World War II there were requests for volunteers to help rebuild the bombed cities. "They were begging for people to come," she said. "I volunteered out of a sincere desire to help rebuild my country. And they refused me. I couldn't understand why until told to my face, 'You are not Ukrainian. You are a Jew, and we do not want your help.'"

Misha H., a seventy-year-old violinist and conductor, underwent a common experience in a Moscow subway. "A man, not intoxicated, unknown to me, said, 'You Jewish muzzle. When will you be deported from Moscow? There are too many Jewish muzzles in this city.' The expression he used was 'Zhidovskaya morda,' which meant I was a dog. A person has a face. A dog has a muzzle." Misha H. might not have taken it to heart but for the fact that a military officer sitting next to the man pretended not to hear and made no effort to shut him up. Nor did he get any sympathy from his neighbor, who said there might be some truth in the man's complaint. She too believed that there were too many Jews in the capital. She remembered when Jews had held important positions and did not think that right. "The Russian people are the owners of this country," she said, apparently expecting Misha to understand her feelings. There were also practical considerations. She reminded him that it was still hard to get a telephone in Moscow. Convinced that most of the telephones belonged to Jews, she was sure that many would be made available to Russians if the Jews left Moscow.

Natasha U., a translator and interpreter at a scientific institute in Moscow, had escaped the usual insults and rejections because of her Russian name and appearance. She was undeceived, however, when it came time to acquire an assistant. The chief engineer for whom she worked gave her permission to find someone, but added, "Please Natasha, don't be insulted—you know how I respect you; but it must not be a Jew. You understand it's not my idea." Natasha, explaining the circumstances, apologized for him. She said, "He was not a bad man. It was just the way it was."

Trying to remember a time when Jews had been treated with respect, Abram A. ironically recalled his years of imprisonment. It was just before World War II, and Jews were appreciated in the brigades because they tried to make the harsh life easier. "A Jew at the head of a brigade didn't work his men to death. He tried to bribe and outwit the leaders and preserve the prisoners. When a Russian became head of a brigade, he'd get a club and beat the members of his own team. He saw himself as a representative of the administration."

During World War II there were half a million Jews in the Red Army. More than a hundred Jewish generals were decorated as "Heroes of the Soviet Union." Though Jews made up a tenth of the army population, they ranked fifth among medal winners for bravery in battle. The facts, however, were buried beneath the propaganda that depicted Jews as weaklings and cowards who sat out the war in Tashkent. Jews were themselves unsure of their history. Only those who were old enough to remember the past could tell what had really happened.

Many émigrés fear that Jews and Judaism cannot survive in the Soviet Union. They worry that official efforts to turn educated Jews into Russian workers will succeed and that Jews will lose their identity. Prohibitions against Jewish study and assembly seem too strong to resist. They tell of Jews who actually seem to have forgotten who they are and behave as if suffering from amnesia, without awareness of what they have lost. In their descriptions of their own reawakening they illuminate the torpor from which they escaped.

Mikhael M. had difficulty finding work as an electromechanical engineer in Odessa and in Moscow. He went to Yerevan, in Armenia, to escape the problems that stemmed from being Jewish. Away from the prejudices of Odessa with its large Jewish population and its restrictions to keep Jews out of the university and places of power, he could relax and forget who he was. His Armenian colleagues were not prejudiced against Jews, but they forced him to think about himself as a Jew. One night he was at a dinner party at the institute where he worked. He was surrounded by Armenians speaking Armenian, singing Armenian songs. "I began to think," he said, "How is this possible? Here was a small nation like the Jewish nation. They looked like Jews. They lived peacefully in their own territory, singing without shame in their own language. I was never at a dinner table in Moscow among Jews singing Jewish songs. We were Jews only at birth, marriage and death."

Awareness of the abnormality of the Jewish situation was especially likely to strike Soviet Jews when they were away from home. An architect who designed hotels, sport centers and cultural houses often traveled throughout the Soviet Union. "As I traveled," he said, "I realized that I can study English, Bashkirian, Azerbaijanian or German without any problem. Studying Yiddish or Hebrew, however, was forbidden to me. I can study Russian history but not Jewish history. I can study Islam, but it is a crime to study Talmud or Torah." He became obsessed with this discovery and began working on a collection of drawings on Jewish subjects. He was not able to show them in any exhibition, but it relieved his feelings to do them.

Emigrés who described themselves as "crypto-Jews," and as "modern marranos," admitted to unexpected bursts of Jewish feelings. They spoke of Jewish identity as if it were a time bomb, ticking away, prepared to go off at some unusual occasion. Men and women who for stretches of time seemed to live without hope, self-denigrating and passive, came to life and behaved in unpredictable ways.

Zinaida T., the art historian from Moscow, saw herself as a member of the generation that had been "crippled for life." She saw herself and her friends as deprived of "spiritual nourishment," lacking traditions, missing a religious rhythm of life. The discovery that Israel could serve as a touchstone to identity filled a void in their lives. Zinaida was sixteen during the Six-Day War and a student in the English school. "We were changed completely," she said. "I remember coming to class the morning after hearing on BBC that the Israelis had reached Gaza. There were several Jewish students, and we discussed it openly. Openly, as we had never before dared to do. We felt so exhilarated. It was incredible. I felt that I was just born then."

Rashel C., a twenty-year-old student from Tbilisi, came from a family that had never celebrated Jewish holidays or exhibited any signs of their Jewishness. She said, "When it was announced that Jews had won the Six-Day War, my father bought wine. My uncle and aunt came, and we celebrated the success and the courage of Israel as if we had taken part in the war ourselves. It was then that we decided to go to Israel."

Men and women who swore they were completely indiffer-

ent to Jewish issues and knew no more about Israel than about
Mozambique admitted that they had rejoiced to hear of Jewish victories and had been depressed by anti-Zionist propaganda. Jewish journalists who were writing anti-Israel pamphlets and articles which they signed with Russian pseudonyms
confessed that they privately delighted in the "excellent victory" of the Jewish people.

Zinaida T. watched her father, an economist, vacillate between his two loyalties. "He went through stages," she said.
"Sometimes he'd carry on about Russia, 'my beloved Mother
Russia.' Then he might for a while be more Jewish, more like
my mother and grandmother, who felt and acted very Jewish."
When pressed to explain what she meant by "acting very Jewish," Zinaida spoke vaguely of "family orientation," of unusual
devotion between parents and children. She was one of many
who spoke of a Jewish style of behavior that separated Jewish
families from their Russian neighbors. "We had Russian friends
in the early sixties, but by the mid-seventies it was no longer
possible. It just didn't feel comfortable after 1967."

It was during that uncomfortable time that Rhya K., then a
thirty-year-old teacher of Russian literature, found herself in
the crowd that gathered near the synagogue in Moscow at
Simchat Torah. She was a woman who had great affection for
Russian culture. She had once believed that there were no differences between the lives of Jewish and non-Jewish people
in Moscow and Leningrad. That was before her Jewish consciousness was awakened by the anti-Semitic nature of Soviet
life. She went to the synagogue in search of Jews and of information. "I came," she said, "to establish my Jewish origin. I
wanted to learn about Jewish culture." She had to start from
the beginning. She saw a *tallis* (prayer shawl) for the first
time. She met Jews who celebrated holidays she had never
heard of. She even picked up two volumes of the *Jewish Encyclopedia*.

In the crowds in front of the synagogue one could find people of all ages who had some interest in the Jewish renaissance.
There were Jews who had kept their identity hidden and were

available as teachers and models. There were newcomers like
Rhya who knew nothing but were willing to learn. Lyosha D.,
a young engineer who came looking for a Jewish girlfriend,
said, "The old people came to pray. The young came to meet
and hear the latest news about arrests and emigration. The synagogue was a symbol of resistance and protest, even for non-
Jewish dissenters. And the police were always there, saying,
'Go home. Go home. It's late.' "

Katya Z., an editor of scientific texts, said there was a hunger
for Jewish culture in Moscow among people who had only the
Jewishness of the fifth point on their passports. She once turned
on her shortwave receiver and caught the voice of a cantor.
"It was some kind of holiday," she said. "Just hearing the voice
thrilled me." Katya deplored the fact that she and her friends
were not "real Jews." "We would have liked to be but didn't
know how to go about it," she said. "I was in college when I
first heard the word 'Bible.' It's a forbidden book. I keep wishing that they'd start smuggling them into the country so more
people could hold one and see what's in it."

She and her friends who had Jewish parents grew up without hearing of Moses or the Ten Commandments. They were
not clear about the differences between Judaism and Christianity and knew only that religion was a form of "spiritual oppression." Many also knew nothing about Hitler's war against
the Jews and had never heard of what happened at Babi Yar.
They had learned, from kindergarten on, that there was no
God and that people who believed otherwise were backward,
uneducated and without scientific understanding. It was a
strong indoctrination. The pressure to disbelieve was so great
and so pervasive that it was not unusual for older émigrés to
describe their parents as "atheists who went to synagogue and
meticulously observed every holiday." A student from Tbilisi
spoke for his generation, saying, "My circle went to synagogue not because they were believers but as a form of protest, for the chance to do something forbidden."

Jewish identity takes as many forms as the people claiming
it. Some, through Jewish observance, say yes to themselves

and their forebears. Others use the same activities to say no to the government, to its restrictions and policies and even to communism itself. For some, Jewish identity is something private, a source of pride and inner strength, a hidden seed that might sprout and flower in freedom. Others see Jewish identity as a public stance, a reason to take risks, to demonstrate and strike, a source of energy that might disappear were there no need for strife and confrontation.

The men and women in this collection of memoirs all have experienced changes in their self-awareness and self-understanding. Some had lived as skeptics, aloof from a system they did not trust. Others had been sincere communists, true believers in the propaganda that shaped them. Some had memories of Judaism to draw upon, but most were totally ignorant. Several generations of Jews have grown up without hearing about Abraham, Isaac and Jacob. The exodus from Egypt means nothing, and the Torah from Sinai is not theirs. Lenin is their only patriarch. "Sarah" brings no image of "the mother of Israel"; it is only an insulting epithet hurled by anti-Semites at women with Jewish faces waiting in line at the bakery or post office. There are many Soviet Jews who have never heard of Rosh Hashanah, Passover or Shavuot. Traditional observances are unknown to them, and the meanings behind the rituals are unfathomable. Their stories, however, reveal what is left of Jewish identity when religion and language are gone. Many find it hard to give up their last ties to an "ancient people" with an "extraordinary history."

Leonid K., a forty-year-old mathematician and the husband of Rhya K., was slow to come to terms with his Jewish identity. Until 1967 he thought "the very existence of Israel a catastrophe for Soviet Jews." He saw them "considered traitors by default." After 1967, however, he watched something unexpected happen. "The more the government attacked Jews," he said, "the more they felt proud about being Jews and having the State of Israel. Many people became practicing Jews." He saw two consequences. "Restrictions against Jews, Jewish emigration and employment problems were blamed on Israel. At the same time, we believed that Jews were still alive and not in Siberia because of Israel and the possibility of emigration."

Those who do not believe that Jews can survive in the Soviet Union point to the high rates of intermarriage. It is assumed that the non-Jewish partner will set the style and the values. Emigré stories, however, tell of the role of the Jewish partners in intermarriages and of the "more Jewish" partner in Jewish marriages. In unusual times, the more passionate and dissenting member of a pair was prone to make decisions and take the lead.

"My wife," said one émigré, "changed my vision. She gave me Jewish literature to read, and it was because of her strong feelings that we began to observe Jewish holidays. She introduced me to families that knew how to celebrate." He described his first Passover Seder in Moscow. "All our friends, Jewish and non-Jewish, sat around a long table. There were soft pillows and we wore skullcaps. My son asked the four questions and I answered him. Everything was as it was supposed to be."

Another said, "It was my husband who had the strong Jewish consciousness. He introduced me to his Jewish circle, and it was the first time I learned about Jews. At first we met to cry on each other's shoulders, to share every insult and rejection. After a time we began to study and to think about Zionism and find out who we are. We were no longer mindless, blind people who could not analyze the situation we were in."

In the interviews, émigrés speak as individuals but find it hard to avoid sweeping generalizations. They have little knowledge about what was happening outside the small group of like-minded people in their own circle. "People were isolated from each other. We avoided any strangers who might disagree with us." Still, it was tempting to believe that one's observations had some general import, that one's family was a typical family and one's group a normal group.

Interviewers, however, discover that each memoir is a mirror of an age, a place, a particular set of parents and grandparents. Men and women who speak about Jewish identity and behavior know only their own feelings and experiences. Those who have deep feelings about their connections to the Jewish people find others who share their history and problems. Those who have severed connections to fellow Jews and Judaism, who have killed the nerve that registers pain and pleasure, assume that others are equally free to ignore the Jewish past and present. They expect no Jewish future and do not prepare for it.

The excerpts that follow are personal views of historical events. They illuminate the complex legacy that Soviet Jews have inherited and passed along "mouth to mouth"; oral *samizdat*, preserving Jewish struggles and accomplishments that cannot be found in official Soviet histories.

The Legacies

 "I WAS BORN on August 22, 1893, in Tsibulovo, a small village in the Ukraine," said Izrael K. "My grandfather was given permission to live there by the Tsar for his bravery and courage in the Turkish War. My father was the accountant in the local mill, and all our relatives lived there as well. The children spoke Russian and played with the Russian children who lived all around us.

"In 1898 my father moved the family to the city of Elizavetgrad, where he became the accountant at a large mill, and the next year I began to study at a *cheder*, where all the courses were taught in Hebrew. I mastered Hebrew quickly and on Saturdays could pray with my father at the synagogue. We were taught about the holidays and went on outings where we could converse only in Hebrew.

"In 1902 I left the *cheder* and was enrolled in a trade school run by an American Jewish organization. The teachers were Jewish, but the language was Russian. They were engineers who were training us in mathematics and technical subjects. And then in 1905 certain things happened that when I recall them now I still shake all over. It was during the time of hunger and strikes. The working class in Petersburg came out into the streets with placards, and the police and army met them with guns and bullets. Three thousand people were killed in the demonstrations. And then the tsarist government put the blame on the Jews. They said the Jews were guilty of everything, and there was a huge pogrom in Elizavetgrad, where we lived. My mother hid with the children in the attic. My father was protected by some Russian neighbors, so he stayed below and sent up buckets of food and water as long as we were in hiding. I was twelve years old and it was very strange and I wanted to know what was going on. So my mother explained about anti-Semitism. I had heard some things from the children in the trade school but didn't imagine that Jews could be killed and beaten. All around us property was destroyed. Everything in the stores was taken. And then after three days or so things calmed down. Everyone could see that the Jews were punished, and life could go back to normal.

"Anti-Semitism in tsarist days had limits. Jews were cut up and killed, but the religion was not touched. Jewish schools kept on functioning. Jewish newspapers in Yiddish and Hebrew were published. In 1906 my parents hired a tutor to prepare me for the gymnasium [academic secondary school]. My mother was set on this even though there was a two-percent quota for Jews and a large sum to be paid. We were a poor family. My father earned only forty rubles a month. My mother went to her father with tears in her eyes to beg for his help. He agreed. When a commercial school without a quota opened up, I was accepted and my grandfather paid the tuition. I entered in the fifth grade and graduated with honors in 1912.

"The commercial school gave me the same right to higher education as the gymnasium, but I could not get into an institute of higher learning because of the quota and the high cost. Meanwhile there were economic problems, and the tsarist government had created the infamous Beiliss case* to encourage

---

* In 1911, Mendel Beiliss, a Jewish workman from the outskirts of Kiev, was arrested and charged with murdering a Christian boy in order to use his blood for making Passover matzot. The case is remembered as an extraordinary frame-up in which officials knew that Beiliss was innocent and that Jews do not practice ritual murder. Protests from liberal Russian people and from outraged indi-

still more pogroms against Jews. I was nineteen, living in Eliza-vetgrad and giving lessons to other Jewish children trying to get an education. When I earned enough money I went to Brünn, in Austro-Hungary,† to take the entrance exam for the Royal Polytechnic Institute. One of my friends was already there, so he showed me the way. I felt guilty about leaving my family while the excitement about Beiliss was going on. I knew that the outcome of the case would affect the fate of the Jews in tsarist Russia. Then a year later, on my way to my lodgings from the Institute, I passed a square where the news was printed on a large placard and I saw: 'Beiliss has been acquitted. Beiliss has been freed.' It is difficult to express in words how I felt when I read that. On the next day I sent my parents a tele-gram to tell them I was coming home. I didn't stay home for long. World War I broke out and I was mobilized into the army."

Izrael K. was discharged from the army for medical prob-lems and persuaded the Minister of Education to permit him to enter the Petersburg Polytechnic Institute even though the 2-percent quota for Jews had been filled. He was in Petersburg when the tsarist government was overthrown. Trotsky came to speak to the students in March of 1917. "Trotsky finished his speech to huge applause and a standing ovation that fol-lowed him out to the streets. A few days later in the same au-ditorium, which held about three thousand students, Lenin came to speak to us about the Socialist Revolution. He said we had to take the factories from the hands of the capitalists and the land from the rich landowners to give to the peasants. The students began to boo and stamp their feet, and the Geor-gian student leader tried to restore order by getting the stu-dents to write their questions down so Lenin could answer them. I put my question in with the others, asking why a rev-

---

viduals throughout the world did not save Beiliss from twenty-six months in jail before he was set free. At stake in the trial was not only Beiliss' life but a government effort to establish legal valida-tion of the ancient libel of ritual murder.
† *Now Brno, in Czechoslovakia.*

olution had to consist of violence and anarchy and the killing of landowners and whatnot. Lenin pulled out a huge wad of telegrams and letters from his pocket and said that the anarchy in the villages was the Revolution. He said, 'I am informed that the peasants are killing so-and-so and the land is taken over in all the cities and this destruction is the real Revolution.' The students were booing and whistling and stamping their feet. The students did not support Lenin."

Izrael was in Petersburg when the courthouse was burned and the women broke into the Filipovsky Bakery shouting, "Bread! Give us bread! Down with the Tsar." The tsarist government, however, had already been overthrown, and anybody who looked suspicious could be arrested. He left Petersburg and tried to continue his studies at a technical institute in Kharkov. "The studies there went badly because the waves of agitation had already swept across the country. The Bolsheviks and the White Guard were battling in Kharkov." He decided to return home again, and during the trip the train was stopped and two armed men got on to check documents and search people. They pulled two Jews off the train, took them into the forest and shot them. The people on the train platform explained that the region had been taken by the Petlyura band, troops from the White Guard who were very hostile to Jews, killing them in great numbers and destroying their property. Certain that he would meet the same fate as the other Jews on the train, Izrael K. slipped away to the village and took a room at the inn where travelers stopped to wait for connecting trains. He carefully scratched his name from his student identity card and replaced it with a Russian name. That became his pseudonym for all his official documents. It saved him on his journey home and many times thereafter. Not until he applied for a visa to leave the Soviet Union did he use the Jewish name his parents had given him.

Lena B., born in 1898 in Mogilev in Byelorussia, came from a Yiddish-speaking Orthodox family. Her father prayed in *tallis* and *tefillin*, and her mother lit Sabbath and holiday candles.

She remembered setting up a *succah* and celebrating Passover. A tutor came to the house to give the children Yiddish and Hebrew lessons, and she studied sewing at a Jewish community school for girls. "We lived in the Pale, in a Jewish kingdom. But even where we were the majority we saw no love for Jews. In the time of Nicolai there were the pogroms, and every Jewish holiday we worried and were afraid to go to the synagogue. My parents prayed that nothing should happen to us on the holiday, that there should be no pogrom and that no one should come to kill us. The fear affected the children as well as the grown-ups."

When she was seventeen Lena followed her married sister to Zurich, where there was a colony of Russian Jews. Some were trying to avoid conscription into the Tsar's army; some were Bundists avoiding arrest. She married a Russian Jew from Poltova when she was eighteen, had a child and earned a living sewing aprons and undershirts at home. Her husband died young, and she married a Bundist from Kiev. They lived comfortably in Zurich until they heard that the Tsar had been killed. Overwhelmed by homesickness, they went back to Kiev. "I was cursing myself for coming back. It was the time of the Civil War and the smallpox epidemic. My husband got the sickness and died. I was left a widow the second time, with all the responsibilities." Later, looking back on her life, she decided that Stalin's time had been the worst. "You worried day and night, and there was agitation and propaganda against Jews all the time, and the KGB held the people so tightly, knowing everything. God forbid you should say a word. We were afraid the walls would hear. There was a telephone in the corridor, and when we had to say something we covered the phone with a pillow. And each person would tell the government about the other. Just dare to say something and you are already in a concentration camp or a house of correction or a mental hospital God knows where."

Maya G., a singer and actress born in Vilna in 1898, had happier memories of the Revolution. Her parents were "modern" people who spoke Russian and greeted the Revolution enthusiastically. Her grandparents lived in a backward village whose houses had straw roofs and no electricity, but her father was a self-educated lawyer, a cantor who sang in the synagogue in Vilna on the High Holidays. Like other Jewish fathers of his generation he was obsessed with giving his children a higher education.

Maya went to high school in Petersburg and could speak in French, German, Polish, Russian and Yiddish. Her mother taught her to read and write Yiddish so that she could send letters to her grandparents.

Maya was a student in the Psychological Institute in Petersburg when the Revolution broke out. Unlike Izrael K., she remembered "the atmosphere of the Revolution as a time of joy, of people in the street hugging and kissing each other. There was a kind of happiness in the air," she said. "We were taught that we would be one nation someday, one people, not Russian, not Jewish, completely intermarried, all atheists and non-believers." She remembers it as "a time of enormous enthusiasm and also of hunger and cold. We'd get one-eighth of a pound of bread a day, and I was always afraid I'd eat it all at once, so I'd give it to my father to hide for me. I'd carry my boots under my arm and use wooden boards on my feet so as not to wear out the boots. We knew we were in for bad times but thought the Revolution a good thing. Before the Revolution you couldn't go to Petersburg. You weren't accepted anywhere. In the schools the quota was set for two Jewish children for every fifty Russians. My brothers got into school under the quota and with a big bribe for the director.

"In those days before Stalin it was no shame to be Jewish," she said. "We had lots of Russian friends. When my mother wanted to bake matzah, my Russian friends came to help her roll out the dough. And in those days I made a collection of Yiddish folk songs."

Sophie M. was the daughter of a country doctor, the only Jew in a small village in the Kaluga province. She had received her early education at home, followed by private school run by a director with socialist convictions. She was eighteen when she entered the Law Institute in Petersburg in 1916. "I was amazed by the active community and public life in the Institute. There were mutual-aid societies and national circles, representatives of various parties. Political life seethed. There were Socialist Revolutionaries and Mensheviks, and the girl students were not afraid to get up and make speeches. I had to get used to this extraordinary intellectual ferment. I didn't know which circle to join, and there was no time to study at all. That's where I was when the February Revolution began. When I recall my student years and think of the student years of my daughter . . . Oh, how dull her years were!"

Shortly after the Revolution, efforts to incorporate workers' evening classes into Petrograd University led to a split in the student body. Many students were opposed to the idea of making the workers' courses equal to their own. Elections were held, with all the political groups putting forth their representatives. After the elections, the entire student organization was liquidated. There was a brief coalition of Socialist Revolutionaries, Mensheviks and the Cadets, the constitutional democrats opposed to the communists. Then the arrests began. Many students were sent to Butyrka Prison and from there to Siberia.

The Revolution is often remembered in personal rather than ideological terms. Raya B., a physician born in Odessa in 1909, had grim recollections of "everybody sitting in the basement and corpses lying in the street." She remembered people dying of hunger, and outbreaks of cholera and typhus in 1921. "We all got sick. My mother died, and then my grandmother died and my sisters, and we had no adults to look after us. We had no clothes to wear. No dresses. No shoes. Somehow we went to school and were caught up in the Revolutionary fervor. There was great enthusiasm in spite of the hunger and cold. People worked day and night as a matter of conscience, as if each person understood that something new was being

built and one could have a personal share in it. We were nour-
ished by the great hopes. Synagogues and churches were both
closed. There were no distinctions between nationalities."

She described her father, a pious Jew from Vinnitsa, as "a
man who could not stand up for himself and his family." After
the Revolution the local committee called him in and offered
him an apartment. "Everything was organized. Workers were
taken care of. Life became better. Schools were opened without quotas. It was a more democratic country than it is now.
My father was pleased that he had lived to see the new era."

Abram A. was born in 1911 in Chernigov, a town on the
front line in the Civil War. He came from a family divided in
its responses to the new era. His earliest memories are of the
relentless shelling of the town of Chernigov during the Civil
War. "The government changed back and forth between the
Bolsheviks, Germans, Ukrainians and all kinds of marauding
bandits. When it became still we knew the town didn't belong
to anybody.

"I ran around with other boys in the streets—picking up un-
used cartridges and abandoned weapons. I remember this very
clearly, as if it were yesterday. I was barefoot, only in shorts,
jumping into the puddles with the boys, when my mother
came running to say we had to leave. The Denikinites, the
White Guards, were moving toward the city, and she was
worried that we would be harmed because so many of our
relatives were communists. She was not a communist but a
Labor Zionist sympathizer. Barefoot and in shorts, I went with
my mother on foot along the highway toward Gomel. We
were walking behind the Red Army units and caught up with
the rear guard. They were mostly Chinese soldiers. I don't
know where they came from, but they were among the most
persistent fighters; when the Denikinites were advancing, they
kept shooting till the last cartridge. For some time we walked
with the units, but then it became impossible to keep up with
them, so my mother and I walked alone along the muddy
roads. This was Polesia, where there are many marshes and

swamps. At last we came to a small hut and decided to rest there. The owners received us kindly, but at night everything changed. A band called the Greens came. They weren't for anybody, only themselves, and they appeared to rob the local population when one group was retreating and another advancing. When the regular army arrived, they disappeared into the forest and became peasants like all the others.

"The Greens came with their regular orgies, accordion playing and drunkenness, and at night they took my mother. They didn't touch me, but they hanged my mother. The main reason was that she was Jewish. She implored them, 'Do what you want to me, but don't kill my son.' That's the way I lost my mother. Her last words to me were 'Go to Gomel and then try to get to Moscow to Aunt Nelli.'

"Still barefoot and in shorts, I set forth alone to Gomel. It was during the last days of summer, and quite cool. I was afraid to be seen, so I avoided villages and hamlets. Once I came to a village and near a church I saw several people hanging from gallows. Local peasants were sitting nearby calmly talking. Saying, 'For us the government is good, but we don't like Jews and Communists.'

"Outwardly I did not look Jewish. I had no Jewish accent and had blue eyes and fair hair. But I knew I was Jewish and had no reason to think they wouldn't do the same to me that they did to my mother. Slowly I moved toward Gomel. I ate berries in the woods and finally came to a little farmhouse where there was a weak old woman sitting outside. I went up to her and she welcomed me. She gave me a piece of bread and two onions to take with me, made the sign of the Cross over me and said, 'Go, son, with God. I don't know where *my* sons are now.' I wondered if her sons were among those who had hanged my mother, but didn't say anything to her about it.

"The next day I was near Gomel. I found my mother's uncle and aunt. I lived with them for a while. Her uncle was the rabbi of Gomel."

The uncle in Gomel was one of several rabbis in the family, and Abram A.'s great-grandfather had been a rabbi in Vilna. In

Chernigov Abram had lived with his grandfather, who "out-wardly behaved like a traditional religious Jew, but only for appearance's sake, in order to avoid conflict with the Jewish community." He was the owner of a fabric shop, was inter-ested in secular things and was very critical of his children, who were active in the revolutionary movement. Abram's grandfather, like others in his generation, believed that Jews should not get mixed up in Russian affairs. In 1921, while traveling to Moscow, he was thrown off the train by the White Guards and was an invalid for the rest of his life.

In 1919, Abram made his way alone from Gomel to Mos-cow. He was eight years old. His aunts were caught up in the fervor of the time, and Abram acquired an extraordinary edu-cation living alternately with his Aunt Nelli, a Bolshevik who became a minister in the government, and his Aunt Chana, whose talents in the black market made her, for a while, one of the richest women in Moscow. Abram's grandfather favored his younger daughter, Chana. He had respect for her talent for commerce and when she was young had put her in charge of his shop. He took a dim view of his daughter Nelli in spite of her position in the government. He was skeptical about the new regime, and Abram heard him say, "What is your entire Soviet power worth if my Nelli is a minister in it?"

Abram found his Aunt Nelli "in a little island near the Kremlin, completely isolated from the entire population of Moscow. She was at the Hotel National, which had become the First House of the Soviets. There were very many well-known people in the National at that time, communists known throughout the world. There were also many parents of com-munists taking refuge in the Hotel National. They were all wealthy people who would not have survived if they had re-mained in the provinces. I don't remember a single worker or peasant among them."

The chairman of the Military Collegium of the Supreme Court had the room across the hall from Nelli's. Playing in the hallway, Abram overheard him talking with a friend, saying, "I'm amazed. Why not open a synagogue in the National, there are so many Jews here?" Too young to understand this as an expression of anti-Semitism, Abram asked his Aunt Nelli why they didn't have a synagogue at the Hotel National for all the old Jews who were living there. His aunt was amazed at his question and his reason for asking it. "You see," she said to her husband, "even among us communists there are so many concealed anti-Semites."

Abram A. was safe and well fed with his Aunt Nelli, but unhappy about his isolated life. The children living in the National couldn't associate with the children outside. They had their own school, where only the children of top officials could go, and special club houses to play in. If they left the National to go for a walk, boys from the neighborhood beat them up. "I had run with the boys from the street and knew how to fight," Abram said. "They did not succeed in beating me; but I felt very uncomfortable at the National. During the Civil War years I had become a street child like Gavrosh in *Les Misérables*, and a regular life of going to bed on time and washing hands and face several times a day seemed of no use to me. So one bright day I decided to run away from Moscow and see the country.

"All Russia was on wheels at the time. People were looking for the best place to live; but everywhere I went I saw hunger, misfortune and sickness. There was real famine in the Volga region, and people were traveling with sacks of food, exchanging one thing for another. At that time you could buy a beautiful Bechstein piano for a sack of potatoes. And with all these sacks around, it wasn't hard for a homeless waif to get his hand into a sack and keep from starving. And that's what I did. It seemed more normal than the life at the National, where there were a good dining room and special stores for the high officials and no one thought of sharing with the people starving in Moscow. I traveled on the trains without any ticket and slept with other children at railway stations. Many times I was thrown off moving trains, but the trains traveled very slowly and I didn't get hurt. If worse came to worst I got a beating, and sometimes went hungry, but I enjoyed the life until the weather got cold. I realized that Russia's climate was not suited for this kind of existence. So I came back, but not as a prodigal son. I arranged to get arrested at the Moscow railroad station, but when I said I had relatives in Moscow they let me go. This time I went to my Aunt Chana, who had no children of her own at the time."

His aunt and her husband lived in a twelve-room apartment in what had once been the home of Prince Gagarin. The last tenant, from whom they had taken it over, was an artist who had gone abroad with only two suitcases, leaving behind a library of books, many paintings and valuable furniture. Most of the apartment was shut off because there was no fuel for heating; they kept themselves warm by burning the books in the library and the picture frames. It was a bad time in Moscow. There was no running water. The streets were not cleared of snow, and food could be bought only in the black market.

Chana and her husband were energetic entrepreneurial types who made their fortune during years of turmoil and starvation. Wealthy people fleeing Russia left behind huge warehouses of textiles, selling the inventories cheaply to them. They, in turn, recruited speculators and black marketeers to remove the stores for hiding in cellars where the Cheka (secret police) couldn't find them. Abram remembered that the bolts of fabric would come to the apartment on a sleigh under the logs for firewood and the pails of water. Then there would be a steady stream of people coming and going. They arrived lean and left fat, weighed down by the fabric wound around them as if they were spools. When Chana went to the market to buy carrots and potatoes she collected money from all the petty traders, never accepting Soviet money, taking only gold.

Chana's husband took every advantage of the New Economic Policy, but remained cautious and distrustful of the communists. He organized the first Moscow mutual credit association, and he secretly ran a textile factory of his own while working as the technical director of a legal mill. He opened stores for his wife to manage and meanwhile transferred money to Swiss banks and had passports ready for a quick escape to Latvia, which was then an independent state.

In 1925 he was arrested. His trial went all the way to the Supreme Court. Abram, who thought he wanted to be a defense lawyer, went to every session. He admired the techniques of his uncle's lawyers, who arranged for his acquittal. But he also saw his uncle leave the courthouse a free man only to be arrested by the Cheka, waiting for him in the street. They gave him five years for the same crime of which he had just been acquitted. His wife hid from the police for two months, but was eventually caught and sent into exile in the Arctic Circle on the Ob River.

Abram oscillated between his two aunts. When one was arrested he took shelter with the other, and he had kind words to say about both of them. He described his Aunt Chana as a warmhearted, generous woman with many dependents and friends who knew her as "a simple, democratic woman with an extraordinary amount of energy" as well as a talent for making money. At the other end of the political spectrum, his Aunt Nelli remained idealistic. Toward the end of her life, however, she told her nephew that she hated thieves and criminals, "but if a person is stealing from the state, he's not really a thief. He's just taking what belongs to him because the state in all its years of Soviet power has mercilessly robbed and continues to rob the people." In this perception the two sisters were ultimately in agreement.

Abram started first grade at the age of eleven under his Aunt Nelli's supervision. He went to classes with the children of Lenin, Trotsky and Kalinin. Too proud and ambitious to be the oldest in the class, he did two grades a year until he caught up with his own age group. He describes himself as a very good student, a devoted Young Pioneer and a loyal member of the Komsomol who at fourteen was elected head of the student government.

He describes his school as a place of great tension and intrigue, reflecting the vindictiveness of the adult power structure. A student accused of plagiarism committed suicide. Two girls were expelled for leaving a broom behind a door instead of in the closet where it belonged. He also worried about the "low-level" students who claimed that "Bolsheviks don't need to know any mathematics." He discovered early that "the serious students worked hard and the others became the bosses, the chiefs and ministers and understood nothing."

He was transferred to a school where the students were children of the aristocracy and the teachers all former professors at Moscow University. He came with a few other Komsomol members "to revolutionize the school," which had an atmosphere not considered loyal to the Soviet system. In an excess of zeal, he used his power as the head of the student organization to call a strike in protest of the arbitrary expulsions of students. He was ultimately expelled from the Komsomol and the school and dubbed a "counterrevolutionary" for his trouble. Not the least of his offenses was getting caught with stenographic reports of Politburo meetings. His best friend at school was the son of the chairman of the Military Committee in Petersburg, who amused himself by sharing information about what was going on. Abram A.'s privileges and problems stemmed from his intimacy with people in high places.

Aunt Nelli's second husband, an old revolutionary and Bundist chairman, urged Abram to study engineering instead of law. He feared that Abram's rebellious character and inclination to say what was on his mind would get him into trouble. Nelli used her influence to get him into the Institute of Chemical Technology. He graduated, went on to graduate school, but always managed to know too much and talk too much.

In 1935, at the age of twenty-four, Abram A. was arrested and given five years in solitary confinement. His uncle, the Bundist, was arrested in 1937 and condemned to exile in Siberia for life. A year later Nelli was arrested for being married to an "enemy of the people" and for bringing up her nephew so badly. She got what was considered a light sentence: eight years in prison camp, with no permission to return to Moscow.

The thirties would be remembered as the years of fear and trembling. Every family had its experience with arrest, exile and mysterious disappearances. Moishe S., a painter born in

Odessa in 1920, had no memories of peace or safety. "From childhood on, we saw neighbors, friends and relatives taken away to disappear forever or come back completely crippled. We took this as the natural course of life."

Zina K., born in Leningrad in 1936, introduced herself as someone born in the generation without fathers. Her father was arrested and shot when she was a year old, and she did not recall any of her contemporaries who lived in what she thought of as a normal family with a healthy working father and a mother at home taking care of children.

Sophie M., a lawyer who came from a family that had welcomed the Revolution, thought the fearful times had begun in 1932, when it became necessary to have a passport to travel to, or live in, Moscow. The people who didn't get permission to live in Moscow were visibly punished for their past, for not coming from the right family, not belonging to the right party. She was a lawyer working in the housing department and witnessed the struggles for the housing left vacant after those who were denied passports left Moscow. There were physical battles over keys. Shootings were not uncommon.

Anastasia N., a psychologist born in Leningrad in 1926, remembered the issuing of passports there in 1933. "Everyone was checked to see if he had owned property before the Revolution, and all so-called former proprietors who had had something before the Revolution or during the time of the New Economic Policy were not given passports. We were among the people called 'the deprived,' and we were supposed to leave Leningrad for some assigned place at a moment's notice. My parents had come from Vitebsk just after the Revolution, but most of the 'deprived' were Russians—former landowners, army officers and shopkeepers. There were practically no Jews in Leningrad before the Revolution, so it was not because we were Jewish.

"I was a little girl then and didn't know what was going on, only that my mother was crying all the time and my father was constantly agitated. Then both my parents were arrested, and I went to live with a distant relative of my father's, whom I called aunt."

Anastasia's father had had a business and a nice apartment on Nevsky Boulevard, which were taken away. She remembers going into a large shop where secondhand goods were sold. "Suddenly I noticed all the furniture from our drawing room—our sofas, our folding screens and little French tables. I cried out, 'Our mirror, our chair!' and this and that, and my aunt started to cry and said, 'Stop it, little fool. Shut up, little fool.' And I couldn't understand why I was a fool and why she was crying so bitterly. I didn't know that our furniture was being sold because we were all exiled to Siberia." (At the very last moment, thanks to intervention or bribes, the exile was withdrawn. Her parents came out of prison and were given passports to live in Leningrad after all.)

Lia K., a lawyer from Moscow, was living with her parents in a colony of scientists and administrators in 1937. She remembered the searches and the arrests of all her friends' parents. "We had one of the two telephones in the colony, so after the searches they would come to our house to call for the car to come to take the people and their possessions away. The houses just emptied out before our eyes. A friend of mine came home at two in the morning and found she'd forgotten her key. She rang and rang and got no response. Then her father came to the door in a white shirt and jacket, ready with briefcase, sure they'd come to arrest him. I should have been traumatized by all that, but I remained lighthearted. I was seventeen. My father lost his job, but he was not arrested. The mother of one of my girlfriends said, 'My husband must have been an enemy of the people or they wouldn't have taken him away.' That seemed reasonable to me at the time."

Raya B., who was a practicing physician in Odessa in 1937, did not remember those days calmly. "I knew many people who were arrested in 1937. What was so painful was that they were the best people in the city. The most honest, sincere, idealistic people were considered enemies of the state. It was on a mass scale, and we couldn't figure out what was going on. We kept asking how it could happen. Had we all gone crazy? I had a girlfriend who had graduated from an industrial institute. One fine day she was arrested simply because her husband had been arrested as an enemy of the people. She was exiled from Odessa. Secretly, however, she stayed for a little while with friends, and she wanted to see me to see if I believed she was involved with something. I and her other friends believed in her and tried to help her even though it put us in danger. In the end she was arrested and exiled. Our efforts were totally futile. In '36 and '37 it was frightening to walk down the street. You'd meet a friend, talk a bit, and the next day he was in prison and just having talked to him threw suspicion on you. You could be accused of being in contact with an enemy of the people. People hid. You couldn't find friends you'd known all your life."

The early arrests seemed more concerned with frightening people than with destroying them. Sophie M., the lawyer in the Moscow housing department, was arrested for a short time in 1925, but her friends among the prosecutors arranged her release. She had already witnessed the arrest of students and had taken it upon herself to collect money from trusted friends to send food and parcels to the Butyrka Prison, where they were kept before being sent to Siberia. Zarisa Y., born in 1943, was too young to have been an eyewitness to the arrests, but she heard about the events from her grandfather. "He was a well-known Soviet scientist, the cream of the Moscow intelligentsia. He'd been educated in Germany and England before the Civil War and was also a gifted pianist. He was arrested in 1928, released in 1930 and lived in fear thereafter . . . always expecting to be arrested again."

Most of the descriptions of the late thirties re-create the arbitrariness and cruelty of the time, from which no one was safe. Lasar R. was only seven when his father was arrested. "It happened in the middle of the night, New Year's Eve 1938, and the next day we were in a vacuum. All our friends and acquaintances had already disappeared. We always knew someone had been arrested when they boarded up the house. The telephone never rang. One courageous person, the deputy director of the Stalingrad Tractor Plant, took me to his home and gave my mother a little money. Everyone told me my father was away on business."

Yuli F., a musicologist born in 1927 in Bryansk, a small town in Byelorussia, was the same age when his father was arrested. "He was taken because of his 'dark past,' because they said his father had been a rabbi. He was actually the cantor in Glusk, not a rabbi at all. But every district had its plan to arrest and execute a certain percentage of the population as enemies of the people. They chose my father because he was Jewish and defenseless. He was a modest, intelligent man who couldn't fight for himself. He was lucky that he was not tried for political reasons like Trotskyism or for bourgeois nationalism, which meant ten years or the death penalty. He was only accused of technical sabotage after a drunken worker had caused an accident in the plant."

Yuli's mother, unlike his father, was a forceful, energetic woman. She went to Minsk and got a lawyer, and after a year of litigation the sentence was overturned. The trial, however, was an important part of Yuli's education. "We could see during the trial that there was no justice. You couldn't prove anything. There was this mighty force over our heads that was always right. We felt pressed down by something very heavy and senseless without any feelings or emotions. Almost every week people disappeared from our village. The first were people of Polish, Latvian or Lithuanian background. There were even devoted communists among them." Yuli remembers his own feelings of confusion. "It was a bizarre mixture of fear, frustration and fanatical belief." He had learned patriotism in school—he had been taught from kindergarten on to love Stalin.

In 1938, Izrael K. was arrested. "An article that came out in the lumber-industry trade paper asked why I was permitted to work as deputy director of the Lumber Trade Management Company when both my brothers had been arrested as enemies of the people." He was first asked to resign, and then, while pleading for his right to work, he was taken away. "It happened without warning," he said. "I was at a lecture at the ministry in the evening. It was on August 22, 1938, my birthday, which is why I remember it so well. I was supposed to present a paper about the condition of the equipment in the factory, but it was delayed and delayed because there were other engineers speaking before me. Then there was a telephone call, and after talking for a while the minister suggested that I go home and make my presentation at the next session. He generously offered me his chauffeured car to save me a bus trip. When I came home, there were three armed agents of the KGB waiting for me."

He resisted giving them his briefcase, but they took it by force and immediately began searching the apartment. "My wife, my son and my daughter were sitting in their chairs without moving a muscle. The men overturned the beds, the couch; pulled everything off the shelves. They took my workbook from my desk, my passports, my letters. They searched for about twelve hours and couldn't find any discrediting information. In the morning they took me to Lubyanka Prison.

"I spent several days in Lubyanka. They stripped me bare, searched my mouth, my ears and even, excuse me, my rectum. Then there were several days in a tiny little room without a table or a chair. Food was passed to me through a little window in the door, and a guard watched me constantly to see what I was doing. Then I was transferred to Butyrka Prison, where I was worn out and tortured for about nine months. They wanted me to sign documents that I was part of an underground counterrevolutionary Trotsky organization and that I had created diversionary acts in the factories when I was the director of the management company.

"I refused to sign. I was twice taken out to be shot, but I still wouldn't sign. A frustrated interrogator beat me on the head so hard I lost my hearing for life. They tried to drive me to suicide, but I wouldn't give in. Later when I was taken to trial before the Supreme Military Consulate I still refused to admit any guilt. I told the judge that I had been tortured, beaten and pressed to sign false documents. The general who was my judge said, 'Well, what else could we do with you when you refused to sign?' "

Izrael K. was sentenced to fifteen years of hard labor in Vorkuta and was grateful that he was left alive. He survived the first part of his ordeal in a cell among diplomats from Germany and Poland, Jews, the assorted people considered to be counterrevolutionaries, who were sent to either Siberia or their graves.

Sophie M., the lawyer working for the government in Moscow, remembered that she and many of her colleagues had been troubled by the confessions that followed the arrests. "We never believed there was any truth in them. Not for one minute did we believe any of it. The only question we couldn't understand was what made people confess. We thought hypnosis was possible, but didn't think there was physical torture."

Her perspective as an interested observer did not last long. "On July 3, 1937, I was out in the country with my mother and daughter. My husband was away and expected to return to Moscow. When I telephoned home to see if he was there, some strange voices answered and I thought I had gotten a wrong number. The next day my brother came looking for us. He had tried to reach us at home and found the apartment sealed. And with that began our life without a place to live. We stayed in the country waiting to hear from my husband and watched the lights go out one by one. We lived on a street where the army officers lived, and they were the first victims. When September came we were the only ones left, very far from the railway. My mother, daughter and I stayed on. We wrote letters and got no answers. We didn't dare try to open the apartment without permission, even though all our belongings were in it. Finally I couldn't endure it psychologically, and my mother, daughter and I went to Moscow to stay with my second brother and his wife and son. So we all lived together in one room, and when my husband returned he found a place to stay with a cousin. A few weeks later, after much pleading at the prosecutor's office, they agreed to open our apartment. Everything was upside down. A real pogrom!"

Sophie M. believed that the arrests and killings of the thirties marked her for life. "For many years after 1938 we lived in fear. We didn't have the strength to free ourselves from it,

and this led to far-from-heroic actions. I was afraid to cor-
respond with a close cousin in Leningrad because she had a
son in Australia and a son in Palestine. She needed my help, and
I did nothing to help her."

Her problems were the problems of a generation. Igor G.,
born in Tbilisi in 1957, said, looking back with youthful confidence, "The generation of my mother that lived under Stalin
are afraid of everything. They're afraid to say something because they remember the terrible oppression and are afraid it
could happen again. Even if they lose ninety percent of those
old worries, somewhere deep in their souls there is still constant fear."

Many émigrés are reluctant to separate Jewish suffering
from the general misery. When describing the arrests during
the thirties they take some small comfort from the fact that
Jews were not singled out for murder. Sarra S., a violinist born
in Odessa in 1924, spoke of the "international" aspect of the
purges. "The purges were international in the sense that they
weren't entirely anti-Jewish. Zionism was just one of the articles used for destroying people at that time." She spoke from
the experience of her own family. Her uncle, a dentist in the
city of Khmelnik in the Vinnitsa Oblast, was arrested and accused of Zionism. In the family he was not known as an active
Zionist or even a serious believer in Zionist theory. "The
charge of Zionist meant that the person was a Jew. My uncle
liked to sing and was known for singing Jewish songs all his
life, and that was enough." It was known, however, that Lat-
vians, Poles, Germans and Ukrainians died with him in the
same camp. That somehow made his fate less threatening.

Lia K., who had had a privileged childhood as the daughter
of a high bank official in the Moscow Ministry of Finance, was
a student in the Juridical Institute in Moscow in 1937. She remembered another kind of response to the events. "My friends
and I at the University were having a good time while everything was falling to pieces all around us. We went skiing,
drinking and singing. We gave ourselves a holiday when our
professor didn't show up to give a lecture because he'd been

arrested as an enemy of the people. We believed the propaganda that surrounded us. It was an ideological hypnosis. It was impossible for us to understand that people were not guilty and were arrested for no reason."

Frieda K., an elementary-school teacher from a poor family in Moldavia, was equally uncritical. "I was the kind of person who paid no attention. It never got through to me that something was so wrong. Every time someone was arrested they said it was for Trotskyism and I believed it."

The "ideological hypnosis" affected even those whose lives were ruined. Larisa P. is an engineer born in Kiev in 1934. Her father worked for the Ukrainian Cheka. He was a major when he was arrested in 1937. "I was only three, and I didn't see him again until 1944 when we were evacuated to Central Asia. He was not permitted to write or receive letters, so we had no contact at all. My mother, however, raised me in a spirit of uncommon devotion to the Soviet regime. She believed in Stalin and in the Soviet regime and does to this day, despite everything that happened. She is a humane person but a split personality. She did not think it so terrible if a certain number of innocent people perished for the sake of the cause."

There were "believers in Stalin" in all the generations, and also anguished skeptics, outraged by events they could not control. The need to have something to believe in was an important element in those who continued to lend Stalin credence. This did not seem to be affected by social position, education, religious or political background, even personal experience of arrest. One hears an undertone of fury, however, in statements like those of Berta R., a government-ministry employee born in Riga in 1910. "People trembled and were deathly afraid from 1936 to 1938. My friend's husband was charged with treason and spying, and it was nonsense. Absolute nonsense. And the wife was exiled from Moscow. Her whole family was arrested, and they had done nothing. Nothing at all. Her husband came back and told how he was beaten but had nothing to confess. And so many died there in the camps."

Abram A., who had seen his mother hanged by the Greens and lived with his Aunt Nelli in the Hotel National, had learned at an early age to distrust the Soviet regime. "I was an enemy of the communist government from the time I was seventeen. I always believed it was wrong to try to make peasants out of the cultivated intelligentsia. I thought sending people to Birobidzhan was very wrong. It was terrible to watch the destruction of educated people."

Abram's disaffection began with his expulsion from the Komsomol. The years at the Institute studying engineering and his friendships with other dissenters did nothing to encourage faith in the Soviet regime. His years in prison taught him "that human strength is determined by a person's spirit and will, the ability to concentrate and have a goal." He studied English during his years of solitary confinement. Though other prisoners died of hunger, he was convinced that he willed his survival to be able to tell what had happened to him. He found out about World War II only after the bombing of Moscow. He was then transferred to a slave-labor camp. Lavrenty Beria, who headed the Soviet Union's internal security system, had given permission to use skilled engineers among the prisoners. Abram became the head of a group building a petroleum factory and was able to pull out fifteen other engineers who were doing manual labor. His knowledge of English became important when tractors arrived from America and no one could read the directions. In 1945, while still a prisoner, Abram A. worked with Americans as a consultant and translator, always careful not to show admiration for American equipment. He said, "Too many people were in prison because of their appreciation of foreign things."

The private terrors of the late thirties were buried, both literally and figuratively, by the outbreak of World War II. Death and disruption reached all classes and places. Ordinary citizens were evacuated to distant, inaccessible areas of the country that brought them close to the prison camps. Engineers and scientists who had been given long sentences doing manual labor were now suddenly working side by side with free citizens for the war effort. The Germans bombed Moscow, Leningrad, Odessa, Kiev and Kharkov relentlessly. Jews were particularly vulnerable. "I would be dead if I had not been evacuated to Sverdlovsk," said a physician born in Kiev in 1923. "All the Jewish people in German-occupied areas were killed."

After 1941 the émigrés' stories of arrest, torture and murder by Soviet agents are displaced by memories of Germans throwing Jews down mine shafts, or herding them into ravines where they were shot down in view of their relatives and neighbors. It was a time of devastating hardship and cruelty for soldiers and civilians alike, for the millions who were evacuated and for the unfortunates who remained in the beleaguered cities and towns.

Frieda K., the schoolteacher from Moldavia who had been able to keep some distance between herself and the fears of the thirties, lost her illusion that "Stalin knew everything and was the ultimate savior and protector." She was twenty-eight years old, married to a soldier and with a three-year-old son when the bombs began to fall on Odessa, where she lived. "The war," she said, "killed everything in me." She lost her parents, her husband and her home. She and her sister were taken by the Germans to do slave labor. Her perception of herself as a woman, a Jew and a Soviet citizen was changed for the rest of her life.

Every émigré alive in 1941 remembered the hunger. Yuli F., the musicologist from Bryansk, recalled that a woman he knew had found a few pounds of potatoes in an abandoned field and was given five years in prison for "stealing from the state." Women remembered the war years as a hopeless search for things to eat. "In Siberia you could get milk but there was no butter. A small rabbit could feed you for three or four days. We grew potatoes and cucumbers if we had a bit of soil." Again and again one hears, "We were dried out from hunger" . . . "yellow as wax." Zina K., born in Leningrad in 1936, said, "I remember the war well. The dead bodies in the street . . . I remember screaming I was hungry, even though

I'm sure my grandmother gave me everything she had to give."

As the German occupation progressed, the concern for food became less important to those who were recognizably Jewish. From the beginning of World War II, Jews found themselves singled out by the Soviet regime as well as Hitler's armies. Ukrainian nationalists, Russian nationalists and Byelorussian nationalists accused Jews of being "double traitors." They had first supported and been active in the Revolution and then during World War II, when there was the possibility of overthrowing the regime, Jews supported it because it was fighting German Nazism.

The regime that the Jews worked and fought for did not trust or support them in turn. Jews speaking Yiddish were in danger of being accused of being German spies. Five or six months after the beginning of WorldWar II, Stalin ordered the replacement of all political commissars of non-Russian nationality; and there have been no political commissars of Jewish nationality ever since.

Yuli F. remembered the Soviet army retreating through Bryansk. "The planes were flying and the sky was lit up with flares. The peasants and workers were ready to celebrate the coming of the Germans. That was a big shock for me. They put on their best clothes and were drunk and very cheerful. The village people were very angry with the government. Ever since the Constitution of 1936 with the terrible sentences if you are late to work, even an hour or two. I knew about it because my father was the manager of a distillery in the village of Kavgary. He was an employee of the Soviet state and responsible for the people who worked under him. There were also a number of men who remembered their captivity under the Germans during the First World War. One man, a mechanic, tried to reassure my father by telling him that Germans were cultured people and very intelligent. He was sure they would establish a better order and that we'd have a better life under German rule.

"On June 26, the fourth day of the war, the Germans were

almost upon us. They were only thirty kilometers away, and my parents took a few suitcases and persuaded the crew of a traveling movie to flee with us. They owned the only car in the village. We went west to Doroganova, the next *shtetl*, and the movie people suddenly changed their minds and decided that they didn't want to leave after all. They brought us back to the distillery, and we felt it was the end for us. But suddenly a delegation of workers came to beg my father to stay. They told him he had been a nice boss for them and they knew he was not a member of the Party. They promised to protect him from the Germans and tell them that he wasn't a Soviet boss, only a good specialist who should continue working with them.

"My father agreed to stay. He had read about German atrocities in the Soviet newspapers but didn't trust Soviet propaganda. Also, he had been arrested in 1938 and falsely accused of sabotage. He'd spent a year in prison and had reason to be skeptical about official pronouncements. I, on the other hand, was a believer, an indoctrinated kid, a good little Pioneer who had been trained to inform on his parents if I saw something wrong in their behavior. I had also seen the Jewish people from Poland who crossed the border into Russia to escape from the Germans, and I believed the stories they were telling.

"When my father said we would stay and wait for the Germans, I began to howl. I burst into tears, grabbed my father around the neck and screamed. I had this vision of being exterminated with the others I'd heard about. My mother supported me, and together we convinced my father we had to flee.

"This time we harnessed a horse to a cart and made our way to the town of Pochep, where my mother had relatives. It was still a Jewish town in 1941. We waited there for a month, sure that the Soviet army would turn the Germans back. I was absolutely confident because we had sung all those songs about beating every enemy, the great victorious Soviets and all that. In Pochep we heard that my sisters, who were study-

ing in Minsk, had survived the bombing of the city on the
second day of the war and were safe in Omsk in Siberia. Later
we heard from my mother's youngest brother, Sasha, about
the fate of our relatives in Minsk. More than twenty of my
mother's relatives died in the Minsk ghetto. Sasha was the
only one who survived.

"Sasha told us how the whole Jewish population of Minsk
was gathered into a huge field in the outskirts of the city. It
was announced that Jews with medical experience and education and craftsmen like shoemakers and tailors should go to
one side of the field and the so-called intelligentsia, the teachers, professors and others from the humanitarian professions,
should assemble on the other side. There was a road between
them. My Uncle Sasha couldn't decide where he belonged. He
had finished three years of medical school but had not graduated and so thought he should not consider himself a doctor.
At the last minute his friends persuaded him to go to the side
of the doctors.

"He was there watching while they machine-gunned the
teachers, writers, professors—all those on the other side. My
cousin Abram, who had just graduated from school and didn't
yet have a profession, was there, the first victim of the family.
Those who survived that day were taken to the ghetto in
Minsk for later destruction. Sasha escaped from the ghetto because he had a blond girlfriend who was passing as a Russian.
She left the ghetto and made contact with the partisans. Sasha
ended up fighting in the guerrilla war in Byelorussia. In this
too he was lucky. The partisans in the Ukraine and Byelorussia refused to take in the Jews who escaped from the
ghettos and camps. Their excuse was that they would be more
severely punished by the Germans if they were caught. There
were rumors that there was an agreement between the German and Soviet authorities about keeping Jews out of the
guerrilla groups in the Ukraine and Byelorussia. It was no
rumor, however, that the partisans shot Jews who came to
join them and refused to leave. My uncle was an exception because he was a doctor.

In the early sixties, Yuli F. went to Minsk to visit the place where the ghetto had been. Survivors had privately collected money to put up "a tiny little monument." The lettering was in Russian and Yiddish.

Every family had its victims and survivors, its heroes who had died fighting on the front or who had been claimed by starvation while they worked seven days a week around the clock in the war industries. Soviet government propaganda claimed that Jews had not fought, that they had hid out in the Urals. Their mass deaths were denied. Alive, they were counted as Jews. Dead, they were counted as Russians. The monuments did not include Jewish names. Only in the Moscow school lobbies where each school had its war dead carved in marble could one find a Jewish name.

The stories told by those who were evacuated from the cities and those who were stranded in them are all tales of fear and desperation. "All mothers and children were supposed to leave Moscow," said Dora M., a seventy-year-old English teacher. "They came from my district and said they could provide transportation and take us to some village on the Volga somewhere. The law was that you had to go if you had a child. But I was teaching, and they said at the office that they'd take me when they evacuated the school. I went to work one morning and found they'd left without taking me and without telling me anything. My husband was an electrical engineer and had been sent to do some work at the airport in Voronezh. So I was stranded. I decided that if Hitler came I'd take my Sasha, go to the Moscow River embankment and jump in. Meanwhile, the bombing of Moscow had begun. There were fires everywhere, and the houses around ours had been bombed. I was at my wit's end."

Leya Y., born in Leningrad in 1936, remembered her mother trading treasured antiques for meat and bread. Her father was at the front, and her mother arranged their escape to Kalkas, trading furniture for whiskey and cigarettes, which in turn were exchanged for a place in a wagon leaving the city. "As soon as we got to Kalkas I got sick, and then the landlady told my mother to leave because the Germans were coming and killing Jews. My mother left me in the local hospital and she, my brother and my grandmother went to Kirgizia in a wagon. She wrote my uncle telling him to find me in the hospital. By the time my uncle came, the hospital had been turned into an orphanage. The Germans came looking for Jewish children, and luckily I had blond hair so the director of the orphanage didn't have to denounce me. They took the Georgians right away because they were dark and had long noses.

"I ran away from the orphanage and just wandered in the streets, begging, looking for scraps in the garbage. For a while a Russian woman took me in, washed me and gave me some bread, but then there was an order from the Germans warning against hiding Jewish children from the orphanage, so she became frightened and turned me out. My uncle came and went without finding me. Later on, after my father was wounded and got better, he came to look for me. He was with Alexei Tolstoy, who was writing a book about the war and had access to the lists of the dead. One day he was crying about his lost daughter to someone who had seen me, and he found me. I didn't recognize him. I was very wild and frightened and wouldn't talk. I was afraid of people and used to running away. Everyone thought I'd lost my mind, that I'd become insane forever. I wouldn't talk even when he took me to my mother in Kirgizia. We stayed there until 1944. That was when we came back to Leningrad and found everything stolen from our apartment. The ceiling was leaking and the windows were open and it was all emptied out. But we survived. We were glad to be alive after everything that happened to us. We had actually survived the siege of Leningrad and the Germans' chasing us. It was a miracle."

Frieda K. described an even more miraculous survival. Frieda was teaching second-graders in a Russian elementary school in Odessa when the war began. She was married to a foreman in a shoe factory and had a young son. She described her husband as "a very sincere, good person from a poor family. He was a Party member and very smart. His father died when he was very young and he had been working since he was nine years old." She remembers June 22, 1941, as a sunny, warm Sunday. They were just leaving with the baby for a walk at the edge of the Black Sea when there was an announcement on the radio. It was the voice of Vyacheslav Molotov telling them, "Hitler's armies have treacherously attacked our Soviet Union. Bombs have fallen on Kiev, Lvov and Odessa." That night the courier from the Military Commissariat arrived with her husband's orders. He was a commander in the reserves. He left the next morning and the day after, June 24, was on the Kishinev front.

Frieda saw her husband again a month later. He turned up at four in the morning. "Our son was sleeping. He tried to wake him up to spend a little time with him. My husband loved the boy very much and was so pleased that the baby was a copy of his father. He pleaded, 'Wake up, Lyona. Papa's come.' He put a record on the phonograph, hoping the music would wake him, and the baby opened one eye, saw his papa and closed it again. So he told me then that it was a terrible war, that they were fighting hard but our equipment was very poor. We had sticks. The Germans had tanks and airplanes. He begged me to leave Odessa as soon as possible. He knew the Germans were destroying the Jews and was very worried for me because he had heard that the wives of commanders were the first to be killed. And then he had to go back to his unit. It was getting light and drizzling, and we stood there in the street, both of us crying. He was wearing high boots and a military cap and had a pistol on each side and grenades and a bag with maps. He really loved me and our son—and that was the last time I saw him.

"Odessa was already being bombed by then. Every three or four hours they'd announce on the radio, 'Air raid, air raid. Take your children to bomb shelters.' My sister and I would grab our children and run to the cellars. We'd sit there for a few hours listening to the din of houses collapsing. We'd come out to see the houses burning, the dead people and ruins all around us.

"When they began evacuating, I went with my older sister and her two daughters, my son and my younger sister with a two-month-old nursing child. The trains were still running, but they told us to leave the train if there was an alarm because an airplane was circling the station. My parents wouldn't leave. My mother wanted to leave, but she couldn't go without my father. 'God is with me,' he said. 'I'm an old man. I'm not a communist. I'll work and I'll live.' We begged and cried and pleaded; we sensed we'd never see them again; but it was no use. Our youngest sister stayed behind to look after our parents, but she left without them later. The trouble with my father was that he had seen the Germans in 1917 and had not found them so terrible. He didn't understand it was a war of extermination. It was not like the pogrom he remembered in Dubossary. He remembered when the Denikinites had caught the rabbi on the way to the synagogue and taken all his clothes, left him naked in the street. He had gotten away and gone to the synagogue, alive. And they thought that was a pogrom.

"My sister and I and the children survived the train ride and were sent to the village of Meshkovskiy because we were teachers. They gave us a room in a small elementary school. They made my sister the principal and me the teacher of first- and second-graders. We had about fifty students, mostly Cossacks.

"The Cossacks were a backward people, and they were waiting anxiously for new rulers. They wanted Soviet rule overthrown so they could become *kulaks* [landed peasants] again and have private property. They really thought the Germans would bring them a good life.

"On June 21, 1942, parachutists landed and we were in occupied territory and the Germans went from farm to farm taking eggs and chickens, plundering everything edible and even taking candles to send back to their wives. The Cossacks were awaiting liberators, but the Germans came as victors and looters. They came right down the street we lived on. We were not far from the railroad station at Millerovo, and they transported the equipment destined for Stalingrad through Millerovo. We stopped teaching and watched the tall young

SS members with the skulls on their helmets. They came on motorcycles and tanks, destroyers bringing death.

"The Germans traveled at night. During the day they plundered and ate and drank. The women were forced to do their bidding and to cook for them. One day they caught a calf, slaughtered it and roasted it out in the street. They ate out there in the road, half-undressed like savages. But these were fighting troops, not engaged in extermination.

"After them came the punitive brigades. They were only after the Jews and didn't touch the Russians. One day they caught a mother and her two children walking along the road. The mother worked in the pharmacy, and we knew the children because they were excellent pupils in the school. The soldiers forced the mother to dig a pit. They shot the children and forced her to bury them.

"After that, they issued an order that all Jews had to gather in a separate house far from the rest of the people. It was a house collective farmers had once used for herding their flocks. There were no doors, no windows, no floor. They brought in all the Jews in the district—old men, women and children, fifty-eight in all—and kept us there for six months. We were forbidden to go into the town, and the townspeople were forbidden to give us food. They refused us medicine, and we buried three old men who died of infection. We ourselves dug the graves.

"I knew a Cossack woman with whom we left our things. At night I would go to get things we traded for cereal, potatoes and other bits of food. One night I came to her house and found the Germans had barged in and were making themselves at home. One of the men in shorts asked who I was, and when the woman said, 'She's a *Zhid*,' he raised his hand to hit me. I didn't know there were such beasts in the world. I ran away after he hit me and cried for days. I never went back to the woman's house.

"In October the Germans took us to help build a railroad to Stalingrad. I was twenty-eight. My older sister was thirty-four. Our younger sister stayed with the nursing baby and the other

children. They drove ten of us Jews out early every morning
in the cold. The snow fell early. We had to wear yellow stars
and worked apart from the Russians. The Germans stood
around us with automatic weapons, and if someone stopped
working they shot him. We worked the frozen ground, preparing the roadbed and laying the rails, and all the while they
shouted, '*Schnell!*' because the railroad was supposed to reach
Stalingrad in two months and the Germans were running short
of food and supplies. We worked from early morning till late
at night. At night we returned to the house, covered the ground
with straw, the holes in the walls with blankets. We gathered
branches and made a little stove. We wore dirty clothes we
could never clean and were covered with lice. My arms and
shoulders ached from the heavy iron pickaxes we used to
pound the earth. We went on that way until Stalingrad was
surrounded.

"We had no idea of what was happening," said Frieda. "We
lived from day to day without newspapers or radios. We had
only potato skins and a little bit of bread we got from the
kolkhozniks [collective farmers] for food. Sometimes we could
get a bit of milled wheat we made into muffins for the children.
When my sister's milk fell off, we had to find a Cossack woman
who'd take pity on us.

"A policeman, a former Party member who had gone over
to the German side, would come to search us for watches, as
if we still had anything. Everything we had had long ago been
traded for food. Still he'd come to threaten to shoot us and
throw us in a ditch. And then the chief bookkeeper of the
kholkoz was betrayed as a partisan. He was a young fellow,
twenty-eight years old, and they brought his mother, father,
wife and children, and before their eyes they hanged him on a
tree. So we didn't know what they would do to us—hang us,
shoot us or what. And then the Red Army came. The tank
came first. When the driver came out, I rushed out and kissed
him. I saw him as our savior, and he was amazed to see us. He
didn't know who we were or what had happened to us. That
night we left our miserable place and went to one of the houses

the Germans had abandoned about three hundred meters away. A little primitive house with a straw roof.

"There was a terrible battle that night, and in the morning we found corpses everywhere. And for the first time people went into the house where we had been locked away, and when they looked in they began to cry. It was inhuman, it was bestial to keep fifty-eight people that way. Six months without water and food, without any kind of help. The little children were all dirty and in the worst condition. Even the Russians, beasts themselves, were convinced it was inhuman.

"Later they told us that the men who had guarded us when we built the railroad had all been shot. There had been a time when I couldn't bear to look at a corpse, but when they gathered up the bodies I gladly dug the pits, and we threw the bodies in. They were frozen, no more than pieces of wood.

"The partisans were dug up and buried in a proper grave in the center of the town. A monument was put up for them. My husband was lost in Sevastopol. All we had was the clipping from a paper telling that he was a hero. When my son was in the third grade he took it to school to show his friends, and he lost it.

"My sisters and I went back to Odessa to the semibasement where our parents had lived. The Russians had already taken their beds and things. We were told they had been driven out, taken somewhere outside the city and shot. A cousin of mine, over forty, had lived in Odessa until the last minute and had seen what happened to the Jews of Odessa. Someone gave him away just before our soldiers arrived. People who knew he was a Jew were afraid they'd be reported as collaborators. The police who worked for the Germans didn't want any eyewitnesses left.

"When we came back to our own apartment in Odessa, it was occupied by the custodian couple and they didn't want to leave. I had written to say I was alive and coming back, and they had tried to sell my things before I got there. Luckily, my brother-in-law was a major and had a car. He drove to the house in his uniform and told them to clear out or he'd give them something to remember. The custodian cried that her son had died in Budapest, but he knew her son had been executed for helping the Germans. The custodian couple left the apartment, but I let them stay on in the kitchen. They had no place to go. I felt sorry for them. They were still people, pitiful people."

It was generally expected that life would be better when the war was over. The purges and arrests of the thirties were thought to be over, even though some men and women were never permitted to return to the cities from which they had been exiled.

Zina K. was only a year old when her father was arrested and shot in 1937. He was the manager of a soft-coal company, one of many Jews of his generation who had joined the Revolution in 1917 and who were destroyed in Stalin's purges twenty years later. Her mother was arrested as the wife of an enemy of the people, and Zina was hidden by her grandparents and saved from the orphanage which was crowded with children of arrested parents. Her grandmother, she said, had a tragic life. Her two sons and two sons-in-law were all arrested. Zina's mother was released in 1939 when Beria freed small groups of women. She didn't recognize her mother and for a long time called her Aunt Mama.

The women released from prison were recruited as informers by the KGB, and only those who were willing were permitted to live with their families in the big cities. Zina's mother refused and had to live in Tomachova, a town a hundred and one kilometers from the big city. "She came to visit us in Leningrad from time to time," Zina said. "It was illegal, and the militia men came each time. She would get pale as a white-washed wall when they turned up." During the war her mother was sent to a collective farm on the border of the Urals and Siberia. She kept the books and wrote letters for the illiterate old Tatars. When the war was over she was taken to Luga with the other people who had to stay over a hundred kilometers from Leningrad. She worked again as a bookkeeper, this time in a brick factory. Zina was in the sixth grade and continued to live with her grandmother in Leningrad. In the summer she would visit her mother.

"The summer I was thirteen I remember going for a walk in the woods, and when I came back I couldn't open the door to my mother's room even though I knew my mother and grandmother were inside. I looked through the keyhole and saw an open suitcase and someone's hands. They had come for my mother the second time. She had been arrested for not informing. She had been at someone's house where the host expressed some heretical thoughts. There had been four people there, and the next day the militia had received only two reports. My grandmother went from one prosecutor's office to another, but the court refused to accept her case. My mother was tried by a special meeting of three and sentenced to eight years. I begged to see her before she was sent away and was permitted. I could see her only through two rows of barbed wire, with a guard walking up and down between us. I think it is probably correct not to let young children see such things. They can never be forgotten."

Many who escaped the accusations and arrests in the thirties were shaken by the campaign against the Jews that followed the end of World War II. It seemed to Frieda K. that "a kind of epidemic against the Jews broke out." In Kiev it was thought that the anti-Semitism had been brought by the Germans. In Moscow, Jews blamed the State of Israel. "If only Israel had stayed in the Russian orbit rather than the American" was the way the reasoning went.

Sarra S., a violinist who had been trained in the Odessa Conservatory, was twenty-three years old when she returned from evacuation in the city of Tyumen in Siberia. She felt that the Germans had reawakened anti-Semitic feelings among Russians that she had not experienced before the war.

As a gifted music student she had led a sheltered life. She came from a religious family and had attended a school in which the overwhelming majority of students and teachers were Jewish. Oistrakh, Gilels, Richter and many others who

became world-famous concert artists were among her fellow
students. The feelings she had as a child about being Jewish
were not unlike those of New York Jews who take their Jewishness for granted, imagining themselves as members of the
majority. Her mother had brought her up with pride in being
Jewish and the awareness that there were a great many Jews
in responsible positions in government, industry, science and
the arts.

The campaign against "cosmopolitans," which she understood to be a synonym for Jews, challenged her feelings of
security. It began, she said, with Stalin's famous toast to the
"Russian people." Until that moment she had imagined that
"we are all Soviets, we all fought against Fascism, we had our
achievements in common and it did not matter if you were
Russian or Jewish or whatever."

Rhya K. grew up in Moscow. Her mother was a doctor and
her father an engineer. Her father had gone to *cheder* in a
small village, but when he became involved in the Bolshevik
movement before the Revolution he had given up Jewish interests and traditions, and his daughter had no Jewish education at all. She did not know that her father had escaped arrest
in the purges of the thirties only because he had been living in
a small city away from Moscow. He told her later that he had
expected arrest then, and he was not surprised when they came
for him in 1948. "He was an old Party member, Jewish and an
intelligent man," said Rhya, "and that was enough cause." An
old friend warned him that he was to be arrested in time for
him to burn a lot of papers and books. He had a large collection of Soviet newspapers going back to the twenties and thirties with reports of the Trotsky trial, the Zinoviev trial and the
Bukharin trial. The government had forbidden the saving of
old newspapers, and Rhya believed that her father would have
been executed if he had not had time to burn the papers. Instead, he received "only ten years."

Thirty years later, she spoke of her father's arrest and her
feelings as a witness as if it were something recent and fresh.
"It was early morning, maybe six or seven. I opened my eyes

with the feeling that someone was looking at me and saw the soldiers in the room with my mother. I began to cry, and they scolded me for crying. After all, I was eleven years old. I didn't know what was going on. I didn't know my father would be arrested. I'd been brought up as an ordinary Soviet child. I liked the Soviet Union. I liked my school and my friends. The soldiers told me to get out of bed. They looked the bed over very carefully, and then I saw all the boxes on the floor and everything a mess all around me. One of the men went out on the balcony where we kept plants and started to look under the plants. Then they demanded to see our safe. When we opened it, they confiscated my French books that I used in school and a copy of Feuchtwanger's *Moscow in 1937*. My father explained later that the book was the most criminal thing in our house."

Rhya explained that Feuchtwanger was a Marxist and he had written about Moscow very positively, but his surprise at finding so many monuments to Stalin had led to the suppression of the book. "My father's arrest was my political education. I knew my father was an honest man. But if he was an honest man, then why did they arrest him, without charges? My mother and brother went to the KGB day after day, waited in line for hours. That went on for three months before they were told that our father had been sent to do hard labor in Kazakhstan for ten years. They said we could receive two letters a year from him and could send him two parcels a year. Later we found out that he was sentenced by a troika—three people who didn't even look at him. They just read his name and called out his sentence, and no questions could be asked. My father wasn't a special case. From time to time we would see the black van near our house and know they'd come to arrest someone else.

"Something had to be wrong with a system that takes honest men off to labor camps in the night. My mother told me the truth as she saw it, and I began to read and think. By the time I was fifteen I didn't believe in the Soviet system at all. When my father returned after six years, I didn't even believe in

Lenin. My father still believed in Lenin and was insulted by
my doubts. 'You think it's so easy to throw everything out?'
he said. 'What did I live for? What did I struggle and suffer
for? If you throw everything out, it means my life was nonsense.' I understood what he was saying, but couldn't change
my mind. Step by step I brought him books to read. He began
to listen to BBC. It was a very sad day for him when he decided I was right."

Many among the memoirists found it difficult to give up
their faith in the system upon which they had based all their
hopes. Some were sure that something had to be wrong with
the people being arrested, only to find themselves taken away
without explanation. Some accused of being "cosmopolitans"
were not Jewish, but the great majority were Jews. The men
and women involved in Jewish cultural institutions bore the
brunt of the storm.

The Jewish institutions and the public who were involved
in them were attacked simultaneously. The Yiddish theaters
were closed, and actors who had been treated as the equals of
Russian actors became pariahs overnight.

Frieda K., the teacher from Odessa, remembered the arrests
of the Jewish writers in her city and the disappearance of the
Jewish writers in Kiev. "The Shtern Publishing House in Moscow was closed and all Jewish journals were discontinued. The
flower of Jewish writers and actors vanished."

When the Doctors' Plot was announced in January 1953, it
was perceived as a continuation, another variation of official
anti-Semitism. "There began to be letters in the newspapers
that Jewish doctors are poisoning people," said Sarra S., the
violinist at the Odessa Conservatory. "We would hear people
on the street saying there's a Jewish doctor in such and such a
polyclinic and it's better not to go to him or to any Jewish
doctor because it says in the paper they're poisoning Russians."

Moishe S., a twenty-eight-year-old painter then working in
Odessa as an architect, also remembered the newspaper propaganda. "We Jews would sit at our drawing boards listening
to our co-workers report on the latest scandal. They'd say they

had nothing against us personally. We were all nice people, but the Jews were all cads and bastards, 'murderers in white coats.'"

Anastasia N. was teaching psychology in Alma-Ata in 1953. Her mother wrote from Leningrad that lists of Jews were made for eviction and resettlement in Siberia, where special barracks had already been prepared. "The public prosecution of the doctors was thought to be the first step of a planned pogrom. We heard it would be followed by public outrage and then Jews would be sent to Birobidzhan. The trains were supposed to be ready for the transportation, and there were rumors of a plan to shoot people and throw them into clay pits. Such talk was very common. Everybody heard it."

Anastasia N. and her husband, who was also an instructor in psychology, took the rumors seriously. In 1948 they had seen many Jewish teachers forced out of the University of Alma-Ata and many students arrested and imprisoned. She had escaped the attacks, but her husband had been accused of "propagating anti-Party views" and expelled from the Komsomol. Her response to the threats was to study dressmaking so that she could earn something in the event that they were driven off to Siberia. She also wrote a disposition leaving her son with a Russian friend who agreed to take him to Moscow to her parents, introducing him as a child she had had with a Kazakh or Gypsy to account for his dark hair. "I was determined to save my child because we were absolutely sure that everything would happen as it had under Hitler and that even children would be killed."

The tension grew. Konstantin S., a journalist and literary critic in Leningrad, was only five years old in 1948, but remembered that "Every morning we'd find out about another child who no longer had a father." His father was a lieutenant colonel in command of the border troops in Kirghiz. "The slogan of the time was 'Beat the Jews and save Russia'—just like the old days."

Dora M., a seventy-year-old English teacher and translator from Moscow, never recovered from her experiences during the days of terror. "It was like walking along the edge of a knife," she said. Her father was taken from his work. Her house was ransacked. "No one told us why he was arrested, where he was taken. Nothing!"

Misha H., a violinist and assistant conductor in the Bolshoi, was expelled from the orchestra in 1951 as a Jew. "To say, 'How can this be happening?' meant you didn't believe the official version. People were arrested for having 'long tongues'—for speaking about things we were supposed to keep quiet about."

On March 5, 1953, the shock of Stalin's death broke the tension. Marsha L., who was seventeen at the time, said, "Everyone was crying when Stalin died, but in my house there was silence. I asked my father what was going to happen and he said, 'It can't be worse.' "

In Kiev, nineteen-year-old Larisa P., the Chekist's daughter, wept until a blood vessel burst in her eye. "It seemed there could be no greater grief in my life. I suffered as if it were the death of the person closest to me in the world. My uncle told me I would someday be ashamed of my tears. I condemned him and wouldn't see him again. He didn't understand my holy tears."

Victoria L., then a seventeen-year-old Moscow pianist who had once had the honor of playing for Stalin at a children's recital, read in the newspaper that "Stalin had geniuslike foresight, that he knew everything that was to happen, like God. My parents didn't say such things. They were happy when he died."

Rashel M., the English teacher from Moscow, said she could never understand why people worshiped Stalin. "They thought he was God Almighty and their Father in heaven, and if anything was wrong they wrote him letters, expecting him to undo the wrong. Well, I was never under his spell. I'd never been under anybody's spell. I knew the worst."

Rita S., a Moscow artist born in 1938, had a friend who was naive enough to write a letter to Stalin. "She was only seventeen and had formed a group of students to help Jewish children. She thought Stalin didn't know the situation and wrote to tell him what was wrong. The answer she got was that her little group of university students were put in jail for nine years."

Young people were trained from early childhood to believe in Stalin and their homeland. Arkady Z., an engineer from Odessa, said, "We knew nothing about life in the West. There was no Voice of America. Anti-Semitism alone was not enough to make one oppose the Soviet government. The great majority blindly believed in Stalin. When the doctors were arrested, I believed they were guilty. There must have been people who were knowledgeable, but everything was kept secret. I was among those who went out to the huge square in Odessa when Stalin died. I saw how people sobbed and wept, and when I came home my mother said she did not know what would happen to us without Stalin."

Whether people "believed" or not depended upon their age, on their education and also on whether the suffering touched them personally. Leya Y., born in Leningrad in 1936, spoke for those who did not, could not and would not know what was going on around them. "I stood away from politics. I was never interested. In Russia I knew nothing. In Vienna I met an editor who gave me books to read and found out that a lot of people were sitting in prison and concentration camps. Living in Russia I had known nothing about it. The government hid that from us. We didn't have any information. I wasn't in touch with people who were arrested."

Dora M., who "knew the worst," mourned the loss of her father all her life. She saved the letters he sent her from Siberia and gave them to her son, Sasha, to read. "He begged me to take them back," she said. "He said, 'I can't read them. It breaks my heart to read them.'" At a young age he knew about his mother's fear and lack of faith in their government. He knew that his grandfather had been arrested for nothing and condemned unjustly to death in exile.

Sasha was among the schoolchildren taken to Stalin's funeral.

His mother described the response to Stalin's death as "a mass psychosis." She claimed that thousands of people died in the stampede. "There were not only thousands of Muscovites but all the people who came on the roofs of the trains from distant places and the people who jumped from roof to roof to get nearer to the House of Columns where Stalin's body was lying in state. People just went crazy. Sasha, my Sasha—it was a miracle he remained alive. He was caught behind an old woman who began choking, and they tried to push her out of the crowd, and Sasha was holding on to her and was pushed out with this dying woman just before the stampede. He came home with one shoe and all the buttons torn off his coat." She was especially aware of the danger because her neighbor's son had been killed in the crush.

Dora's sister-in-law was a violinist playing with Oistrakh and other musicians close to Stalin's coffin. They played through the day and the night. She heard one of the members of the Politburo come up to Oistrakh and say, "Don't play so sadly. Play more optimistically, more cheerfully." Oistrakh looked up wide-eyed and speeded up the tempo. Everyone was weeping. The cannon were shooting. They began to play the anthem normally and finished at a gallop. Her sister-in-law came home and described it all, asking, "What can it mean? Why did he tell us to play more cheerfully?"

Three years later, the De-Stalinization Congress of 1956 would provide official explanations. Official history would be rewritten to fit the new facts. Ordinary Soviet citizens, even those who had not been Stalin worshipers, were expected to change with the times and give up old myths for new truths.

Larisa P., the Chekist's daughter from Kiev, spoke of those years as the time when "What had been bad became good. What had been good became bad." Her father, who had carefully kept his opinions to himself, had known what was wrong all the time. "He had even known about Israel. My mother said that he was a Zionist in his soul."

In Georgia, people took to the streets to protest against Khrushchev's speech against Stalin. Igor G., who came from

Tbilisi, said that people had grown up with the idea that Stalin had given them everything. "He was their pride, their love, their life. It was a great shock to hear that everything they had believed in for thirty years was a lie. They couldn't accept the loss of their father figure. They didn't believe Stalin was responsible."

Michael F., who was born in Moscow in 1947, recalled that period during his childhood termed "the thaw." He still remembered the poems to Stalin he had recited. "I joined the Pioneers to be true to his name. We were told he had defeated fascism—not the Soviet people but only the people under Stalin, because he was so great. We never knew that fascism had been crushed with the corpses of our people, or that we had lost the war because Stalin had destroyed the military leadership, or because we hadn't known how to fight and hadn't been prepared for war. We were taught only that we had attacked victoriously and retreated victoriously. Worst of all was when Khrushchev said that Stalin had harmed the communist system and way of thinking, that he had been essentially a criminal who destroyed enormous numbers of people. In the courtyard, children a little older than I were told to destroy the monuments to Stalin, and I watched them smash them as if they were idols."

Moishe S., the painter from Odessa who had agonized about the anti-Semitic accusations during the time of the Doctors' Plot, spoke of a "softening" after Stalin's death. "There was talk of restoring Leninist norms. We thought that there were some norms to bring back." Some young Jews were encouraged to find new opportunities in television, theater, film and music, even though the possibility of entering institutions of higher learning was diminishing. There was "access without nationality restrictions" in situations where people had special talents and were desperately needed, particularly where there were not enough Russian applicants.

Returning prisoners, and the rehabilitation of those who had died in exile, forced everyone—those who had believed in Stalin and those who had never been taken in—to confront the

monstrousness of the crimes that had been committed. Historians now called upon to rewrite Soviet history to fit the new
era joked that "We can never tell what will happen yesterday."
It was no laughing matter for the prisoners, who were broken
in body and spirit. Many lived out their lives as voluntary
workers in the places where they had been slave laborers. They
married, had children and accepted life as it was.

Yuri B., an economist born in Moscow in 1928, said his father had been taken away when he was very young and did
not wish to see his family when he was released. Yuri received
word of his father's rehabilitation and the message "My son
didn't see me when I was a real man. Now I'm too old and
broken to be seen."

Papers of rehabilitation were not issued automatically. Zina
K.'s mother was arrested as the wife of an "enemy of the people" in 1937, released without permission to return to Leningrad in 1939, rearrested for "not informing" in 1949 and released again in 1955. "It took another year and a half before
she obtained legal exoneration for herself and my father," said
Zina. "I was a college student then and used to come to Moscow to try to help her get her rehabilitation papers. When I
went to the Central Committee of the Communist Party, I felt
that the people there really wanted to correct the mistakes that
had been made. I also have to say that my teachers all the years
I was in school knew that my mother was in prison camp and
were very sympathetic. They did everything they could to
help me get a gold medal even when I didn't see the importance of it. I was lively and energetic in school in spite of my
traumatic life."

Zina, until she was personally chastised by the regime, was
able to believe that there were real regrets for the errors of the
past and some hope for the future. Rashel M., perhaps because
she was eighteen years older, was too angry for such faith. "I
don't understand people who are all-forgiving. I can't forgive.
I see people who have no malice, who suffered bitterly and
know the names and faces of their oppressors and still have
no anger. If I knew who killed my father, who actually did it,

I think I could strangle him with my bare hands. Luckily, I
don't know. I see these people acting like saints. All they need
is a halo. They have no need to fight back. It's something I
can't understand. My husband says that their backbones were
broken and they are now lost people. They have no normal,
human emotions. The spirit of resistance is knocked out of
them. I've heard people who were in camp say, 'I don't like to
look back. Maybe I *was* guilty. After all, I never supported the
regime, never liked it. So that's what happened to me.' "

There were many rehabilitated old communists who spoke
that way. They came back and were given apartments, jobs if
they needed them, a little bigger pension than the others. Their
children were not denied admission to the university on their
account. It was more than they had had reason to hope for before Stalin's death.

Izrael K., the engineer who was born in the Ukraine in 1893,
was arrested in 1938 and freed in 1953. He remained in Vorkuta
as a "voluntary worker" after his release in 1953. He had begun his imprisonment carrying logs to a cutting mill. Then he
was sent to work as a machinist at a power station, then to the
construction of a boiler room to supply thermal energy. He
received no pay for his work, but was permitted packages from
his wife and son. When they arrived, half the contents were
taken from him. Letters were withheld; he did not know when
his son was killed fighting the Germans. His experience as an
engineer, however, was well used, and he was even sent to give
lectures to free Party members who didn't know how to run
the turbines in the power station. He was in an unusual position for a prisoner. When he was released he was named the
director of steam and power for several mines, but could not
leave the area. In 1955, an order restored his civil rights and
provided compensation for some of his inventions during his
imprisonment. He could enjoy the company of his wife, who
was a doctor; see his daughter and granddaughter. He had permission to return to Moscow and enjoy some well-earned
happiness.

Back in Moscow in 1956, he received a call from the prosecutor's office. He was told his case was being studied, and he was asked by the colonel in charge to tell in detail about everything that happened to him in Vorkuta, as well as about his arrest and trial. He was disturbed by the request, because he had signed a document before leaving Vorkuta promising not to reveal what had gone on there. He was reassured and given the number of the law that made it necessary for him to describe his ordeal of fifteen years.

"He gave me a pad of paper and closed the door behind me, and I wrote from ten in the morning until five o'clock at night. I wrote about who had investigated my case, how they had interrogated me, how they had beaten me. I told everything. I mentioned other people who had been imprisoned with me and because of that their families received pensions even though they had died. So I did a good deed by telling of the horrors that went on in Vorkuta.

"A few months later, however, there was a knock on the door. Three men came in. I was lying on the couch, reading. I got up quickly, thinking, They've come again to take me away. They were representatives of the Communist Party in the city of Gorki. They had come to ask me to repudiate the story I had written for the military prosecutor. I was terribly upset. I picked up the picture of my son who was killed in the war. I fell down on my knees and said, 'I swear on this picture that everything I said to the prosecutor is true, not one word is a lie and I will not repudiate what I said.' One of the men said, 'We didn't even touch your wife or your family as we could have.' I said that that didn't matter at this point. I would not repudiate what I had signed. They sat for a few minutes longer and then left and went back to Gorki.

"It was because of this that my daughter and my grand-daughter decided to leave. They decided to leave the anti-Semitism and escape the destruction of the Jewish race that the Soviets had undertaken. They went off into the unknown, not knowing what America held for them, and once they had left, my wife and I followed."

Zina K. said she had kept her faith in the future in spite of her mother's long imprisonment. She was active in the Komsomol until the Hungarian uprising in 1956. She was attending a textile institute and had a circle of older, more sophisticated friends. They would come together to discuss the events in Hungary, which they saw as "an open return to Stalinism." A well-known dissident was among their acquaintances, and they were all called as witnesses at his trial. Zina was eventually accused of disagreeing with the Central Committee of the Communist Party, which had sent tanks to Hungary. She had the support of many students and was expelled from the Komsomol at a meeting of a district committee rather than at a general meeting. This took place just before graduation and the assignment of jobs. Though she graduated as a laboratory technician, she was assigned to a laundry as the foreman in an ironing shop. It was intended as a warning, a reminder that it was not wise to question the decisions of the Central Committee of the Communist Party. After a few months she was able to leave the laundry and look for more suitable work. A "high-placed acquaintance" helped her find a place appropriate to her training, and a year later she was promoted to junior scientist. She was able to get into graduate school by correspondence and ultimately had a successful career. She never, however, forgot her experience in the laundry.

Leonid K., who was her contemporary, a gifted mathematician accepted at the University of Moscow the year after Stalin died, also remembered his feelings at the time of the Hungarian uprising. "I felt betrayed," he said. "I was not alone in this. Many people around me were hoping for the relaxation of tensions inside the society, and we were encouraged by the things going on around us. That abrupt change caught us unprepared. And then things got better. The early sixties were probably the best time ever in Moscow. And then it was all over after two events."

Most Soviet Jews were awakened as Jews by the Six-Day War in Israel in 1967. Leonid K. claimed that it did not make any impression on him. He was, however, devastated by the Soviet invasion of Czechoslovakia in August of 1968. "It became apparent to me and many others that it was hopeless to expect things to change. And the last straw was the famous trial of the so-called hijackers in Leningrad. It was all so disgusting, so anti-Semitic."*

Leonid K. had grown up in a Yiddish-speaking family. As an adult he would remember them as "pleasant, tender people." He was thirteen when the Jewish doctors among his neighbors were taken away. As a college student at Moscow University, however, he was more concerned to separate himself from Jews and Jewish issues than about sharing their troubles. He was careful to rid himself of a Jewish accent and to dislike the Jewish foods his family preferred. He made light of the anti-Semitic experiences that touched him when he was trying to enter the University. The invasion of Czechoslovakia, however, touched the nerve that had been numbed. He read the newspapers with Jewish eyes. He was over thirty, older, wiser.

Leonid spoke like many young Soviet Jews born in the thirties. They knew about the purges of the thirties and the forties from their parents, but imagined that the bad times, like the war, were over. The brief glimmer of hope magnified their disappointment.

The generation born in the forties grew up with other disappointments. If they lived in Moscow or Leningrad they were less likely to be burdened with Yiddish-speaking parents and relatives with embarrassing accents and gestures. Konstantin S. described his father as "a very Russified, assimilated Jew. He was a Soviet Jew, not like the Jews in the paintings of Marc Chagall. My father was a military man, a member of the Communist Party, a lieutenant colonel. In his youth he was a guard who served in Stalin's guard and also Bukharin's."

His father was not touched by anti-Semitism until 1943, when it was forbidden for Jews to take part in partisan combat. Konstantin's father retired in 1949 after thirty years of

---

* *In June 1970, a handful of desperate Jewish dissidents who had been refused exit visas attempted to hijack a plane to get to Israel. Their plan failed, but the strident anti-Semitism that accompanied their arrest and trial led thousands of Jews to apply for exit visas.*

army service and spent the rest of his life mourning the deaths of his friends and colleagues. "My father suffered a lot from those losses," he said. "He once showed me a picture and said, 'This one was killed and this one and this one'—all murdered by the NKVD, the secret police. He wanted me to know that they hadn't died in the war but at the hands of the Soviet regime."

Konstantin grew up with a father who hated Stalin, hated Beria; who thought he might have liked the regime of Bukharin. He suspected that his father had saved himself at the expense of others. He had heard the accusations when he was a child. Though early in his interview he described his father as a very assimilated Jew, he later added that his father owned Sholom Aleichem's books in Yiddish as well as other Yiddish books published by Deremus, a Jewish publishing house in Moscow that was closed down in 1948. When the Yiddish poet Lev Kvitko was sentenced and shot, his father brought people together and read his poems aloud.

"My father," said Konstantin S., "was not religious, but Jewish culture was very dear to him. He identified very strongly with Jews, and yet when I was sixteen he urged me to write on my passport that I was Russian so that I could avoid the problems of anti-Semitism. I wanted to write the truth, not because I felt so Jewish but because I was uncomfortable lying."

Another variation on the issue of identity was expressed by Andrei P., who was born in 1943. He introduced himself by saying, "My grandmother was shot by the Germans. My grandfather and uncles were arrested in 1937. My father and mother met in a concentration camp, and that's where I was born." He would feel that his identity was irrevocably fixed by the time and place of his birth.

Every émigré expresses the fear that the Soviet Union cannot and will not change, and the conviction that Jews will never be secure because of the fifth point on their passports. The history books are easily rewritten, but the unwritten legacies are not lost or forgotten. Along with the fear that nothing changes, one discovers that children in every generation resist their parents and generate changes in spite of official policies. The interviews with Soviet émigrés born in the fifties are strikingly different from those of their elders. They are different not only because they did not experience the Stalin era and World War II but also because they want to separate themselves from their parents. In spite of all the efforts to force them into an obedient Soviet mold, they speak as independent individuals.

Olga D., born in Kiev in 1957, sees herself as one of the new generation who are determined to learn from the mistakes of their parents. She feels fortunate in having grown up under Khrushchev when foreign books and films became available, when foreigners could come to the Soviet Union. "We could see that foreigners have two feet as we do and they can speak and see as we do and they are not wild wolves as Stalin pictured them." During her youth Jews could participate in art, science and literature more freely than before. She believes that the Soviet people began to think about their place in the world and to wonder how to live with people who didn't want to be communists.

Olga is convinced that her parents were mistaken in rejecting their nationality, their Jewishness. "If someone is trying to think about the good life for all people, he must first seek the good life for his own people. Jewish people can be independent only as Jews, not as Russians or Ukrainians. They cannot be 'international.'"

Olga D. sees herself as a kind of survivor of the efforts to destroy Jewish life and traditions. "I have seen a photograph of my grandfather and know he was very religious. My parents were the first generation of irreligious Jews, but they kept the traditions within themselves, so it's not too difficult for me and my generation to return to the ways of our grandfathers. It's not so far from us in time." She was in touch with other young people who met secretly to study Hebrew and Judaism because of their grandparents. "They came to Judaism because there was something Jewish in their hearts," she said. "They didn't know what it was, but when they began to study Judaism they understood that what they felt was religious."

Marc T., born in Moscow in 1956, came to similar conclusions from very different circumstances. His grandfather was a Soviet general, an establishment Jew who took part in the anti-emigration campaign of 1968 and who still appears on television warning Jews against emigration and vilifying Israel. Marc's father is an aircraft engineer, still in the Soviet Union. His mother is an employee of Aeroflot. Marc developed his political and Jewish consciousness outside his family. He and his friends walked out of an anti-Israel lecture in high school. He made friends of dissidents and attended unofficial art exhibitions in 1974. He had contacts with Western correspondents and was proud to have been arrested five times. He thought his most important connection was with an illegal *yeshiva* in Moscow which brought old and young people together. The generation who had studied in *cheder* taught young people who had only just discovered Judaism. Marc had himself circumcised at the age of eighteen, and at the hospital where this was arranged he met the people he called the "secret Hasidim."

The "secret Hasidim" in Moscow can't be recognized in the street. They don't wear side curls or black coats. They do wear ritual fringes under their clothes and avoid taking off their hats as much as possible. There are old-timers and new converts among them. Many have only recently been circumcised. (Soviet antipathy to circumcision is so strong that a chapter of the Russian edition of Dr. Spock's *Baby and Child Care* was deleted because it claimed there were advantages to circumcision.)

The styles of rebellion vary from city to city, but émigrés offer variations of the possibilities available. Igor G., who was born in Tbilisi, Georgia, in 1957, describes his city as a place "where people look for material things, for money and independence. Life can be enjoyed in Tbilisi if you have the right attitude and enough money." He describes himself as "a spoiled child, the only child of divorced parents who was brought up by an indulgent grandmother." The grandmother, he said, lived like a European. She collected antiques, had a maid and a butler. People came to tea. He was sent to a government kindergarten for privileged children in which there were groups of seven or eight rather than the usual thirty to forty. He went by taxi in the morning rather than by bus like the others. He was aware even at an early age that it was more important in Tbilisi to find a way to make money than to have a career.

Igor G.'s mother was a doctor. His grandmother was a dentist. Though born in Tbilisi, she had studied medicine in Petersburg. She was the daughter of a rich father who had owned a chain of jewelry shops. She gave her grandson the kind of strict but privileged education she remembered from her own time. He went to a special English school, and though his family had memories of celebrating Jewish holidays, he was forbidden by his grandmother to go to synagogue or talk about Israel. "I was ten years old when the Six-Day War took place, and maybe because I was a rebellious child I began to speak about what was forbidden. I became very violent about it. I would shout, 'Let's go to Israel!' and my mother would burst into tears and my grandmother would be furious and frightened because I said, 'I don't want to live here. Let's go!' There were four other families living on the second floor with us and they could hear me shouting."

In this rebellious spirit, he went to synagogue whenever he had a chance. "I was looking for my origins. It's necessary to feel you have some roots, something that goes down deep in the centuries. I was a student. I was not supposed to be religious, but deep down there was pride in knowing that there are people who are my people."

In 1977, while a student in the Foreign Language Department at the University of Tbilisi, he took part in the student demonstrations to keep Georgian the official language in Georgia. "Jews did not participate," he said. "They were afraid because the tradition of hating Jews is so strong in Russia. I was strongly influenced by the Georgian students. They were nationalistic, and they didn't have the fear of their fathers and mothers. We had no memories of 1938 or 1948. When we went out to demonstrate, we weren't afraid we'd be shot.

"It felt great. We felt our power as students for the first time. In Moscow and Leningrad students are too worried about their careers to risk a demonstration. In Tbilisi we could take chances. Parents were wealthier. Jews had lived there for many generations without much anti-Semitism. Moscow and Leningrad were far away. Many Georgians wished to be a separate country, free like Switzerland. I hated Soviet power. It was the power that made people weak and frightened. It was the power that didn't let me study where I wanted. It didn't let me read the books I wanted to read. It didn't let me go anywhere."

Alexander A., the son of Abram A. and Irene A., also went to a special school, where French was taught from the first grade on. The students were the sons and daughters of Soviet diplomats, journalists and trade representatives who worked abroad. They were being groomed for study at the Moscow Institute of International Relations. By the eighth grade he had proved himself unreliable by refusing to inform on his fellow students. He did not therefore go on to study at the Institute of International Relations.

His mother, an actress born in Irkutsk, where her father worked in the gold mines, had married Abram A. without knowing much about him. "That he was a former prisoner was to his credit," she said. She knew that "the very best people were arrested and shot" and that those who were sent to Siberia as political prisoners "were good people who had suffered for nothing." She sympathized with them all. She was satisfied with life in Siberia and had no wish to go to Moscow. "If they wanted to exile him farther," she said, "there was no place farther to go. Siberia was exile and we were already there."

Abram A., however, was rehabilitated after the death of Stalin. He earned a doctorate and an appointment as a full professor at the U.S.S.R. Correspondence Polytechnic Institute. He was able to arrange privileged schooling for his son; but he kept no secrets from him.

"I knew all about my father's having been a prisoner and

how he was arrested," said Alexander A. "He told me all about it when I was seven or eight, and he advised me not to talk about provocative subjects with any of my friends. He said, 'If somebody starts saying something provocative'—and I knew that 'provocative' was about being a Jew or having a father who had been in a concentration camp—'stop the conversation.' He told me that the principal of my school and the teachers were anti-Semites who didn't like us. I trusted none of my friends. I had one friend, a brilliant student, who wouldn't tell anyone but me that he considered himself Jewish, but I didn't trust even him.

"I knew I was Jewish," said Alexander, "and that Jews were persecuted. I'd learned Jewish history from my father and knew there had been a few generations of rabbis in the family. My aunts talked Yiddish all the time. I'd never been in the Moscow synagogue until we applied for an exit visa. I was sure I shouldn't even come close to it. I was twelve at the time of the Six-Day War in Israel. That was when Russian people became more anti-Semitic and we Soviet Jews became more proud."

The Actual Life

 "I WANT TO TELL about my actual life," says the memoirist, looking for the words that will separate propaganda and gossip from his own experience. He is determined to distinguish what he has been told should be from what actually was. This is not such a difficult task for those who have seen and thought about the discrepancies for a long time. Many émigrés, however, had coped with difficulties by *not* thinking. In their accounts, they grope for words to express and explain what they themselves are only just beginning to understand.

The accounts they give of their lives are diverse, affected by age, education, work, by the cities in which they were born and lived, and most of all by what they call their "level" in society.

Nadya K., a thirty-year-old scientific editor, was aware of "several levels of status in the Soviet Union. There are the intelligentsia, the workers and the people who are involved in business. These are all different worlds, and as a rule they have no contact with one another. They are different people with different needs." Eleanora S., a movie critic and a researcher in a theater museum in Leningrad, is her contemporary and shares her perspective. She said, "I was always aware of the sharp divisions between the intelligentsia and the common people. They read different books, have different opinions. The common people believe what they read in the newspapers. The intelligentsia are skeptical. The common people listen to Soviet radio. The intelligentsia listen to BBC."

The separations in terms of work, however, began early in life. "From the age of three," said Minna M., "my son was taught by his kindergarten teacher that his mother doesn't work, that only the laundress works. I was a music teacher, and his father educated him in the spirit of intellectuals." A thirty-year-old schoolteacher said, "One can distinguish between the children of the intelligentsia and children of the proletariat by the age of seven. The children of the intelligentsia were cleaner, better behaved and better dressed. They didn't yell."

Differences and divisions that are considered perfectly normal in Western countries are perceived differently in the Soviet Union. Efim S., interviewed as a student at Boston College Law School, explained the problem as he saw it. "Officially," he said, "we are taught that we are all equal and that everybody is striving toward the communist goal. We are given to understand that the individual in the Soviet Union is nothing. We are taught that the Soviet people, all of them, want this, like this, hate that, don't need this. Every aspect of life is categorized and compartmentalized. You are supposed to be ready to live in this community of like-minded people. The family is supposed to die out under communism. The objective is to have a huge commune of people, an integrated social structure. At home, however, we hear very different things. In the street and in school we find out about the prejudices against educated people. We hear that the only labor that is real work is done with one's hands. Since my parents were both teachers, I was unhappy to find that working-class people thought of them as bloodsuckers, leeches, good-for-nothings who were fed and supported by workers."

Katya Z., an editor of scientific texts, twenty years older than Efim S., offered the perspective of her generation. "I sort of had a dual personality," she said. "I think all Soviet people have. One is for yourself and the things you really think, and the other is an outer face for the public that conforms with policy. You have to comply with the rules and walk in step. You have to vote 'for' when you are asked to vote. You just vote 'for,' never 'against.' That's what I now think of as herd behavior, but then I just took it for granted. That was the way I was brought up and what everybody did all around me. It didn't enter my head that it could be any different."

A Moscow pianist of the same generation did not search for reasons to explain Soviet behavior, but noted that "Russians are restrained, cautious, always afraid of saying something wrong. We always worry about what people will say. You have to know the right way to speak to your boss, how to bow, how to flatter."

Sergei S., a Moscow heating engineer born in 1939, traced the problem to the discrepancies between official statements and reality. He saw not only the need to keep one's thoughts to oneself but a pervasive resistance to obeying the law. "In the United States, a law is a law, not to be circumvented. People understand this. In Russia nobody understands the meaning of law. The law causes no other response than the wish to get around it." He explains that there are rare exceptions. His own father was an atypical man. He remembers him as "a noble person, poor, honest, even though he was the chief of the supplies department of a large radio center in Moscow." His father had been raised in an older tradition in a small town in Moldavia. He had worked hard from the time he was fourteen until his death at seventy-five. He was the last man to take risks with the law. "Usually when they mention a head of a supplies department, it is understood that the man is a thief," said Sergei. "If a woman works as a waitress it is assumed that she is a prostitute." Whether it was true or not mattered less than the fact that people perceived it this way.

Nadya K. was aware of the levels of status in her country and attuned to the expectations of her own group. She knew that they would reject her if she broke their rules. "A person from my circle in the Soviet Union would never go to work as a salesclerk. That represents the end, the collapse of all ideals. For an actor to work in a restaurant is the bottom, the sewer, the same as working as a garbageman. In the United States, people can work collecting garbage and nobody dies from it. For us to work in the low jobs means the end of the line."

Nadya K. is in her early thirties and has no memories of war or hunger. Her sufferings as a child were caused by the bedbugs in the corner of the room her family shared with another family in Moscow and her futile struggle to enter the University of Moscow. She was too young to remember Stalin or the war. Her parents' generation could set their present difficulties in perspective by comparing them with what they had lived through. "Remember how we suffered in the war?" said a sixty-year-old engineer from Leningrad. "Do you remember the Revolution?" said an older doctor. "Whatever happens these days is nothing compared with how it used to be."

Nadya K. and her husband emigrated even though they had jobs that other people envied and a decent place to live. "I just felt I could no longer live there," she said. "It was a physical sensation of disgust. It was as if the air became too heavy to breathe. . . . There was this weight pressing down on us."

Sometimes older émigrés, with memories of a faith they no longer had, were able to explain how Russians coped with the deprivations that were part of Soviet life. Itskov R., born in Leningrad during the Revolution, is an Orientalist and linguist. He graduated from the University of Leningrad when Jews made up a large proportion of the faculty and student body and served as an intelligence officer for the military for nine years. He told of the role of traditional Russian pride in enduring the hardships of present-day life. He said, "Russians know that their living standard is very low. They understand that they do not have democracy or freedom of speech. They are very proud of being a part of the Great Soviet Empire. They're proud of their history, of the wars with the Tatars, the Swedes, the French and the Germans. There is no criticism of the treatment of Afghanistan because it is considered good to be feared by neighbors." He spoke for Russians who remember Stalin as the great statesman who opposed Hitler and who governed in the tradition of Ivan the Terrible and Peter the Great, for Russians who thought Khrushchev too humane and Brezhnev too weak.

Zakary K., an actor and director born in Kiev in 1939, had no such beliefs. "When we ask, Why do we live so badly? we are told that it is because we're encircled by capitalist countries who are trying to destroy us. From childhood on we're taught that we are under a constant threat. . . . The only thing is that people no longer believe this." He had once carried a picture of Stalin in his right pocket and as a child had eagerly gone looking for spies. He had not believed in Khrushchev, had hated him "for being such a clown." He remembers the time of the "thaw" as a wonderful time for the Russian theater, a brief respite from censorship. What was left of that time was a collection of anecdotes and a way of speaking in hints and double meanings, what he called "Aesopian" language. It was the secret language in which newspapers were written, the language of literature and theater. "The most important thing," said Zakary K., "is to know how to read it. For those who understand it, everything becomes clear."

Konstantin S., a thirty-five-year-old journalist, divides the world between "ordinary" people, who cannot read this secret language, and the "others," the small minority who share his wish to be an individual. He sees ordinary people in the thrall of a censored press. "Anti-Semitism is a theme in government propaganda. Xenophobia and dislike of America and China are shared by the press and the people. Most Russians see China as the major threat to their national existence . . . and the majority supported the invasion of Czechoslovakia in 1968. They say, 'What's this? We freed them from Hitler and now they want to be independent?' The Russians saw the Czechs as traitors."

He found, however, that even "ordinary" Russians, whether they were writers or readers, sometimes formed their own opinions. Ordinary Russians supported Israel in the Six-Day

War. They liked heroism and displays of strength and force. In spite of everything they write and read, they feel a grudging affection for America. They know it is a rich country. They are willing to pay 200 rubles for a pair of its jeans. They see it more as rival than as adversary. The press had to try to minimize the fact that Americans got to the moon first. It would have been considered a national disgrace not to be first in space, sports, chess, Olympics. It was crucial for national honor to be the country with the most medals.

All the memoirists had had some higher education. Some had been born into educated families and continued the traditions in which they were raised. Others were the children of parents who had had no opportunity to study themselves but were obsessed with the idea that their children transcend them, leave the factory and the marketplace for the institutes, the universities, the world of the "intelligentsia." If this meant working all day and studying all night or acquiring advanced degrees in correspondence courses that might take eight or nine years, it was considered worthwhile. "If you want to live, if you want to be a person," said Nelly B., "then you have to finish university." She was born in Kharkov in 1935. Her father was the manager of a store, but she studied to become an engineer—a less lucrative but more respected profession.

Again and again one hears that Jewish parents, more than others, were passionate about education for their children. Larisa P., the daughter of a member of the secret police in Kiev, also became an engineer. She said, "The main thing was to receive a higher education. In a Jewish family, a young person without a diploma was considered an unfortunate. That mentality exists to this day. Young people know that higher education now will give them nothing in life, but the attraction remains."

In the years just after World War II, the percentage of Jews graduating from the institutes (technical schools) and universities was higher than that of any other nationality. It fell sharply in the fifties, when they were accepted in fewer and fewer numbers. In elementary and secondary schools, however, the children continued to compete for gold and silver medals, for the chance to win a place in an institution of higher education. What they believed to be at stake was more than the kind of work they would do or the money they could earn. Nadya K. was convinced that work in the Soviet Union was not important as "a means of making money, since everybody earns the same amount. The importance of choosing a job is that you should like doing it or because it gives you some prestige. Your job determines your place in society."

What is meant by "place in society," however, is amorphous and constantly shifting. It changes with each generation, differs in every city and is drastically different in urban and rural areas. The very idea of a "place in society" seems a leftover from pre-Revolutionary times or the brief periods when it was believed that a talent for learning and a capacity for hard work ensured a place among peers.

The memoirists also describe their discovery of their vulnerable place as Jews. Misha H., a violinist and conductor born in 1910 in Leningrad, said, "I didn't pay attention to nationality before World War II. I was too young to understand what went on and believed that all nations were equal in the Soviet Union. Later I understood that it was best to be Russian, the second step lower was Ukrainian, the third Byelorussian, then Uzbek, and so on. At the lowest step of society were the Jews."

In the 1960s, Jews found that it was possible to avoid this reality by finding a place in an institute or by gaining acceptance into the Academy of Arts or Science. It was possible among the intelligentsia to find people without conventional prejudices, people with independent political views, often in opposition to the government. Nina S., who did research at the Institute of Oriental Studies, described the intelligentsia as people "who use their work as an escape, as a narcotic to save them from the harassments of ordinary life. They continue the Russian tradition from the eighteenth and nineteenth centuries of disregarding material things and making spiritual and intellectual problems the center of life."

Another option open to Jews is to seek out the industries

and schools that have low status and poor pay. They become Jewish industries because the people who have choices and privileges don't bother with them.

The stories of Soviet life in this collection are told by men and women who attended institutions of higher education and who think of themselves as members of the intelligentsia. Some were members of prestigious institutions. Others were engineers in obscure factories. The memoirists differ from each other as much as they do from ordinary workers. Some were able to lose themselves in their work. They expressed their search for moral values in a passion for intellectual and aesthetic theories. They use the word "culture" as it is transliterated from the German *Kultur*, not in the sense in which it is used in English. They associated culture with truth, wisdom and morality as they take form in literature, art and music. The feelings invested in cultural interests are not very different from those associated with religious observance. The disdain of the "cultured" person for those who are unmoved and ignorant of "spiritual" things is not unlike that of a pious person for an unbeliever.

Others were concerned with the problems of everyday life, the ordeals of finding food, housing, schooling and jobs that were difficult at all levels of life. One by one, émigrés describe the special problems of living in a society in which there is no conception of a need for and a right of privacy.

"I cannot find an equivalent word in Russian for 'privacy,' " said a forty-year-old violinist from Moscow. "If we want to speak of privacy we use the English word. The very idea is foreign. You can say you want to be alone, but that's not what privacy means. It means that you can close your door, that you have the right to be able to do that. In the Soviet Union, however, they pretend that you are such an enthusiastic member of society that you do not need a door to close."

Efim S. had vivid memories of his childhood in Moscow. He and his sister and their parents and grandparents lived in three rooms of an apartment shared by twelve families. "The right to privacy is not given in the constitution and is in fact contradictory to the spirit of Soviet life," he said. "In America I see that everything is done under the aura of individuality. You have to make it by yourself, and your individuality is a big thing for you, protected by law. The protection of legal rights begins with protecting the individual. The individual gets no such respect and consideration in the Soviet Union."

The obsession with finding and keeping adequate living space is at the root of many other issues and problems. Relationships between parents and children, marriage, having children, finding work, conformity and dissidence all depend in some degree upon having a floor, a roof, a door of one's own, whether open or closed. The prejudices of city people against rural types, and the anger of provincial people who are offended by the arrogance of those raised in the larger cities, are exacerbated and confirmed when families of different backgrounds, styles and values share the same kitchen and lavatory. Mentally and socially they may live in different worlds, but physically they often live on top of one another. This can make for great tension.

Men and women who were brought up to strive for higher education, for the honor of belonging to the intelligentsia, found themselves caught between different value systems. A violinist from the Moscow Philharmonic spoke of an "older mentality" that had valued education and the people who acquired it for its own sake. He saw a younger generation more tempted by money and power, less respectful of learning, less willing to lose themselves in scholarly or creative work. "When the goal of life is to have an apartment of one's own, earning the money to pay for it becomes more important than a prestigious job at a low salary."

A forty-year-old magazine editor from Moscow was sure that her generation was more concerned about earning money than about anything else. The older respect for the learned professions remained only in this: that people often lied about what they actually did. A waiter might claim to be a teacher. A salesgirl might introduce herself as an engineer. Waiters and salespeople earned more money and had more power than teachers and engineers. It was only the wariness about sinking to a lower level of society that made it hard to admit the reality.

Sergei S., the Moscow heating engineer born in 1939, tried to describe the communal apartment in which he had grown up. "When I talk to Americans," he said, "they can understand food shortages, anti-Semitic harassment, problems with getting into a university, but they don't understand how four of us lived in nine square meters. It lies beyond their comprehension. And yet that was how I lived until I was ten years old. I didn't think it was unusual because everyone lived that way.

"We lived in a communal apartment in a house in the Zariadye District of Moscow near the Rossia Hotel. A real slum. The courtyard of the house was filled with people who had come to Moscow from the villages. I remember one thing from that period. My brother who was six years older than I was reading a novel by Balzac, and there was the line 'Everything began to go wrong and the Countess had to live in an apartment of only five rooms.' And my brother was taken with the poor countess who had only five rooms and there we were in nine square meters sleeping on chairs. But the most astonishing thing was that my father said he liked our home. He was grateful for his small space, his own bed. In 1951 my father received a room of eighteen square meters in a large wooden barracks close to the Radio Center where he worked. That room, when we moved into it, impressed me more than the three-bedroom house I have here in the United States. It was twice the size of the slum we left and had a large window. We lived there from 1951 while I went to school and after I got married. Our son was born there. We didn't get our own two-room apartment until the barracks was torn down. But it was not until my father died in 1969 that I found out why he was so content with his small space. Talking with the people who came to his funeral, I found out that he had spent time in prison and for the rest of his life was grateful to the State for freeing him and letting him work till he was seventy-five. I'm often tormented by the fact that I knew nothing about his life before I was born. I had never been able to buy him even the smallest gift, and he worked to help me until the last day of his life."

The older émigrés have even worse stories to tell. Sophie M. came to Moscow from Leningrad in 1922. She was a young lawyer who worked for the housing division. She said, "The housing situation was disastrous in Moscow in the thirties. Nothing was being built, and there were huge lines in housing departments everywhere. To live in Moscow everyone required a passport, and many people were refused passports. To get a passport one had to come from the right family, the right party and the right past. I knew well the story of three architects who graduated from the Architecture Institute in Leningrad and were sent to Moscow, where they waited for three years for a room. The first to get approval was about twenty-eight years old. He received the official notice, went to see the room and found it sealed by the local militia. He was told to come back in a week, when he could have it. When he came back, the room was open and there was a trunk in it. The militia responsible for the census had decided they were the real bosses and one of them had taken the apartment for himself."

Sophie M. met the young architect when he came to the housing department to make his complaint. She said, "At that time the head of the housing administration was also the deputy chairman of the Moscow Soviet and was not about to let a local militiaman spit on his order. He sent his assistant to force the militiaman to give the architect the room that had been promised him and to tell him to come to the housing administration to apply in the usual way for his own place. Well, when the assistant got there the militiaman refused to give up his key. All this was done in the middle of the night, you understand, and in the argument the militiaman shot the young assistant. When he was tried, he said he was sorry. He was sorry he had shot the wrong person. He had meant the bullet for the head of the housing administration."

Such stories did not reach the public then any more than they do now, but those who worked in the housing administration knew only too well how much suffering was caused by the lack of living space. Emigrés describe those days in a dry, mocking tone appropriate for people who survived the most trying times. Sophie M., when she came to Moscow, had half of a sixteen-square-meter room which she shared with a friend who was also a lawyer. "We had a couch and pushed a few chairs together. There were no central steam heating and no conveniences. Just a little stove for heating. . . . One day I came home and found a suitcase near the door. A friend had come to Moscow to see her fiancé, who'd just been arrested and was to be sent to Siberia. She had no place to stay, so we took her in. I took everything off the desk and put a blanket down, and that's how I slept. I was the hostess, after all, so I gave her my couch." Ten years later, though she still worked for the housing administration, Sophie M. had a sixteen-meter room without conveniences, for herself and her husband and young daughter. That administration was low on the prestige ladder, and its employees had few privileges. It was not until the housing administration was raised to the level of other administrations in the Moscow Soviet that she was able to have two rooms, a country cottage and the right to eat in one of the special restaurants for privileged people.

How people felt about themselves and their place in society depended upon whether their material life improved or deteriorated. Frieda K., a librarian and elementary-school teacher, had lived in the same small room in Odessa for forty years. "My rent was low," she said. "Only six rubles. I used little electricity. There were no conveniences. I had no bath, no gas until 1972. Before that I used a Primus stove. I was a war widow on the waiting list, but they couldn't satisfy everyone. They were building new residential neighborhoods, but for the most part the young couples moved into the new housing and the old people stayed behind in the old homes." Frieda K. was fifty-eight years old in 1972 and thought of herself as an old woman with no expectations. There is a Russian saying that forty years is a woman's life span. At forty she hears "Why are you trying to act young? Look your age." At fifty-eight she is expected to assume a grandmother's role. When Frieda's building was declared unsafe because the second floor had caved in, her 6-ruble room was demolished, and like other grandmothers she went to live with her son and daughter-in-law. She shared their two rooms and looked after her grandchild. She knew of people who made demands and fought for privileges, but she "didn't like to go and ask for things." Her salary as a librarian in the Radial Machine Tool Plant in Odessa was 90 rubles a month, with an extra bonus of 25 rubles if the workers fulfilled their plan. "I lived modestly and poorly," she said, without complaint. "I lived from payday to payday, with never an extra kopek to put aside, but I had my piece of bread, enough so I didn't have to borrow. If I wanted to do something special for the children, I went to the bookkeeper for a loan and paid it back little by little." She was not the kind of woman who would make a fuss about small inconveniences. She had memories of *shtetl* life in Moldavia, had lost her parents and husband in World War II and been taken for forced labor by the Nazis. She was proud of having emigrated from Odessa, which she described as "a real European, cultured city, one of the best in Europe." Though her personal share of its space was less than comfortable, it pleased her to have lived in "a pretty city, where Pushkin and Gogol had been."

Dr. Alexei G., an orthopedic surgeon from Moscow, was the son of a famous surgeon who nearly came to grief over his struggle for a place to live. In 1930, he said, when he was only a year old, his father was a surgeon in the clinic at Gorki. "At the age of thirty-four my father managed to get his own apartment for the first time. The head of the NKVD, however, also claimed it, evicted us by force and moved into it himself. My father tried to seek justice through Soviet legal channels, but was told that one cannot sue the head of the NKVD and that he had endangered himself and his family by trying. A few years later we moved to Moscow, where my uncle who worked in one of the ministries gave us a room in his apartment. So my father, a famous surgeon, decorated during the war, chief surgeon of the Army Tank Corps, had to wait until he was sixty years old for his first private apartment in Moscow."

Alexei G.'s own experiences were no easier. He was sent to

the city of Petrozavodsk, in the Karelian-Finnish Republic, when he finished medical school. There he rented a small room in a peasant's house for which he paid a fourth of his salary of 60 rubles a month. He could not even afford to feed himself on what was left and depended upon the food packages his parents sent from Moscow. After completing his three years of internship, he came back to Moscow in 1959 and moved back into the twenty-square-meter room he shared with his parents and old grandmother.

Alexei did his residency in the Botkin Clinic, which he describes as "the largest and best hospital in Moscow." He worked with great physicians, 90 percent of whom were Jewish, but earned only 80 rubles a month. He met a young woman he wanted to marry, and they did marry and have a child, though they lived apart. She remained in the small shared room in her communal apartment, and he in his. In the summer his aunt went to her *dacha* in the country, and they borrowed her apartment for a short time to be together. It was not until his father was granted a three-room private apartment that he and his wife could take over the room in the communal apartment and live together with their son as a normal family.

The stories of "normal" family life are difficult for Americans to imagine.

Galina K., an English teacher from Leningrad, born in 1941, said, "My husband, my son, my mother-in-law and I lived in one room for six years. It was a long nightmare—but I had friends who were worse off. Some were in one room with nine other people. Our single room was part of an eight-room apartment in which forty people lived. I went to the public bath every week . . . waited in line for two hours."

Julia V., a physics teacher in Moscow born in 1931, shared half a room with her mother. "The room was eighteen square meters and divided in two by a carpet we hung lengthwise from the ceiling. There were a door and one window in the room. We had the window and our neighbor, the pediatrician, had the door. When the pediatrician's husband came back from prison, we traded our half of the room for her husband's small room so we could have both a door and a window."

The violinist in the Moscow Philharmonic said, "I could reach every wall without moving. I could take a teapot from the cabinet without shifting my chair. We were four people in that small space and could not get permission to move to larger quarters. I would go to the housing clerk to beg for a place, and I can tell you it takes nerve to do it. You feel you are taking your life in your hands, and I'm a nervous person who doesn't take things calmly, but I still kept going and begging."

It was no easier to find housing in Kiev than in Moscow. Leo S., an engineer born in 1935, was married in 1959. "My wife and I lived with my wife's aunt and uncle in a room of sixteen meters. There was no space in which to stand. In our tiny place the only guest we could receive would be a cat."

Irene A. was an actress born in Irkutsk in 1924. Her father worked in the gold mines. When her parents separated, her mother took her and her ten-year-old brother to Novosibirsk in the hope that life would be easier. "But there was no place to live when we got there. No rooms, no apartments. We rented a corner of a room from the wife of a railroad man in Nehalavka, just outside the city. My mother would go off every day to try to sell some of our belongings for bread, and my ten-year-old brother and I, eight at the time, would sit all alone in the house waiting for her. There was not a crust of bread, nothing to eat. The frosts went down to forty degrees below, and we had no warm clothes."

Twenty years later Irene married Abram A., and they had a son, Alexander. Her husband, who had lived in the National Hotel with his Aunt Nelli, was one of the rehabilitated prisoners who had been permitted to return to Moscow and was promised a place to live within half a year. Apartments, however, were being given out for bribes, and they waited two years for a room in a communal apartment. "The only place we could find while we waited was a tiny room and a shed on the outskirts of town that belonged to a railroad worker." She set up housekeeping in a room that was only about four square meters. "It had a couch, a wooden bench, a tiny cradle for my son and a kitchen so small you couldn't even walk into it. The cradle was near the stove. I'd have to move the cradle to get the stove going. I'd get in between the cradle and the stove, climb over the bench and push the wood in. I'd protect the cradle with a sheet of iron so it wouldn't catch fire. We lived in this hovel for two years. My husband spent the whole day in the library. I'd get out only to do a little shopping. I'd put the baby in a sled and go the long way to the store. That is how it was until they gave us a room. We got the room just after my husband finished graduate school and had begun to write his dissertation."

The room in the communal house was hardly worth waiting for. "One of the neighbors couldn't stand Jews," said Irene A. "He'd come into the kitchen and shout, 'What are the kikes doing here? What are they cooking there in the boiling water? We should kill them as soon as they're born . . . suffocate them when they're still small, choke them before they have a chance to grow up.' He was a young man, maybe thirty-two years old, and a fierce anti-Semite. I and my little son had to listen to that day after day . . . for eight years."

In the summer she escaped to a little house in the country. She would take her son, a bench and a portable typewriter into the woods and spend the day typing her husband's dissertation. "I couldn't stand the way we were living. I couldn't go on. The anti-Semitic abuse . . . the child couldn't open his mouth when his father was writing. Nobody could visit us."

When Abram A. received his candidate degree, the equivalent of a Ph.D., he earned 320 rubles a month, but still could not afford the down payment on a cooperative apartment. His relatives helped him. "It was the height of my dreams," said Irene. "After all the years of suffering and wandering, I had my own place. We bought an apartment that had three rooms and a kitchen. I had a room for my son, a quiet place for my husband to write another dissertation to become a professor. In our old age we had everything we were aiming for."

Eugenia S. was born in 1931, a third-generation Muscovite, in her grandparents' apartment on the Arbat. It was in the neighborhood of embassies and elegant old apartments where doctors, lawyers and other educated people lived before the Revolution. It was a street described in Tolstoy's *War and Peace* and often mentioned in stories and novels. Her grandfather had graduated from the chemical-pharmacological department of Yuriev University and had first worked as a pharmacologist and then became co-owner of a company that made him a wealthy man by the time of the Revolution. She had heard he could have lived in a more elegant place than the Arbat, but he was content with his nine rooms which included space for a maid and a cook.

When the movement began to create communal apartments* to be shared with the people living in basements and cellars, her grandparents were forced to give up six of their nine rooms, which were thereafter populated by strangers. They were able, however, to keep three rooms, familiar possessions and memories of more luxurious times. Her mother was born and married in that apartment, and Eugenia S. grew up in it, was married there and lived in it with her husband and son until 1968.

"It was a communal apartment by the time I was born," said Eugenia. "We shared the kitchen with six or seven other families. My grandparents and an unmarried aunt shared two adjacent rooms. My mother, father and I had a small room. We even had a maid, who slept on a folding cot in the corridor. That was permitted before the war. When it was forbidden after World War II, the maid slept in the room with my parents. There were different maids at different times, but my mother could not have managed without them. They saved her from the brawling in the kitchen."

The apartment's only resident besides the original owners who belonged to the intelligentsia was a bachelor, a nobleman from Leningrad who occupied a five-square-meter room that had once been the maid's room. He filled it with books and a remarkable collection of French and Russian porcelain. The

---

* *The communalization of apartments began a few years after the Revolution. Millions of people had come from the provinces to the cities, and there was no new housing for them.*

rest were peasants and *kulaks* who had run away from the collective farms.

"In this mélange of people," Eugenia said, "we were 'the Jews.' We'd hear our neighbors say, 'Borrow it from the Jew. Call the Jew to the telephone. . . . Here is a letter for the Jews.' For such people the Jew connoted something different, something unusual. Before the war there had been no antagonism or unpleasantness, just the awareness that Jews were different, didn't belong. It was a traditional way of speaking, not an insult. Our actual relationship was friendly, helpful, even pleasant. If anybody needed advice or medicine they came to my parents. If there were documents or questionnaires to fill out, we helped them. They came to my mother and father for personal advice. They were respected—and of course we did not participate in the intrigues, the jealousies, the kitchen quarrels. There were battles about cleaning the common areas, about paying electric bills and gas bills. People came to blows because of wash soaking too long in the tub or hanging too long on the ropes stretched across the kitchen. It was only after World War II that antagonism toward our family flared up. During the trial of the Jewish doctors and the Jewish writers there were direct insults as well as glances and hints that interfered with living calmly together."

Efim, the son who was born in 1956, remembered that apartment as "a world providing all the experiences of life." He saw births, deaths, weddings and fights. He saw "the whole gamut of life, everything out in the open. The doors were not closed. Everyone was on top of everyone else. The skirmishes and scandals were all visible." He was in direct contact with thieves, prostitutes and drunkards even under the safety of his parents' roof. He also could not escape the fact that he was Jewish and different from the others.

Every description of communal life is full of the yearning for a separate place, away from parents, from neighbors. "I have very nice parents," said a forty-five-year-old librarian from Leningrad. "They loved me and I loved them; but we couldn't live together peaceably in two rooms. We had thirty-two square meters, with my husband and me in one room and my father, my mother, my daughter from a first marriage and a housekeeper in the other." There are routine descriptions of the fights, the need to call the police, the petty thievery of clothes and food within a communal apartment. Konstantin S., the Moscow journalist, was convinced that "crime, disease and divorce were caused by communal apartments."

He said, "It is the dream of every Soviet citizen to have his own apartment. When a house is being constructed or renovated, women try to get pregnant right away to put their names on the list. Some even pretend pregnancy, but the government knows this and sends them to the doctor for proof. Women get pregnant to get a bigger space and then have an abortion when the apartment is secured. You can't imagine how unpleasant it is to live in a communal apartment with strangers who become your enemies."

Gennady P., a forty-nine-year-old journalist and editor, considered himself a privileged person because he had the right to buy his own cooperative apartment. Another equally privileged member of the Writers' Union explained the details. "For three people you can get two rooms in a communal apartment or a two-room apartment. If the child is a girl you get the communal rooms; if it's a boy you get the separate apartment."

Masha B., a Moscow art historian and silent dissident, believed that cooperative apartments were bought only by members of the intelligentsia who valued privacy enough to be willing to pay for it. In their own quarters, they could listen to forbidden radio broadcasts, read *samizdat*, entertain friends. There was always a long wait. Special permission was required. If one had lived in a communal apartment with parents, it was necessary to take the parents along to the co-op "unless you're clever enough to get around the ruling that says only seven square meters are permitted per person."

The descriptions of the new co-op apartments show them to be something less than dreams come true. Katya Z., an editor of science texts who acquired one, said, "It included one room of twenty square meters and one of ten square meters. You went through the bigger room, which served as living room and dining room by day and bedroom by night, to the smaller room, where the child slept. The rent was a sixth of my salary. The real problem with living in a new development was that there were only two stores in it. You could buy liquor, some bread, maybe some cheese. You had to get up very early to find some milk. I had to do my shopping at lunchtime, downtown. That was where I stood in line for the piece of meat or fish, and I'd drag whatever I could find back in my net bag at the end of the day."

The obsession with buying a co-op was not confined to members of the intelligentsia. There were many like Leya Y., a forty-year-old engineer in Leningrad, who said simply, "We lived with my husband's parents for a year. It was terrible. We fought constantly. They were just hard people to live with in one room. They made my life unbearable." To get away from them, she moved to a new development where there was no road, no telephone, no buses, no one to care for her child when she went to work.

Leya Y. had neither the strength nor the patience to go through the usual channels. "Usually," she said, "you waited in line for ten years to be accepted as a member of a cooperative and then another year and a half while they were building. But I got friendly with the head of the cooperative, and we gave him two hundred rubles under the table. I had the connections through my father, who did everybody a lot of favors, and when he needed something he would be paid back."

Leya described her father as "a very smart man. He had a very good job in an organization that made up the budget for a small factory. He saw all kinds of ways to make side money, and he took the opportunities. Our family always had everything. We lived well. But it was dangerous. The police were always watching us, so it was very hard to sleep peacefully. The law in the Soviet Union is that you are not supposed to do business, but you had to do it to live. When my father got sick and died in 1970, he left us some money. He looked after us to the end of his life."

Nadya K. described what happened to her uncle and to her family when he was caught by the police for illegal dealings. "My father," she said, "was the youngest of three sons and an ordinary Soviet man. His older brother, my uncle, was not typical. He was the head of administration for a construction trust in Moscow. The two brothers had grown apart because my uncle was adventurous and my father was the person who made molds and braces for dentists, a kind of dental technician. Their opportunities for moving up and making money were very different. In addition, my uncle was married to a Russian woman, and my mother, of course, was Jewish. Anyway, this uncle rose very nicely up the Russian ladder of success. He lived high, had mistresses, his own car, a *dacha* and a great apartment in downtown Moscow. He did this by helping people get state-built apartments. He helped lots of people and was paid well. When we came to Moscow he helped my father find a place to live. When he was discovered, the whole family had a terrible time. He was sent to prison as a common criminal, and we were kicked out of the apartment he got for us. A Soviet policeman came and announced our fate. They threw our things out into the street. It was winter, and cold. I was about eight years old, but I remember it well. I remember the building and our Russian neighbors looking out the windows, happy that Jews were caught. My uncle served a long term and then was released during an amnesty. They confiscated everything he had owned. Of all his beautiful things, he was left with no more than a chair and a table."

The struggle to find an apartment in Moscow created an infinite variety of illegal solutions. Fictitious marriages were arranged for the hefty sum of 1,000 rubles so that someone from another city could acquire the right to live in the capital. More common and less expensive was the kind of solution arranged by Alla G. Alla was attractive and ambitious. Unhappy with teaching, she found work as an airline stewardess in Magnitogorsk. She knew a lot of people, had good connections and arranged for a better job in Moscow at the Doma Madevoda airport. Since she had always lived in Magnitogorsk with her parents, it was her first experience in finding and renting an apartment.

A friend found her an unofficial apartment illegally owned. "The police came every day and I had to pay them. I could never relax. There was always the fear that the police were coming to be bribed not to report me for living in an illegal apartment. I lived this way for three years, but I could find no other way to live in Moscow."

Parents and Children

Itskov R., an Orientalist born in Leningrad in 1917, saw nothing but trouble in the fact that "Traditional patriarchal views and economics kept three generations together under one roof. It's a tragedy for all of them," he said, "because eventually they will have to hate one another."

The stories and anecdotes that turn up in the memoirs are not so much about hatred as they are about intense relationships, about the need for dependency and the struggles for independence in a society that offers no space for maneuvering. They reveal struggles, ways of coping under the most difficult circumstances and a variety of accommodations. Adolescents need to rebel and separate themselves from their parents in totalitarian societies as well as in democratic ones. Parents are loath to give up their illusions of control. Children find themselves at different times of life shifting from what the state demands to what they feel to be right and what parents and grandparents urge and teach. Such normal struggles take place, however, in an atmosphere in which parents may be punished if their children misbehave and children may be denied opportunities for education and work because their parents are out of favor.

Old patterns of concern and control are still transmitted

from one generation to the next. "I worked all my life so my children should be dressed well and have a good education," said Lena B., an eighty-two-year-old dressmaker from Kiev. "I wanted to give my Flora piano lessons—she was good on the piano; and when my grandson was born I looked after him. Later Flora did the same for her own grandson and taught him to play the piano. I wanted to give the best that I could to my children, and my daughter was the same with hers."

Mother and daughter, both widows, had lived together in "a nice one-room apartment without neighbors." When Flora's son and his wife and child left for America, Flora and her mother decided to stay in the Soviet Union, where they had pensions and friends. Flora, however, could not stop longing for her grandson. "She lived for the letters from Chicago," said her mother. "When she heard they had a car she was afraid of an accident. She lived on nerves until we decided to get our visas and join the children."

A twenty-five-year-old English translator from Tbilisi said, "The older parents have no life of their own. From the time they have children they give all their time to their children and so prefer to live with them till the end of their days."

The grandmothers include a few who had interesting professional lives. Raya B., a physician from Odessa, was old enough to be in the generation in which educated and emancipated children took care of their parents. She had been a dutiful traditional daughter and cared for her sick father till the end of his life. Remembering how she had felt about her responsibilities, she was eager to raise children who would be independent of her. She was proud of the fact that her son lived in another city, that they could visit each other on occasion and not exert the kind of pressures that existed between parents and grown children.

Albert D., the forty-year-old journalist from Odessa, believed that the older generation, the people over fifty, were visibly more idealistic, more willing to make sacrifices for their children and also more fearful and anxious. His own generation and those a little younger were both ready to exploit the grandmothers and also ready to complain about their meddling and their old-fashioned anxiety.

"If there is a grandmother," said Olga D., a twenty-two-year-old nurse from Kiev, "then she will make dinner and look after the baby. She will do the shopping and cleaning. Otherwise the young mother must stay at home or give the child to a kindergarten where the teachers are not good people."

Olga was grateful for her grandmother's care. "I had a good childhood," she said. "I was born into a Jewish family. My mother and father were both Jewish, and I had a grandmother who was always with me. I didn't go to kindergarten. I went to school when I was six and didn't enjoy it at all. I was a home child and didn't like the way children were fighting and quarreling. I also didn't know how to fight. Later on I learned and wasn't so afraid to be with children."

Igor G., a student from Tbilisi, had not yet overcome his resentment about the way in which his grandmother had raised him. "She never allowed me to do anything childish. It was 'Don't do this and don't do that' and 'Why are you making noise while you eat?' and always 'Don't get yourself dirty.' She taught me to use a knife and fork, and I always envied children who could eat as they pleased. . . . No children ever came to play with me. I would just be taken for a walk every day and then put down for a nap. I had no experience with other children until she died. Then I went to a Georgian kindergarten and after that to a Russian school with Armenians, Kurds and Jews. They all seemed uncivilized, uncultured, altogether different from me. But the real difference was that they were children and I was never permitted to be a child. I did not run and play. I didn't eat with my fingers. . . . All because of my grandmother."

Victor C., a professional hockey player and gym teacher in Kiev, saw the consequences of grandmothers' raising children very clearly. He said, "Jewish children were good at everything but sports. Jewish families pay no attention to physical development. The main thing is that the children be learned and well read, that they sit home quietly with a book or play the piano. By the time a kid came to school he had no love for the active life. It was hard to work with those children. They couldn't move. Their grandmothers had stuffed them, so they were chubby. In all my teaching practice I had only two Jewish students who came to me physically strong and healthy. Mostly they were too fat, and I would try to help them get rid of their extra weight."

In spite of all the disadvantages, parents seemed to agree that the most impatient grandmother was a better caretaker of a young child than a nursery school or kindergarten. Eleanora S., the movie critic from Leningrad, said that the real problem was that the children got sick in the nurseries. "There are twenty-five kids to one teacher. Nursery-school teachers are paid sixty rubles a month, so no normal person takes a job like that. If somebody does, it doesn't mean she likes children, only that she can't do anything else. Some are so mean they open the windows to make the kids catch cold so the next day they have twelve instead of twenty-five to take care of."

Anna D., a physician from Moscow who worked with children, corroborated the dismal picture of the public nurseries. It was never possible for a single caretaker and one nurse to look after twenty-five babies. "So the babies were left wet and unchanged. No one talked to them. They do everything late and get more sicknesses. It's only for mothers who have no alternative. The studies show that children brought up collectively before kindergarten do not do well. They look unhappy and uncared-for. Unmarried mothers, however, have to work. They get only a five-ruble allowance for a child. If they have no mother or aunt to help them out with the baby, they have no choice." A Moscow English teacher said dramatically, 'It's torture for a woman to have a child and have to leave it in the kindergarten." Working mothers could get five days' paid sick leave to care for children who were not well, but after that they lost their pay and had nothing to live on.

The caretakers in nursery schools and kindergartens wore aprons with large pockets. It was customary every morning for the mothers to leave money in the pocket in the hope that their children would be singled out for extra care and concern. It did not change the basic problem. The sophisticated parents knew that the caretakers did not have a college education. They had no knowledge of child psychology and didn't understand the differences in children. Any sign of independence was seen as badness to be punished. "If a child behaves badly, the parents are blamed," said Anna D. "The parents' work boss may be informed. The Party organization is involved. In a good family where parents pay attention to children, they develop well. Meanwhile, the psychiatric hospitals have 'quiet' divisions for children who are not sick, but bad."

Attentive families, however, caused other problems. "Russian children are spoiled," said Maria P., a thirty-five-year-old translator from Moscow. "It's not only from the higher levels. Even workers' children are spoiled because their parents survived the war and want their children to have all the things they didn't have." Katya Z., in the same generation, thought that "Jewish children were even more spoiled than the Russians if they lived with their grandmothers. They have to act properly in public and do as they're told, but at home they can throw tantrums and nag and cry and whine. Parents give in to maintain peace for the sake of the neighbors. Walls are thin. If you raise your voice everybody hears."

Among the men and women born after 1948, one heard evidence that parents succeeded in making their children feel privileged and cared-for in spite of shortages and poor housing. They also made great sacrifices to help their grown children after marriage and childbirth. It was not unusual to hear "I waited in line for three hours to get a piece of fruit for my daughter that I wouldn't even taste." Parents fought to get their sons and daughters into universities, worked hard to buy them apartments, country houses, better clothes than they themselves wore. Mothers who were content to be housewives brought the daughters up as Soviet princesses. "I was the treasured Soviet child," said Nadya K. "I lived with my parents. They housed and fed me. All the money I earned I spent on myself." She pitied young Americans who worked while going to school, who had no devoted mother to wash and cook for them. One heard men say, "My wife did no housework. Her mother took care of everything until she died in 1971."

Parents were torn between their wish to protect their children from suffering, especially that due to anti-Semitism, and their obligation to help them live in a society in which they expected to remain all their lives. Some tried to protect their children from the world and others tried to prepare them for it.

"We learned how to live with the government," said Irina G., a forty-year-old schoolteacher from Odessa. "We never talked about anti-Semitism in front of our kids. We never spoke about the government. We taught them to support their teacher and to cooperate with people. When my son worried about going into the army after we applied to emigrate, I said, 'You will go. This is your country. Your father, both of your grandfathers and five of your uncles died for this country. So you too will go if they call you.' "

Felix B., a conductor from Moscow, knew that what parents said and didn't say reflected the political climate and their own state of anxiety. "Parents," he said, "were so afraid of their children because they could unthinkingly say something that would destroy a family. We had an example of a family perishing because of what a child said to a teacher in school. This little girl said she liked the music of Wagner, and because of her the family was accused of sympathizing with the fascists. The family was exiled from Moscow. It was a Jewish family, so it made no sense at all."

Yuli F., the musicologist born in Bryansk in Byelorussia in 1927, said parents had good reason to fear their children. "As a child I was ready to go and inform on my parents if I felt something was wrong with their behavior. Do you know about Pavel Morozov? He was the little boy from Siberia who denounced his father and was killed and became a kind of Saint Paul for us. We were brought up with him as our ideal and our idol, and I wanted to be just like him. It tortured me to love my parents and yet know that Stalin and the state were more important to me than they were. The propaganda and education were very strong, impossible to resist.

"Parents, to be close to their children, tried to accept our mentality and our point of view. Little by little I saw my parents become Soviet citizens even though they could not forget their pre-Revolutionary experiences. My father kept from me his Zionist beliefs because he was afraid I might inform. He didn't scold me too hard when I mocked my grandfather praying and tried to disturb the Passover *seder*. It was very confusing for me because my grandfather clearly loved me and played with me. He talked to me and hugged me even though I behaved badly with him."

By the time Yuli F. became a parent himself he had acquired different values and loyalties. "I didn't want my daughter to repeat my way of life. I didn't want her to be a deceived person who understood only half of reality." He had to battle with his wife and mother-in-law, who thought she was too young to be burdened by contradictions, too young to keep two points of view in her mind. He wanted his daughter to pretend in school that she accepted what they were teaching and not tell about what went on in the family. "They were afraid she would denounce us in school. My wife and my mother-in-law were afraid they would lose their jobs. They were terrified that she'd repeat the jokes we told about Lenin and Khrushchev and we'd all end up in prison. My daughter never denounced us, but my marriage broke up after five years in a tiny room with a strong mother-in-law and endless arguments about how to raise a child."

The fears were not unreasonable. The dangers of speaking out were known, and the problems were not just between parents and children. Minna M. told about her nephew, a construction engineer in Leningrad. Early in the seventies he was sitting in a restaurant with two friends, joking and chattering, and said, "I don't think Nixon is any stupider than Brezhnev." Three days later he was thrown out of his division because he'd lost his clearance. Dora M., the English teacher and translator, was so fearful of speaking her mind in public that she chose an unusual way of coping. "I was very sly," she said. "I didn't want to speak to people at work, so I pretended to be deaf and made people shout when they talked to me. It's not easy to gossip if you have to shout, so everyone left me alone. Nobody talked to me. I was happier that way and I didn't have to worry about saying something wrong." There were many others who did not choose such extreme behavior but who shared her feeling. "It is a matter of survival in Russia not to expose your point of view," said Mikhael M. from Odessa.

Danielle I., born in 1943, a music teacher in Moscow, could not keep her thoughts to herself. "I talked openly to my daughter. The worst thing would be if our daughter grew up with different ideas and attitudes from her father and mother. I think our critical ways helped her. We were not ideal parents, but *my* parents—her grandparents—played that role. They took my daughter to their home, took her to the theater, to concerts. She got all the warmth, much knowledge and excitement from them. There was nothing in Moscow she could want that they wouldn't give her, but we taught her other important things."

Nina S., an Orientalist from Moscow, behaved in a similar way. "My son was brought up after Stalin's death. Khrushchev had made his speech denouncing Stalin, and it was probably the best time of my life in the Soviet Union. It was a time of relative freedom, and people started to talk to each other more freely. That had a big impact on the relations between parents and children. I never lied to my son. We discussed a lot of things as friends. I would still say, The situation is thus and so, but don't mention it in the classroom. I explained everything to him, as I understood it. I gave him *samizdat* to read and told him how I felt about Party membership. . . . My mother, of course, was against this. She was still frightened. Her generation was frightened once and for all. Only emigration could cure her."

How young people responded to their parents' discretion and indiscretion depended upon their strength and the circles in which they moved. A film director in Leningrad, born in

1937, spoke of her father with pride. "I had a hardworking father, an engineer. He was a very special person who opened my eyes to everything. He told me, 'Don't believe the newspapers. Don't believe the radio. Don't believe everything they tell you.' When I came home crying about the Jewish doctors, he said, 'Don't be foolish. Let me explain what this is about.' He had lived through the siege of Leningrad. He knew literature and art. A very interesting man! My father was not religious, but he told me about the Jewish holidays at his father's house. It was too dangerous to observe anything in Leningrad."

Eleanora S., also in Leningrad, was not comfortable with the challenges her parents offered. "My mother talked freely to me," she said, "but she always added, 'If you want me to be in prison you will tell what I told you.' I was only five the first time she said that to me. My father used to listen to Voice of America on the radio. I was very uncomfortable about having such parents. I couldn't invite friends to the house. It was not good that my father listened. I didn't trust it. I knew it was impossible to hear the truth from the Russian media and didn't believe anything heard on the radio could be true. It didn't make sense to listen, especially if it put you in danger."

Boris F., a space engineer and computer worker from Kharkov, resisted his father in different circumstances. "My father," he said, "was a military man, an officer who was proud of his accomplishments. We broke apart from each other not only because we live in different hemispheres but because he was so persistent in his desire to shut his eyes. Since childhood I protested against his wish to make me not see what was going on. I was the only Jew in my group at school. I heard the stories and the anecdotes from kindergarten on and then again in elementary school and in the Pioneer camp. I felt it a kind of subjugation to an assault from the outside. My father refused to admit this could be."

Parents who insisted that there were no real differences between Jews and Russians if both were members of the intelligentsia often created what seemed like unreasonable demands that their children choose Jewish partners. Albert D., a journalist from Odessa, saw the practical reasons for the problem. "The mother of a Jewish girl marrying a Russian fears the anti-Semitism of the Russian relatives and worries that there will be problems with children who will not obey the parents. The mother of a Russian girl marrying a Jew is sorry for the grandchildren, who will have Jewish problems." Leo S., an engineer from Kiev, said, "My father advised me against marrying a non-Jew. I myself knew of a Ukrainian woman married to a Jewish officer who wrote her mother in the village, 'Everything is okay. We are living well. But my husband still smells of *Zhid*.' You know she said it without malice. She meant no harm. But she left the letter on the table and her husband saw it. He refused to stay with her any longer. He said, 'We are different beasts. We cannot live together.' He drove her away with 'Go smell your own kind.' It was a pity. They had a two-year-old son and had been living quietly together. She had not meant to make him so angry."

Itskov R., the Orientalist born in Leningrad in 1917, married a Russian woman in 1945. "Some people told her then that she was wrong to marry a Jew. Her father was in a concentration camp until 1956, and he absolutely disapproved of her choice. When he came out, he did not relate to his Jewish son-in-law. My parents, however, were dead, and my relatives approved of my Russian wife." Itskov R. believed that it was only the Samarkandi, the Bukharin, the Ukrainian and Georgian Jews who opposed assimilation and intermarriage.

The stories that the memoirists tell, however, recount the strong opposition to intermarriage in Kiev, Kharkov and Tbilisi, and of similar problems in Moscow and Leningrad. In spite of regional and generational differences, the same anxieties and conflicts kept turning up as variations on an old theme.

Marsha L., a forty-year-old pianist and Latin teacher from Kharkov, said, "My father wanted me to marry only a Jew. My mother didn't press me. When I was twenty-two I had a Rumanian boyfriend. My father wouldn't greet him, wouldn't even say hello. I couldn't sleep in those days and couldn't talk to my father at all. I told him that all people are the same to me, all equal. I didn't care if a man was a Jew or not as long as he was a decent person, and my father would say that when life became difficult he would call me a 'kike.' I couldn't understand why my father was so hostile to my friend. We had never discussed Judaism. We had never even mentioned that we were Jewish. It all came as a blowup. Still I kept choosing non-Jewish partners. I didn't marry my Rumanian. I married someone half-Jewish. My Jewish feelings were changed by the Doctors' Plot. I talked to my friends about it. I was shocked and scared. I couldn't believe such a thing could happen."

Danielle I., another pianist, was born in Moscow in 1943 into what she called "a purely Jewish family." Her grandfather was a well-known Soviet scientist who had been educated in Germany and England before the Revolution. Her grandparents had taught her English, had taken her to concerts from the time she was five or six. They had a library of thousands of books which she could read when she was old enough. Her other grandfather was an important Party official, the chairman of the secret service. Her parents were both scientists. Her father was the designer of large plants for oil production, and her mother did scientific research at the Academy of Science.

Danielle I. grew up as a privileged child in a family that believed in "internationalism," by which they meant the equality of all Soviet citizens. She was not prepared for the distress of her parents and grandparents when she married a Russian. The marriage fulfilled all the stereotypes, all the warnings about the dangers of mixing people of different backgrounds. "He was a very talented musician," she said, "but lazy. He didn't need to achieve anything in life. . . . My husband just couldn't understand that things were difficult for me because I was Jewish. The longer he couldn't find himself, the more apparent his negative attitudes toward Jews became. We did not reach the point of Ivanov in Chekhov's story, but we came very close." (Ivanov, in that story, threatens to use the insulting word for Jew, the word that hangs in the air, a symbol of uneradicable difference.) Danielle I. blamed her divorce on "the problem of different backgrounds, different attitudes and understanding of history."

Olga D., the twenty-two-year-old nurse from Kiev, was opposed to intermarriage because the Jewish–Ukrainian marriages she had seen were disastrous. "Children don't know who they are and which side to take. A little bit of Jewish nose or Jewish eyes create too many problems for them." She had a Ukrainian aunt, a teacher at the University of Kiev, who didn't want her children to see their Jewish cousins. She knew the Ukrainian wife of a Jewish doctor who wouldn't let her husband help his mother when she was in need, who brought up her children to see their Jewish father as a misfortune and threatened to denounce him in the newspaper when some of his relatives left for Israel.

Naum L., a young student from the Carpathian Mountains, said that Jews in his area had no choice. "Jews who marry outside their nationality are forced into a shell. They suffer and can never lead a normal life. If a Jew marries into a Christian family, the Christian family does everything possible to cause a divorce. In my father's circle, the intermarrying person is totally isolated, punished for the rest of his life and never accepted in a non-Jewish circle either. Intermarried Jews are not accepted anywhere in the small Carpathian towns."

In the seventies, an upsurge of marriages of Jews with non-Jews who were eager for Jewish passports so they could leave the Soviet Union led to the passage of a law that one had to wait five years after marriage before getting permission to emigrate. In the 1980s Jews avoided marrying non-Jews because of problems with emigration.

Marriages among young people were often entered into casually, after brief acquaintance. Divorces were easy to obtain. Sometimes divorced couples lived together to avoid going back to their parents. Common-law marriage was equal to legal marriage until 1944. It is not always possible to tell from the memoirs whether marriage meant the decision to live together or whether the marriage was officially registered. This issue was likely to be mentioned only in passing. For example, Zina K., while telling of her father's arrest and murder, said, "My parents were not formally married, as was the case with many people in the 1930s, but that didn't save my mother from being arrested as the wife of an enemy of the people. The only time she had to prove she was the wife of her husband was when she was rehabilitated and was able to obtain legal exoneration for herself and her husband so that she could receive a pension."

The belief that marriage was necessary and desirable, however, survived the casual system of certification and the lack of celebration. "In order to be a person, a full person, a complete person," said Irene A., "everyone got married. Friends and family urged me. I think I got married to please everyone around me." Irene A. was an actress performing in Irkutsk and Novosibirsk. She was attractive and intelligent, but at the age of twenty-eight had no boyfriends and was not particularly interested in men, at least the men available. "In the theater," she said, "men had an irresponsible attitude toward girls without husbands. They felt they could do anything they wanted with them."

Friends arranged her meeting with Abram A., who was working in the same area in which he had served his term of imprisonment. "He was forty-one, thirteen years older than I," said Irene. "There was no time for courting. We were married two weeks later. He suited my requirements. I did not fall in love. I've never been in love—but I was twenty-eight and didn't want to be different from everyone else. I wanted an educated man. I thought he was kindhearted, and I was not mistaken. It was important to me to have a Jewish husband. Jews are proud in Siberia. They think only a Jew can be a good husband, that only a Jewish husband won't be a drunkard. There were no mixed marriages in my family. Later my sister married a Russian and was very sorry. He was not a decent person. There were not so many choices in our generation. So many men had been killed. After the war there were only cripples.

I was lucky that my husband had been saved by being in a concentration camp."

Dora M., the English teacher from Moscow, described her marriage in the thirties in the course of remembering the desperate housing situation. "My family had three rooms in a five-room apartment. Two other families had one room each. So my father asked me, 'Look here, are you going to get married?' and I said, 'No, I don't think so.' And he said, 'Look here, you have to make up your mind. If you don't get married we'll have to give away the third room to the housing authorities.' There were only four of us—my parents, my sister and I. My father said, 'If you get married, Yasha will come and we can keep the extra room.' So I said, 'Look, I don't know. Must I get married because of the room?' He said he didn't mean it that way, but that it would be nice if we were planning to get married anyway. So I agreed to ask Yasha. We had known each other a year. But he didn't know what to say except that if we did marry he would not be able to register at our place because then his mother would have to give *her* room away."

In shared rooms, children were often sent out to the movies on Saturday so the parents could have a few hours alone. When the children grew up and married it was customary for them to give their parents presents of tickets to concerts and plays, as far from home as possible, so that they could have a few hours alone.

The émigrés also discussed the division of labor within marriages. Tamara S., a micropaleontologist, thought "It's unrealistic to expect a Soviet woman to be a wife, mother and housewife and have a career as a serious scientist. She has to have a mother, aunt or maid to look after her children. She has to have someone to shop and do the cooking."

When Zina K. became a successful engineer in the textile industry she did a lot of traveling. She was able to get help from her husband. "When I was away, I of course left a refrigerator full of prepared food, and when I got home I would have to do a general cleaning, but my husband nevertheless had many chores. My husband was more capable than I at marketing. In the Soviet Union you have to have a special skill to find out where to wait for 'what is given.' My husband had more patience for this than I. He used to spend hours in lines reading his newspaper. I couldn't stand to do that."

Dora M., the English teacher and translator, found that few husbands were willing to help. "No matter what position a woman holds in her office, she goes home to another day's work. After standing in line, she feeds her family and washes her dishes without hot water. There are conveniences in some of the big cities, but all over Russia women struggle just the way their grandmothers did and the men sit in the park and play cards and dominoes and chess. That's considered manly work, while women do their chores till two in the morning."

Katya Z., another translator and editor, described a typical evening in her life. "I'd get home about seven. First I'd drop the two bags and try to get some blood circulating in my legs because I'd been standing in that beautiful Moscow subway for an hour and a half and then walked from the subway and climbed up to my fourth-floor apartment. There was not much time to relax, so I'd jump up and start cooking supper, or maybe heat the leftovers from the night before. And then it's already after eight o'clock and time to think about putting the child to sleep. So I'd check my daughter's homework and put her to bed. Then I used to clean and press her school uniform for the next day and sew on a fresh white collar and add the white cuffs and get my own clothes ready for the next day. We used to wear the same blouse or dress for a week. Then on Saturday I'd wash it. On Sunday I'd press it and Monday I'd put it on again. So by the time all that work was done I had to go to sleep because I had to get up at six in the morning to get to work on time. On Saturday or Sunday I might take half a day off to go for a walk, or skiing in the winter. But I still had to do the same things when I got back. Never went to a restaurant. They were all the same, anyway, and much too expensive. But everybody would drink every day. There was vodka everywhere. There was no meat, no fish—just vodka to drink out of big glasses."

Drinking was a daily escape for many people. The pervasive longing was to be somewhere else, away from the deadening routine and the press of people. The most privileged people had access to summer places in the Crimea, the Caucasus or in the countryside outside of Leningrad and Moscow. Konstantin S., a journalist born in 1943, placed high on his list of privileges "the luxury of a single room with sink and bathroom in the special summer home for writers." The usual summer accommodations were for five people in a room. The high point of his career was the permission to travel to Belgium, Luxembourg, Sweden, Finland, Czechoslovakia and Yugoslavia. He even boasted that he had refused to cooperate with the Security Committee. "I just told them I was not going to watch anybody and not follow anybody. I was going for a vacation and to see the architecture, not to see how the Soviet group conducted itself."

Ordinary engineers and teachers had a hard time getting away even for a weekend. Tamara S., the paleontologist, had a summer house about an hour's ride on the suburban train from Leningrad. "My husband and I worked very hard to build the house, and we made a nice garden. We grew strawberries and had beautiful flowers; but the transportation was a terrible problem. In September, when we were harvesting, there were fewer trains. The trains were so crowded that they could hardly close the doors. We once waited on the platform three hours before we could get into a train, and then when we finally squeezed in I had to stand between the cars. People were so crowded up against each other that a man standing next to me looked as if he were going to die. His face turned completely red, and his eyes bulged out of their sockets. And all the people in the trains were angry because they'd been working in the gardens all day and had large, heavy bags to carry. There were all kinds of quarrels and conflicts on the way home. And this was called the weekend rest. We finally decided to sell the house. Like many things in the Soviet Union planned for relaxation and pleasure, it had turned into a heavy burden." Instead they saved their money for a vacation in the Crimea. "It was very expensive. We had one room for my husband, me and my daughter. We'd run down to the beach in the morning and then had to face the long lines to buy something to eat. Dinners in restaurants meant even longer lines. There was no way to rest."

Leya Y. had heard that things were easier in Bulgaria. "After a gallbladder operation I decided to try to get permission to take a vacation in Bulgaria. I needed permission from the director of the factory, the secretary of the Party and the workers' union. The director wouldn't sign the reference. He called a meeting and asked me political questions about the constitution, all because I wanted to go away for two weeks. It was a two-hundred-ruble trip including fare, hotel and meals. It was very expensive for me, but I had saved the money and planned it with the agent from the KGB. But you see, they see vacations abroad as dangerous. You can see other people living better and may want what they have for yourself."

Kira G., a biologist from Moscow, had set her heart on a trip to the Warsaw Bloc countries. She found that there was a three-month wait for permission. "You needed a car," she said, "and also the signature of your boss, the director of your institute and the Party council. They wouldn't permit me to go to Yugoslavia, and we had to leave our sixteen-year-old son as a hostage. After two and a half days of traveling we reached the Hungarian border and were told we couldn't go any farther by car. We were told we had to travel by train and stay in hotels; but we had no money to pay for hotels. We called Moscow and cried and begged for permission. It was very unusual to get permission."

In spite of the difficulties and obstacles, the struggles to get away went on. Sergei S., a gas engineer from Moscow, said that families focused on different obsessions. "For some people the most important thing is to be able to buy a set of furniture. Some take it into their heads that they must own a crystal chandelier. In our family the most important thing was to take our son out of the city every summer. We waited all winter for the chance to travel to the Volga or rent a house at the Baltic or Black Sea."

Rhya K., a teacher of Russian language and literature in Moscow, found a way to escape the city even though she had no car and no money for hotels. "If you are not rich enough to go to the Black Sea, where it is so crowded and expensive, you have to find some other way to rest. So we decided to go to the north. We were told it would be difficult. There are no hotels and no food. But we went anyway, to Vologda and Akhandinsk and even farther. We traveled on foot with our knapsacks, hiking as much as fifteen miles a day, sometimes twenty miles. We carried very little with us. A pair of pants, some T-shirts. Mostly we carried tins of meat, because the only things we could buy were sugar, salt, maybe cookies. That was what we found the first year we went north. But then we came back many times. We liked the area for many reasons. First, because it was not crowded and we could see virgin forests and pure lakes and listen to the deep silence. Secondly, we found great art—Russian icons, folk art, beautiful old Russian churches we liked very much. And the people were altogether different from the city people we were used to. They saw us as strangers, foreigners. Americans or Europeans would be closer to us than we were to them. They know nothing about modern facilities. They know nothing about international affairs. They are not even sure who is the big guy in Moscow. They know about the Soviet system because they live on a *kolkhoz*, but the collective farms were different in the north country. A farm united five, six, maybe seven villages, as much as twenty miles apart. The people knew only the others in their village, and mostly they were old people because the young people refused to accept the loneliness and the hunger of the life of the north. Young people want modern conveniences and think the farm life too boring. So mostly they were women whose husbands had disappeared during collectivization or during the Second World War. They earn enough money to live but cannot buy milk or fresh fruit or vegetables.

"The only culture in the north," said Rhya K., "was from the old movies. But the people were very hospitable and very talkative. They never said, 'Show us your passport.' We could just knock on any door. It didn't matter if it was in the middle of the day or late at night—they'd say, 'Come in.' Even the old women were not afraid of strangers, and when they saw that we were travelers they'd ask us what city we were from. When we told them we were from Moscow, we could see that it would have made no difference if we'd said Paris or Rome. They never asked about politics. They never asked about the places we came from or what we had seen on the way. Their questions were always very fundamental. 'Do you have family? Do you have children? Do you own a cow?' is what they asked. A woman might ask if I liked my husband or what we ate in Moscow, but that was all. They did not seem to envy us our city life, and anyway couldn't imagine it. They had lakes and forests and their own little houses made of wood that didn't cost anything. When people left or died, the houses remained and were just taken over."

Rhya K. found that the old people were usually religious. "They would ask us to come to church, and when we would tell them we were Jewish they didn't react at all, as if to say, What difference does that make? and just ask again, 'So do you want to come to church?' We collected icons and old dishes, and if I noticed something and said it was beautiful they would want to give it to us. I would sometimes bring things to trade. They liked aluminum pots better than their worn old things.

"These travels showed us there were other ways to live, more fundamental than our own. The strangers we met made us feel like guests and would not take money if we stayed overnight. It was as if we had gone back far in time. In one village we talked with a man who was the head of his brigade. We noticed that his pants were held up by a piece of rope instead of a belt, and we were surprised to see that. After all, he was the boss and surely he could afford a belt. When we asked him about it, he said, 'Of course I can buy a belt, but why should

I?' He said he was not sure of what would be tomorrow and thought it better not to make any changes in his life. He wanted only to 'keep this life as it is and wait to see what will be.' "

Getting an Education

 It was generally believed that the most crucial support in life came from a good education. It had certainly been true in the past. In tsarist times students, even in rabbinical schools, had been exempt from conscription. Education has given Jews places of power in the Revolution. In spite of arrests and purges, Soviet Jews had made their way into the circles of privileged people by working in the institutes and academies, by joining the Writers' Union, the Artists' Union, the music conservatories.

Times had changed but Larisa P., a forty-five-year-old engineer from Kiev, maintained that "the old mentality exists to this day. People know higher education now will give nothing in life, but the attraction remains." A young person in a Jewish family who had no diploma was pitied. A portfolio full of diplomas and certificates, however, was no guarantee of work. "We still need decades of unhappy lives, broken fates and miserable salaries before people understand that education in and of itself does not make for a good life."

Frieda K., born in Dubossary, Moravia, in 1914, spoke of her education in the glowing terms of her generation. She had been one of four children, and her parents had hired a rabbi to teach them until they were old enough to go to the state school. The whole family had worked on their two-acre tobacco farm, which provided a meager living. "My father was religious but sharp-witted and determined to educate his children. Mama could read Yiddish but not Russian and she too wanted us to study." When she was nine years old Frieda went to a state school run by a Jewish nationalist who thought Jewish children should learn only Yiddish. She studied mathematics, Russian history and literature and Yiddish literature and planned to become a teacher in a Yiddish school herself. The Yiddish schools of that time, of course, were run in "the communist spirit," and children were forbidden to pray. Frieda went on to the Pedagogical Institute in Odessa, where there were Russian, Ukrainian and Yiddish sectors. She majored in Yiddish literature. The Yiddish sector also had departments of biology and history. The Jewish teachers in the Institute were educated in France, Germany and Italy because it had been difficult for Jews to get into Russian institutions of learning.

Frieda was at the Pedagogical Institute during a time of famine. "We got salt, a roll and a glass of tea every morning," she said. "We divided the roll into three parts and had a few bites in the morning, afternoon and evening. . . . We sat up all night writing and studying in spite of being so hungry." She remembered the names of her teachers, the Yiddish writers and poets who came from Moscow to discuss their work, the professor of Russian literature who taught Pushkin, Lermontov and Gogol and the Yiddish professor who knew thirteen languages. "The three years in the Institute gave me a great deal in personal development, culture, contacts with people and understanding of life . . . in spite of the fact that we were starving and living in horrid conditions." When the Yiddish writers and poets were killed she mourned them as acquaintances, rather than distant public figures.

The Jewish schools and institutes were closed in 1938. Frieda K. was in the transitional generation. She had begun teaching at the age of eighteen because there was such a desperate need for teachers. "We were the new generation, the first builders of communism." When Yiddish was no longer a language for teaching she shifted to Russian. In 1949 she couldn't find work as a teacher in Odessa and took a job running the library in a machine-tool plant where 40 percent of the workers were Jews. With five thousand workers at a plant far from the center of the city, she had twelve hundred readers to serve. She enjoyed her involvement in worker education. "I loved literature and encouraged people to enjoy reading. I set up discussions and lectures, invited poets and writers and actors. The workers read Dreiser, Jack London, Tolstoy, Gogol, Dickens and Galsworthy." Though the salary she received was only ninety rubles a month, Frieda K. kept her job as factory librarian and her faith in education until she emigrated to America.

Georgi S. was born ten years later than Frieda in Moscow into a much more sophisticated family. His father was a pediatrician, his mother a dentist. "My parents were assimilated. We observed no Jewish customs. There was nothing Jewish about us," he said. "My mother spoke Yiddish to her relatives only when she didn't want me to understand something." He went to an ordinary neighborhood school. His parents, like other educated parents, wanted him to have special advantages that would help him enter a university. They enrolled him in a French-speaking group that met after school. "I was nine years old," he said, "and a big patriot. The old woman who spoke French to us didn't like what was happening in the country. It was 1935, during the trial of Zinoviev, and she talked very carelessly to the children about it. I argued with her a lot. At that time we lived in a big communal room. Our neighbors were all workers and Party members. They were my heroes, and I talked to them a lot and told them about the French lady. One fine day they took me to the Party office in their factory and I told again about the French lady. I didn't even know her name; we just called her Madame. Then they brought me to the NKVD office and I told about her again. So they arrested her. They summoned my mother and questioned her, and right after this I knew I had done something bad. My mother was summoned to Lubyanka Prison, the most frightening place. You see, I hadn't told my parents anything; the neighbors told me not to tell, so I didn't. And I felt like a great hero, a regular Pavel Morozov.* Later I kept having the same dream over and over. I'd be riding on a tram and I'd see the old Frenchwoman. I'd be terribly ashamed and try to hide from her. The truth was that I never did know what happened to her. But that remains the strongest memory of my school years."

Eugenia S.'s parents sent her to a German-speaking group before she was seven. "Before the war," she said, "there were many groups led by German women from the Baltic countries. The children met at a different home each day. The maids or their mothers would bring lunch. We learned German songs and poems and played games in German. We would draw pictures, embroider and take long walks on Gogolov Boulevard with the teacher talking German to us. It was all oral. There was no writing or reading."

The early efforts at enrichment of education were followed by attempts to enroll children in one of the model schools, the special schools for the privileged children of privileged parents. Eugenia's son, born in 1956 in Moscow, described his experiences as a "privileged kid" of academic parents. "The first school I went to was very prestigious. It was an English experimental school for children of parents who had taught them to read and count, who read stories to them and provided special learning experiences at home. They had such schools for children with unusual talent in math, foreign languages, music, art, sports. Later on, however, I went to a common school for four years with the so-called basement people who had poured into Moscow just after the war. That was where I came in close contact with the new Muscovites, the barely civilized villagers with the village mentality, the coarse manners and habits."

In education, as in all other aspects of Soviet life, there was official policy and there was a spectrum of possibilities and al-

---

* *Pavel Morozov, fourteen years old in 1932, reported that his father was hiding grain from the state. He was murdered by farmers who opposed collectivization and immortalized by the Party as a hero and model for young people.*

ternatives created in response to official policy. Anastasia N., a fifty-year-old psychologist from Leningrad, explained that there had been a time when children were placed in different classes according to their level. The literate were separated from the illiterate, the fast learners from the slow. There were tests and grades to determine how they were to be assigned. In 1936, however, the Central Committee denounced "Pedology" as a "false, bourgeois science." From that time on children were not tested before entering schools. There were no longer divisions in graded classes. All children were to receive the same education. The books, the curricula and the teachers' plan books were the same everywhere. In 1936 all first-grade children recited in unison, "Yezhov, ruling with an iron hand, is our savior and catches all our enemies." (Yezhov that year was appointed Commissar for Internal Affairs.)

Everything was standardized but the quality of the students and teachers. The curriculum that was rigorously followed in Moscow was treated more politically in Magnitogorsk. In Tbilisi, Dimitri T., still a student, noted that children had to go to school in their district, and parents used all their connections to find housing in a better neighborhood with a better school. The gifted children tried to get into a special English, French or German school. The luckiest got into the handful of show schools, the schools to which foreign dignitaries were taken. The only trouble was that after the freedom of the special school, it was very difficult to go back to the ordinary school, either as a student or a teacher.

Rhya K., a forty-two-year-old teacher of Russian language and literature, compared her experiences teaching in a special school affiliated with Moscow University with the standardized education all over the country. Teachers are normally given a program they must follow, with strict rules about discipline and homework. She could in her unusual situation treat her students as if they were a friendly circle enjoying art, music and literature together. She could even, in the context of an art-history course, speak about the Bible, Homer, French Impressionists. "My students in secondary school had never heard

of Bach or Mozart. So we listened to music together, went to
museums and read world literature together. When the director asked why I gave them readings from the Bible, I told him
it was impossible to speak about Western paintings without
knowing what is in the Bible." In the class she ran as "a
friendly circle" she encouraged her students to ask questions,
to ask their parents and grandparents about their memories of
the moral questions in the Bible. One student even brought in
a few pages left from a confiscated Bible.

Such freedom for teachers and students was very unusual.
It was much more common to hear "You have no choices in a
Russian school. You have to follow the program, which is the
same for everybody regardless of your talents, commitments,
your hobbies and affiliations."

Irina G., a forty-year-old science teacher in Odessa, said she
would not have dared to make any changes in the program she
was given to follow. "The principal comes to listen. If you
don't follow the program you lose your job." Marsha L., a
Latin and music teacher from Kharkov in the same generation,
said, "The whole educational system from day-care center to
the end of a person's life is saturated with ideology. All the
teachers in Russian secondary schools use the same textbook.
All students learn that Mayakovsky is the greatest poet of our
time. They never hear about Pasternak, Mandelstam and Akhmatova. Students are discouraged from thinking for themselves.
Right from the beginning, when the nursery-school teacher
says, 'Now the children will draw a flower' and everyone
draws a flower, the initiative is destroyed. The child who
wants to draw something else is in trouble."

Rita S., a Moscow artist, saw the school discipline in Moscow as resembling that of the army. Anna D., a doctor who
worked with disturbed children in a psychiatric hospital, blamed
many of the disturbances on the harsh discipline in the schools
and the inability to accept individual differences. "School children are disciplined by scolding, humiliation, beating and deprivations. There is no fear of traumatizing children. The idea
is to raise them up to be socially responsible. If a child behaves

badly, the school informs the parents' place of work. Then the Party organization takes over."

Dr. Anna D., as head of a division for children with problems, saw children from the ages of three to sixteen. Some were brought in because they slept badly or did not behave in school. They were all children who deviated slightly from the norms set for them. Children who fought with their parents were sometimes put into disturbed divisions with schizophrenics. There were runaways to Afghanistan, stowaways on planes and early adolescents who were picked up for chasing after foreigners and asking for trinkets. The hospital was free. Mothers were sometimes happy to get rid of difficult children for a few months. It offered a respite from the worry of what they might babble to their teacher in school. They would be fed and observed by doctors and drugged if they became obstreperous.

Alla G., the mathematics teacher from Magnitogorsk who became an airline stewardess, told of her disillusionment with Soviet propaganda and the problems that surround standardized education in a country with a heterogeneous population. Alla was born in Magnitogorsk in 1951. Her parents, who came from Kiev and Vinnitsa in the Ukraine, were evacuated to the Urals during World War II, and her father remained as a worker in the metal factory for twenty-seven years. She was an unusually good student and also had help from her parents, who were very eager that she have the education they missed. Alla went to a special school for mathematics students and was ultimately, in spite of problems with anti-Semitism, accepted at the University of Magnitogorsk. She graduated in 1972 prepared to teach mathematics.

Most students tried to get teaching assignments in a city, but having no contact with anyone with influence, Alla was sent off to a village school a hundred kilometers from Magnitogorsk. There were two hundred children in the school in the village of Cilo. "Most of them were Tatars," said Alla. "Warm water and soap had never touched them. They had never known clean clothes. Seven- and eight-year-old children spoke the most terrible words, the coarsest slang and swearwords. The twelve-year-olds came to school with bottles of vodka to drink and cigarettes to smoke during the lessons."

Alla was supposed to teach math, physics and chemistry. "I tried so hard," she said. "I was honest and serious. I came every day with my lessons prepared and tried to explain to the students that they must learn everything and get good marks. I had promised to stay in the village for three years, and for a whole year I went to the school every day and came back to a peasant house to sleep and cry at night. Every two weeks I went to visit my parents in Magnitogorsk, so depressed that I told my mother I'd kill myself if I had to stay in that village for three years. It was absolutely impossible to be a teacher there. The students just came out and told me that I might be good in mathematics but I was stupid in life. They knew that it was not important for them to have an education. They had no passports and could not leave the village. When the boys were old enough they went into military service, and when they were finished they had to come back to work with the cows and drive the tractors. The girls began trying to get married when they were ten. At fifteen or sixteen they'd be pregnant. In my class I had a fifteen-year-old pregnant woman. Just to look at her depressed me. Once in a while an unusual student was given a stipend to study outside the village, but then he still had to come back. The passports were held by the head of the *kolkhoz*. Otherwise everyone would try to run away. There was nothing to keep them there. They didn't even have enough food to eat. Sometimes I'd think they did not live like people, more like animals. But I knew they weren't born this way. Life made them like that. They were the children and grandchildren of the people who were rich *kulaks* before the Revolution. They had once had houses and money and land, but they had been sent to the Urals, where they had nothing.

"It was a big education for me to teach in the village. I went there as an idealistic child who'd been taught about the nice life in the village where everybody is happy and good. I came back to Magnitogorsk an older, wiser woman who had learned that the communist propaganda about the happiness and well-being of all people is a lie."

Alla was aware of well-known model villages in which life was comfortable, but she was convinced that "in ninety percent of the villages the people still have the same life I described." She did not last the three years she had promised. Her mother came to her rescue. She took a job in a restaurant, where she met influential leaders of the Communist Party. By going out of her way to make reservations for them, she found the person who could help her daughter transfer to a city school.

At the end of one year Alla returned to Magnitogorsk to teach, and there she learned other lessons. "I learned how important it is to be a member of the Party and have some protection. If you have people looking out for you, everything is well. If not, anything can happen. I watched the teachers trying to get the best classes, the best hours, the best students. I had just a regular job, not the best students or the best hours, but after my village experience I was happier than anyone else. In the city school I learned that it was not so important to educate the children because you cannot give bad marks. If the children get bad marks the head of the school will say you are a bad teacher. So teachers never give children bad marks because they are afraid it will reflect on them. For the eighty rubles we were paid it was not worth getting into trouble."

Alla G. was also troubled by the discovery that the teachers accepted money and presents from parents. "The children knew that they must bring a present to the teacher to get a good grade. I didn't want to lie to the children and make up to the parents. I saw teachers giving the wrong information to the head of the school and knew I was expected to do the same. I remembered how my parents had sat over me to be sure every paper was perfect, encouraging me to be serious and learn well to get on in the world, and I just felt depressed. The schools I taught in destroyed my faith. I lost my belief in Russia. I lost my dream that everyone was equal, that there were no rich and no poor and that all people are on the same level no matter where they live."

Alexander A., the son of Abram and Irene A., was only six years younger than Alla, but he grew up in a family that was realistic and outspoken, and he had no illusions. "I was no more than seven when my father told me about his experiences, how he'd been arrested and kept in a concentration camp. He also advised me not to talk about provocative subjects with my friends, and even as a little child I knew what a provocative subject was. It was about being a Jew and having a father who'd been arrested." Though Abram A. had wrested rather than earned his education, he was determined to arrange easier and happier experiences for his son. As a professor at the Polytechnic Institute in Moscow, he had the connections to help him enroll his son in a special school. He tried to get him into an English school, but there was none available. He compromised by sending Alexander to a special French school.

"When I was seven," said Alexander, "I began going to this show-off school where they used to bring French-speaking foreigners and lots of delegations. They'd bring all these people to show them a typical school. It had all this modern equipment that was available in only a couple of other places. It was supposed to be a neighborhood school, but only five percent of the students came from the district. The rest had parents with connections. They were the sons and daughters of Soviet diplomats or of people who worked abroad as trade representatives or journalists. We were four Jewish kids in a class of thirty. Later, after we turned sixteen, there were fewer because some of us managed to get passports that said Russian or Polish."

The school was not subdivided into elementary and high school divisions. It was a ten-year program called the Moscow Special School Number Two, which took students from the ages of seven to sixteen. French was taught from the first grade on, and the students became proficient in speaking, reading and translating the language. They were being prepared for entrance into the Moscow Institute of International Relations.

Alexander A., as a Jew, was not eligible, but he shared the ambitions of his classmates. "We all wanted to become diplomats and journalists, to be among those going abroad to work in other countries. Most of the students knew that their parents lived much better than the average Soviet citizen. They had access to foreign countries and could bring back things they could sell on the black market. They had a much higher standard of life than ordinary people."

The Moscow Special School Number Two was not run as a permissive "friendly circle." The principal was a KGB man, the former chief of Smirsh. Alexander A. explained that Smirsh was the military intelligence who were behind Soviet troops during combat. They carried machine guns, and the Soviet soldiers who would not fight were cut down by the Smirsh soldiers. When asked how he knew all this, Alexander claimed that it was no secret, that it was spoken of boastfully, with considerable pride.

In the eighth grade students began to be obligated to inform on their classmates. It was a test of loyalty to find out which students would be acceptable at the Moscow Institute. In the tenth grade, however, a wave of rebellion among the students caused a scandal. A few students refused to report on the behavior of their friends. The administration, in turn, gave them bad résumés and would not let them take the examinations for entrance into a university. Alexander A. experienced the excitement as an observer. He had not been asked to inform because he was not trusted in the first place and was therefore saved the ignominy of refusing. He was a cautious member of the Komsomol and a personal friend of the local leader of the Komsomol, who was also Jewish.

He described 1971 as a tense time for Jewish students whether or not they had protection from high-placed friends. The official anti-Semitic campaign was under way. Moscow University and the medical school were closed to Jewish students. In the hope of acquiring special qualifications that would counteract the possibility of getting a bad letter of recommendation from the Moscow Special School, Alexander A. enrolled in special classes at the Mendeleev Institute of Chemical Technology. Courses in chemistry, physics and mathematics were given at night for talented tenth-graders who wanted to enter the Institute without taking entrance examinations. The experience served him well. He passed his examinations with high grades, but then entered the medical school in Irkutsk, the city from which his mother had come. It was far enough from Moscow so that no one knew that his father had applied for an emigration visa. Alexander did not believe that they would actually get permission to leave, but he knew that if he had pursued his education at the Mendeleev Institute, where his name was known, he would have been expelled and inducted into the army.

It was not unusual for Jewish students who could not apply at the major universities to find a place for themselves in Irkutsk, Novosibirsk or Magnitogorsk. Those who had prepared themselves for the competition in Moscow or Leningrad found the entrance examinations for less prestigious schools easy to pass. They also found less concern for quotas, less anti-Semitism and less fear of informers. Alexander A. found the standards in Irkutsk the same as those in other schools and also found good professors. He also found the kind of Jewish community life that was not to be experienced in Moscow. The Jews in Irkutsk did not go to synagogue and did not celebrate any holidays, but they were a closely knit group, knew each other and helped each other.

Emanuel D., a civil engineer who had grown up in Kharkov, went to graduate school at Akademgorodok, thirty kilometers from Novosibirsk. He had heard that it was an unusual place, a haven for intelligent people, beyond the reach of Soviet power. When he came to it in 1970, he was told it was no longer as free as it had been when it was founded in 1958. He still found it different from any place he had ever seen.

"It was isolated, far from any center. Akademgorodok was on the bank of a man-made lake, surrounded by a forest of birch and pine. The sky was clear, always blue." Emanuel D. found a few beautiful tall buildings and also the standard buildings constructed during Khrushchev's time. It was the people, however, that he found so unusual. "I had found," he said, "that the majority of progressive unorthodox types were in physics and mathematics, not in the humanities. There were many open-minded young scientists at Akademgorodok. I can't explain the reasons for their freedom, but there was no question about the unusual degree of independence. There was even the remains of an intellectual club where interesting people came to sing and read poetry. There was a high concentration of Jews at all levels among the scientists, students and graduate students. More than the intellectual work of my dissertation I enjoyed the relationships between people. They were more natural, less restrained, more kindhearted and open than I had ever seen before."

Emanuel D. was accustomed to the nervousness and the bitterness of Soviet citizens who'd been beaten by the harshness of their lives. He had come to expect "the rigidity and fierceness, the boorishness and vulgarity." The Jews in Akademgorodok came from the Ukraine, from Odessa, Kiev and Kharkov, the most anti-Semitic areas of the Soviet Union. They found the atmosphere so pleasant, so free of harassment that many would have liked to stay forever. They had to leave, however, once they acquired their degrees, because they could not find work in Siberia. In any event, the sanctuary did not last. An anti-Zionist campaign destroyed the atmosphere from within in the middle seventies. From without, the peace and quiet were ruined by the Torgoble Central, a shopping center provided for the scientists which brought people from miles and miles away to shop for things unavailable in Novosibirsk. The once-quiet forests were filled with picnickers. It became impossible to walk for the crowds. People tried to go back to Moscow and Leningrad. They began to leave for Israel if they could.

Educational havens were invariably temporary. Galina K. described an experimental English school in Leningrad as a kind of paradise for teachers and students. The English classes were taught in groups of ten. The teachers were unusually tal-

ented and the students carefully selected. The high point of
the school year was a full production in English of a play by
Shakespeare, Shaw or Oscar Wilde. She was an English teacher
in the school for ten years and watched the American and English delegations come to admire the lively atmosphere and the
educational accomplishments.

Galina saw the school as an escape from the harsh realities of
life in the late sixties and early seventies. "We managed to create our own little world," she said. "It elevated and purified
us." The students were the children of teachers at the University of Leningrad, and they were groomed to become students
and teachers at the University. Unfortunately, the success of
the school led to its demise. In 1976, it was reorganized. The
standard curriculum was restored. The English classes and theater productions were forbidden, and the faculty and students
were deprived of their special atmosphere. When Galina K.
left to teach in a conventional school in Leningrad, she found
the atmosphere "dismal . . . a striking contrast" and with no
safety from the anti-Semitism of the teachers and students.

When asked about their education, many émigrés answer
that they began their schooling at the age of seven in "a typical, dull Soviet school." After graduation there were the usual
years in an institute studying subjects that were not necessarily
interesting, and then, if they were lucky, the first assigned job.
The unlucky people received a free diploma, which meant
they had to go hunting for work.

The passionate stories, however, are told by those who were
looking for more than a "typical experience." Education in
the Soviet Union is compulsory and free. Even workers in factories are urged to attend classes at night in order to "achieve"
a diploma. Only privileged people, however, have choices. The
struggle to get into a special school which may open a door to
a university or a prestigious institute begins in early childhood.
Success in school is seen as the first step to success in life. Parents make the decisions for their children, because there is too
much at stake to risk a wrong move. There are special strategies for Jewish students, who are restricted by quotas, oral ex-

aminations designed to make them fail and even grades that are altered so that they will not receive the gold or silver medal that normally guarantees entrance into a university.

The barriers inspired a dogged stubbornness, the kind of determination that might never be visible in a less restricting environment. Polina N. had decided at the age of fifteen to become a physicist. Her father, however, was missing in action in World War II. Captured soldiers were expected to kill themselves, and since there were no witnesses to prove he had died honorably, he was considered a traitor. This created a problem for his daughter when she applied to the University of Moscow. Parents were responsible for the behavior of their children, and children, in turn, were punished for the sins of their fathers. Polina came to Moscow from Chelyabinsk to take the entrance examination and came out with one of the five highest grades in the group of more than two hundred students. It was decided that it was impossible for a student from the provinces to do so well in a competition with the best students in the Moscow school. She was rejected for cheating. "They could not say it was because of my father or because I was Jewish. It was their way of making my rejection legal."

She was ashamed to return to Chelyabinsk as a failure. "The whole school and all the neighbors knew I was to go to the University in Moscow. I didn't go back. I went straight to Leningrad to take the entrance examination there at the Institute of Optics, which had a Department of Nuclear Physics. Again I received superior grades, and this time nobody accused me of cheating. I confirmed that I really was good in mathematics and assumed that I would be accepted. I didn't even think to check the registration list until the day before classes began. When I did, I saw that my name was missing. I went to the secretary to say there'd been a mistake and was told that I'd not been accepted in spite of my high grades. So then I came to the chairman of admissions to ask for the reason. All he would say was that it was the decision of the committee and that he was not authorized to tell me why I had not been accepted. I had the card showing that I'd been rejected. There was nothing written where the reason was to be given. I begged him to fill it in, and he wrote, 'No dormitory space.' I told them I would find my own space, though I had no idea how to do that. I was only seventeen, and away from home alone for the first time in my life. They wouldn't change their decision, so I applied at the Shipbuilding Institute, where they were looking for students because too few had applied."

Polina N. remained as a student in Leningrad for only a year. She was disappointed in the Institute, and her mother became ill in Chelyabinsk and needed her help. She took a job as a manual laborer and studied mathematics by correspondence in a university in the Urals. It took her nine years to get a degree. She went on to do research in molecular spectroscopy, fought for the right to defend her dissertation and ultimately became the physicist she had wanted to be at fifteen.

The years of schooling were usually described as a series of trials and competitions, made more difficult by unwritten restrictions and unadmitted prejudices. "The Jewish quotas were not published, but they were always there," said Edward K. "You had to have the right connections to be able to reach the person in charge of the entrance examinations. You had to know who was to be bribed." He asserted that the problems with getting into a university had begun as early as 1945. What happened in the late sixties and seventies was only an intensification of an old pattern.

Professions were chosen less because of individual interests and talents than because of their "access without nationality restrictions." If it became known that there was a director of an institute who was not anti-Semitic, Jewish students would apply. Interest in the work itself was a secondary consideration. There were many engineers like Boris F. who wanted to be doctors. "In 1967 it was impossible to study medicine or law. Only the engineering fields were open to us. If you were a Jew you had to be an engineer. There wasn't anything else. I heard of a friend who was able to enter medical school, but his father was an attorney with powerful connections. It was very unusual." Ilya K., an engineer in the design department

of Soyez Lift, said that 90 percent of the engineers working
with him were Jewish. There were many talented and well-
trained men among them who had been fired from their jobs
in military research. When they went looking for work in an
undeveloped industry, they discovered the elevator industry,
in which the Soviet Union was at least thirty years behind
West Germany, England and France. Jews entered a new design bureau and were able to bring their unemployed relatives,
friends and students with them.

Conflicts between parents and children were exacerbated by
changes in the opportunities available. Parents trying to spare
their children the pain of rejection met with resistance from
young people who found it hard to believe that the indoctrination of their schooling was nothing more than official propaganda.

Mikhael M., born in Odessa in 1935, said, "I couldn't believe
that people weren't getting into school because they were
Jewish. I discounted what my father told me because he didn't
even have a high school education. What would he know? He
was not a developed person. I was always trying to find legitimate explanations for the difficulties. It was my way of trying
to survive morally and physically. When I was not accepted at
the Polytechnical University for being too young, I wrote to
the Ministry in Moscow, sent copies of my certificates from the
mathematics Olympics and said, 'I'm sixteen and want to be a
scientist. Please permit me to be enrolled.' When I received
permission, I knew I had been right not to listen to my parents." He was a good student, a silver-medalist with great expectations. "It was prestigious at that time to be an electromechanical engineer, more prestigious than to be a mechanical
engineer, so that is what I wanted to be," said Mikhael. "Of
course, it was more prestigious to be a mathematician, but all
the graduates of the Mathematics Division at the University of
Odessa became teachers, and that was not prestigious."

He entered the university as the only Jewish student in the
freshman class and was suspended in December of 1952 when
the Jewish doctors in the Kremlin were jailed. "There was an
announcement on the wall that two hundred students were ex-

pelled and my name was there. I was expelled for being a hooligan, for lack of discipline, for using coarse language with
teachers. My father knew why I was expelled, but even then I refused to believe that I could be expelled from the university for
being Jewish. My father let me go to Moscow to fight for justice, and in Moscow I was told to be patient and quiet. It was
'This is the situation. We have papers that you are a hooligan.
We understand you are not a hooligan, but we have the papers
that say you are. You are a good, smart boy. Go home and sit
tight.' I went to the Ministry every day for three months, as if
going to work. At eight o'clock every morning the basement
window opened and a little boy outside called out, 'Jew, Jew,
Jew' and then closed the window. It was like morning exer-
cises. . . . And the last month of my stay in Moscow, Stalin
died. I went back to the Institute in Odessa, where I was told
that the situation had not changed and the best thing for me to
do was go to work as an unskilled laborer in a factory and acquire references that I was a good worker." A year later he returned with the references and was taken back. At this time he
was no longer the only Jew in his class. He was in another department in which 50 percent of the students were Jewish.

After graduating, Mikhael M. worked in a design bureau
that was known for hiring Jews. The director was a Ukrainian,
but he had a reputation for taking on Jewish engineers in good
and bad times. "It was like being in a synagogue," said Mikhael.
He went as far as he could go in the bureau, had some inventions of his own and twenty-two patents, but was not accepted
at the university as a postgraduate student. He went to Moscow to apply and found there a replica of the Odessa "synagogue," where he was accepted, defended his dissertation and
earned the equivalent of a Ph.D.

An ordinary worker earned more than an engineer, but acquiring an advanced degree could double an engineer's salary.
It was not unusual to hear, "Engineers are the poorest educated people in the Soviet Union." They cannot supplement
their earnings like doctors and lawyers. They have no way of
getting more than a salary.

Professional Life

 DESCRIBING THEIR EXPERIENCES in acquiring an education, the memoirists divide themselves into two major groups. Men and women both turn up as potential mathematicians, physicists and scientific researchers, even though they may not have had opportunities to work in the professions for which they had prepared themselves. There are also those who describe themselves as "humanitarians," meaning humanists, who studied history, languages, Russian culture, art and music in the hope that they would find work as performers, teachers, writers or researchers in the state-sponsored academies.

In both camps one can find practical men and women who looked for an opportunity to earn a few extra rubles and privileges and unworldly types who looked for an escape from the culture of a restricting society by losing themselves in creative and scholarly work. Polina N., the determined physicist from Chelyabinsk, was so enamored of the process of doing independent research that she spent her own hard-earned money on lab materials when they were not otherwise obtainable. "My colleagues thought me a kind of nut," she said. "But my research was my big love, my hobby."

Nina S., an Orientalist who wrote her dissertation on Buddhism in Ceylon, spoke of a "crazy involvement with scientific problems and cultural problems. We talked only about ideas and books, never about the ordinary things of life. We had no life beyond our work. Once, working late in the library, I said to a friend who was also staying as late as possible and who would be back the next day and the next that we were involved over our heads. It was a kind of escape, a kind of narcotic for us."

It was hard to tell whether special privileges were awarded to the people of the highest status or whether simply having privileges conferred the status. Writers, artists, composers and leading scientists in the Academy of Science were envied their opportunities to obtain housing, special foods and vacation homes. Seventeen-year-olds trying to get into a university or the network of institutes that trained them for a specific industry or service knew that the rest of their lives were determined by that first step. A forty-year-old magazine editor from Moscow was sure that the most important factor in choosing a profession was how much money one could earn. She thought teachers and doctors were to be pitied because they were paid so poorly. Polina N., the obsessive researcher, cared less about earning money but more about doing work that was of interest to her. For her, to teach meant failure. "I felt as if I will sink if I have to teach. I will be as if drowned in the river."

The most envied people were those who had a special talent that was publicly rewarded. A twenty-two-year-old said that he wanted to study medicine, but his parents had objected and insisted that he study music instead. A violinist from the Moscow Symphony told of his conflicts with his father because he wanted to be a physicist and his father saw no prestige in anything but music. It was believed that in the city of Tbilisi, 90 percent of the Jewish children took music lessons. The parents hoped to discover some liberating talent. The children, however, saw the music as a way to independence. "It's something you learn without your parents' interfering," said Dimitri T., a student from Tbilisi. "It's a way to escape your parents' control." Musicians might have opportunities to travel, and they could earn small sums beyond their salaries. They were accorded high status even though their salaries were low. The status, of course, came only within the small world of performers and music lovers, but it was enough to separate them from ordinary workers and tradesmen. Musicians and artists were on another level, supposedly serving the cultural needs of the population. The parents who brought their children to the conservatories for lessons wanted to save them from the drudgery of medicine, law, engineering and teaching.

Rima M., a forty-five-year-old dentist from Moscow, said that doctors and dentists in the Soviet Union had no more prestige than barbers or beauticians, even though they received gifts from their patients that tripled their basic salary. Law was no better. Emanuel D., the engineer from Kharkov, was the son of a lawyer. He said, "My father was a typical Soviet man, leading a double existence, trying to be honest when it was impossible not to make compromises. From my earliest years I heard that jurisprudence is not a profession, not a science. To be a lawyer is to have a sorry profession." Florina R., a Moscow lawyer, valued only the free time that was possible in her profession. She said, "I decided to get away from criminal cases because no matter what I did I couldn't help anybody."

The wish for the power "to help somebody," the need for meaningful work and some dignity and integrity in professional relationships, seemed at least as important to some people as salaries and privileges. In their stories about earning a living and in their reasons for leaving one hears about frustrations that could not be resolved by acquiring more money or the right to shop in a better market. There are as many complaints about what they call "the ideological aspects" of work as there are grim tales of trying to feed a family on 120 rubles a month—the salary of an ordinary worker, a biologist or an ordinary engineer.

Teachers of all subjects, musicians, artists, writers, scientists, actors and lawyers, as well as the law enforcers, are considered ideological workers. This aspect affected the lives of the most talented and the least talented, the famous and the unknown in all the professions.

Victoria L. was a Moscow pianist who took the normal restrictions as a personal affront. "For entrance into graduate school," she said, "I had to pass exams in piano, music theory and 'The History of the Party and Marxism.' We studied the works of Lenin, Marx and Engels in the schools as in tsarist times they studied God's law. We had to memorize everything and answer questions like an automaton. You could get A-plus for music and be refused entrance to the Conservatory if you could not show by your answers that you were a good Soviet citizen. Before traveling abroad to give concerts you had to get permission from the Party committee. You'd be asked questions about the lead article in *Pravda*, about the latest propaganda about China or America, and if you couldn't answer they wouldn't sign the reference and you couldn't go. No one ever asked me if I was ready to perform. There were only the questions that had nothing to do with music or me."

Musicians complained that they were expected to inform upon each other when traveling. Teachers at the music conservatories were warned against training Jewish students to become prize winners and urged to find Russian students who could win the competitions. "Music is a form of diplomacy, a way of making political points," said Misha H., a violinist and assistant conductor of the Bolshoi Theater until 1961. He had a long memory of the shifting attitudes toward composers, pieces of music and performers and the harassment of Jews, who were unwelcome and distrusted as ideological workers.

The violin was considered a "Jewish instrument," and the major conservatories had once been run by famous Jewish teachers. After World War II there was an open campaign to limit the enrollment of Jewish students. Victoria L., who at thirteen was a student at the Gnesen Music School in Moscow, remembered that the rector of the Conservatory said openly that the goal of his life was to create a Russian conservatory free of Jewish teachers and students. This was said when David Oistrakh and Leonid Kogan were on the faculty. The Jewish music director was fired. Jewish children were not chosen for performances in spite of competitions in which they excelled. The policy was to let the old faculty die out and to keep new Jewish musicians from entering it. Musicians who received invitations to perform were unable to get permission to travel. Students who asked to study with a Jewish teacher were sent to another. It happened gradually, so that there was a time lag between the policy changes and the public awareness of what was happening. There were always exceptions which led people to hope that they might be among the ones chosen and that the climate that changed might change again in their favor.

It was hard to know when one began an education whether it would be useful when it was completed. A violinist in the Moscow Philharmonic admitted that it was very difficult for Jewish musicians to get into the orchestra, though many Jews did. "The difficulties made us try harder. Teachers would take on only students with a lot of talent who could be pushed and driven. They were very strict and authoritarian. Getting into an orchestra was seen as winning a competition. One doesn't get in. One wins the right to play."

The working life of orchestra players was difficult and poorly paid. Their schedules could be changed without notice, so they were unable to add to their income by teaching. The conductor, however, received 1,000 rubles for each performance. The assistant who conducted when the main conductor was ill received 300 or 400 rubles. A soloist touring within the Soviet Union could earn 1,000 rubles for ten concerts. Victoria L., when teaching at the Conservatory, was proud to be earning 300 or 400 rubles a *month*—as much as a full professor at a university or institute. If she bridled whenever the Ministry of Culture refused to permit her to play abroad, she knew she was not alone. Sviatoslav Richter was not permitted to play outside the Soviet Union until he was forty-five, and then he could go only to Socialist countries. The French had recorded him when he played in Poland and sent him a car, a Citroën, as a present.

The majority of the graduates of music conservatories did not win their way into major orchestras. Singers, soloists and conductors were obligated to give a quota of concerts a month and were sent out to the hinterlands to fulfill their responsibilities. Felix B., a violinist and conductor, had graduated from the Music School for Gifted Children in Moscow. He was there during the purge of Jewish teachers and remembered competitions in which the difficult pieces were given to Jewish contestants and the easier ones to the Russian musicians and the title of "People's Artist of the Russian Federated Socialist Republics" was not given to Kogan, who deserved it, but to a Russian musician who could not be compared to him. Felix B. saw musicians as struggling, unappreciated people. "Musicians and performers get very small salaries. A miner or an ordinary construction worker has a minimum salary that is four times that of a musician. A clerk, an ordinary clerk, earns one hundred twenty rubles a month. A performer in my theater gets seventy or eighty rubles a month.

"We were supposed to bring music to the outlying areas," said Felix B. "When I was young I liked touring. I liked to see the scenery and meet different kinds of people. We were a group of youngsters traveling together, having a good time. We didn't mind sleeping on beds full of bedbugs and eating peasant food that endangered our health. We lived for weeks on those miserable cans of fish and loaves of black bread so hard you could hammer a nail into the wall with them. When we traveled to Kharkov or Novosibirsk from Moscow we'd try to find some food and the stores looked as if they'd just been robbed. No sugar, no butter, no fresh bread, let alone meat. Fifteen kilometers from the big-city centers, that's how it was. But what got on my nerves even then was that nobody wanted us and nobody needed us. We were sent by the Party committee with all our papers and certificates to serve the cultural needs of the population. We had an accordion, a singer, a guitar and a violin and we were to play folk music. We'd arrive at some *kolkhoz* to give a concert and before we got permission to play there'd be a battle because the chairman of the *kolkhoz* would say that there was no reason to distract the people and he'd send them off to work, so we had no audience. We'd hear, 'What the hell do they need culture for? They need to go into the fields, and here you are with your culture.' So we'd go out into the fields and set up our stands. We'd play and sing, and the peasants would gather around and listen for a few minutes. Their interest didn't last, and the leader would say, 'Stop! That's enough! Go back to work!' We'd be cut off in the middle of a piece, in the middle of a phrase. We knew they'd have gotten a lot more pleasure if they had been drunk and playing their own accordions. They knew the songs better than we did. After all, it was their culture.

"We had such experiences almost everywhere we went. We'd come to some old-age homes. Horrible places. Everything stinks. People no longer look like human beings and are treated as if they were animals. It was as if we were in the world of Hieronymus Bosch. We'd play a little bit and get out as fast as possible. That's how it was for musicians touring in the sticks. We went to the depths of Siberia and the far east. In Birobidzhan I met Jews unlike any Jews I'd ever known. Totally assimilated, they spoke only Russian. They were broken by the cold and the hard work and had lost any kind of distinction, cultural or otherwise.

"As I got older," said Felix B., "I became less enthusiastic about touring. You can imagine how I felt when I was sent alone to give a violin recital. I was welcomed with 'We don't need that. What do we want with violin playing? Don't they have any jugglers or any magicians?' I could see that it was possible to give a proper concert only in a big city where there was an audience that listened with pleasure. You could give yourself over to them and feel that you were a necessary person. Still you had to give at least sixteen concerts a month to keep your standing in the union. You went wherever the Party sent you. Most of the concerts were given outside the big cities."

Felix B. ultimately made his living as the conductor of the orchestra for a children's theater in Moscow. He was more than a little bitter when the theater traveled throughout Europe and went to Canada and Australia without him. He was the main conductor in Moscow, but it was impossible to get permission for a Jewish conductor to go beyond the borders. The deputy director had said, "If only you were Russian, Felix, I could send you around the world."

It gradually filtered back that studying music offered Jews no escape from ordinary life. Ella B., a pianist and music teacher born in 1954, was convinced that the "craze for music education" was over. "The competition was high when I began to study. You really had to have ability to be accepted. Of course, there were bribes and protection, and a word had to be put in for you, but there was a good selection of talented children. By the time I finished music school it was over. Parents stopped sending their children. There was no longer a need for music teachers, and the selection of children available was poor. In spite of that, if they had to choose between a gifted Jewish child and a not-so-gifted Russian or Ukrainian, the non-Jew was always preferred."

The Jewish musicians documented the changes in policy and opportunity. Each individual remembered every competition, every triumph and rejection and every battle for permission to travel abroad. Marya L. had opportunities to perform because her last name was Ukrainian rather than Jewish. She remembered playing for Stalin as a little girl. She studied at the same time as Vladimir Ashkenazy and won first place in a competition selecting contestants for the international competition in Warsaw. Only the Russians were permitted to go to Warsaw. Ashkenazy had a Russian mother and used her name so that he could compete. Victoria L. stayed home. Later she was permitted to go to Paris and then to America for the Van Cliburn competition. "They tried not to send Jews to competitions, but then realized there was no point to that. The important thing was to defend the Soviet Union and win. It's like sports, chess or gymnastics. So they send the one who plays best. Of course, if a Jew and a Russian play equally well they send the Russian. If the Jew is much better they will send him. But after the competition they will not give him concerts to play. The Ministry of Culture decides who plays where, who will be famous and who will be ignored. There's nothing you can do if they decide against you. You can't make your own arrangements." In explaining her own decision to emigrate she was also explaining why so many other musicians had defected. "The best have left," said one of the émigrés. "No musicians of importance are left."

Actors and directors had stories to tell about their own problems. The theater was even more vulnerable than the concert stage. The actors and directors among the émigrés were enthusiastic about their schooling in Russian theater. They praised its subtleties, its intellectual and philosophical qualities. Directors in Russia had the right to change the texts of plays, eliminate parts and do whatever they thought would improve the work. Moscow had thirty theaters with permanent repertory, producing twenty to thirty plays a year. "If it were not for the censorship," said Zakary K., an actor and director from Kiev, "Russia could have the best theater in the world."

Peter V., a theater actor, director and star in many films, agreed that it was very difficult to work under permanent control of the government but that there was strength to be derived from the pressure. Conservative officials, however, opposed everything new. Anatoly Efros, the best director, did classical plays, and there were not many new good ones. To be produced, a play had to be approved by the censors on the artistic council. Directors were expected to produce plays on subjects assigned to them, and the approval of the Minister of Culture was required before any production could be staged.

The most difficult problem for Zakary K. was the "unwritten understanding that there should be no Jews in ideological work, and there were all kinds of excuses for keeping them out." The actors and directors who were too young to remember the Yiddish theater thought their troubles had begun in 1967. Three Yiddish actresses among the émigrés remembered auditioning at Mikhoels' theater in Moscow. Their careers paralleled the flowering and the demise of the Yiddish theater, and they knew that problems for Jews in the theater began long before 1967.

Zakary K., born in 1939, was also convinced anti-Semitism

had not existed before the Second World War. He had no contact with actresses like Reveka K., who had seen sixteen theaters banned and who remembered when the district constable disrupted Yiddish performances and the actors shifted into broken German to keep the performances going.

Reveka K., born in Warsaw in 1908, had come to Moscow to study acting at the Mikhoels theater in 1929. She came from a family of actors; in the twenties Jewish actors had the same status as Russian actors. Jewish theater was unconventional, a new art form enjoyed by non-Jews as well as Jews even though the language of performance was Yiddish. The Jewish department of the Communist Party was responsible for the Yiddish theater. Reveka K., though not Moscow-born, claimed that she saw herself as "a Muscovite. I felt absolutely no difference between myself and other Muscovites." The theater went on as usual during the purges. When the war began the theater was evacuated to Tashkent, where the Jewish actors and the local population got along without friction. The illusion of safety was maintained when they returned to Moscow because Mikhoels, the director, had a high position as chairman of the Art Commission for the Stalin Prizes. New performances brought large audiences. The most successful postwar play began with candles burning in memory of the people who had perished in the war. The play was a statement about Jewish survival and tenacity, a testimony to the uncrushable Jewish spirit. It ended with a traditional Jewish wedding, with dances and folk tunes. For several years there were lines of people waiting outside the theater on Nikitsky Boulevard for tickets.

"And then it was over," said Reveka K. "Mikhoels was killed in a planned accident in Minsk. They brought his body to the theater in a metal coffin. They put makeup on his face to make him look like one of the comedians he liked to play. He was a national actor, a knowledgeable, thoughtful man and a man devoted to the Soviet state. Zuskin, the director who took his place, was arrested. Bergelson, Fefer, Dobrushin and Galkin were taken away, and the families of Zuskin and Markish were exiled from Moscow. There were no sentences and no trials. People simply vanished and never returned.

"Spectators began to be afraid to come to our theater. There were rumors that we had a secret printing shop backstage. Meanwhile we kept on preparing performances. Other Jewish theaters closed before ours. I remember Tairov standing in front of his theater crying the day he received the notice. In 1949 or 1950 we received no salaries. We were told the theater was no longer profitable and we were free to do as we pleased. The actors began to study crafts. We made little boxes and painted flowers. I sold books at a newsstand."

Reveka K. was among the actors and actresses who kept on rehearsing at night and for years sent in applications for permission to perform in public. The applications were rejected by the Moscow Concert Administrator and the Ministry of Culture on the ground that there was no longer a literature or an audience in Yiddish. "In 1963," Reveka said, "we managed to get a permit. When we went on tour we found that we had an audience, even places where children spoke Yiddish. We had packed halls in Leningrad, in Zhitomir, in Magnitogorsk, where we gave two performances in a single day and the young people came with bunches of flowers." The troupe at this time included eleven actors, an orchestra of nine musicians and a staff. They performed Sholom Aleichem's *Enchanted Tailor* and *Tevye the Milkman*, Lermontov's *The Spaniards* and Gordin's *Beyond the Ocean*. Playwrights promised to add to the literature so the theater could continue.

"We worked under the hardest conditions," Reveka continued. "We existed even though they did everything possible to prove we were not needed. We were given no publicity and no chance to advertise. We had to go out ourselves to post the notices. We came to Kishinev by bus and found all the tickets for our performance were sold. People looked forward to our coming as to a holiday. But when we arrived there was no place for us to sleep. The officials said there were too many actors on tour and no room for them. We were told we could go back to Moscow if we didn't like it. In Zhitomir, after we

had traveled so far, they would not let us perform. We could
go only to the small towns in the provinces where nothing was
prepared for us. We were made to feel like second-rate citizens. We were once proud actors. I love my art more than my
life, but in those conditions I felt only shame for what we
were doing. We had become pariahs. It was as if we were
living on an uninhabited island. In 1974 we were allowed four
performances in the concert hall of the Sovietskaya Hotel in
Moscow. There were no performances in the five years before
I left. Our last performance in Moscow was at the time of
Nixon's visit to the U.S.S.R. They made up a show of a Yiddish theater for the West. The actors who have the strength to
put on those shows of a nonexistent Yiddish theater are true
heroes."

The older Jewish actors and directors spoke of themselves
as Russian conservators of Yiddish culture. They were Rus-
sian-speaking, secular and often only marginally Jewish. The
Yiddish theater recognized no Jewish holidays or Sabbaths.
Maya G., a concert singer as well as a trained actress in Mikhoels' theater in Moscow, sang in Russian, Italian, French and
Hungarian. She also collected Yiddish folk songs and had
more than twenty in her repertoire, but did not dare to sing
them in public. When the careers of the Yiddish-speaking actors and singers were cut short, they felt it was because they
had chosen an obsolete and unfashionable medium for their
talents.

Younger actors and directors, however, were thwarted by
open anti-Semitism. Their names, their faces and the fifth
point of their internal passports kept them out of the professional theater. They speak of a few exceptions, such as Lyubimov and Yefremov at the Moscow Art Theater and Efros and
Zakharov, but are convinced that no amount of talent and
study will help them scale the barriers set up to keep Jews out
of the professional theater in the Soviet Union. The profession
they chose in the hope that it would offer a magical escape
from ordinary Soviet life was not what they had hoped it
would be. The belief that there was safety from anti-Semitism

among intellectuals and creative people in the arts was under-
mined by the pronouncements of the new Russian right, the
Obshehestvo Rasiya. There were open attacks upon the Jewish
people and Jewishness in any form. Having talent only made
Jews more vulnerable. They were spoken of as "parasites who
corrupt and spoil the cultures to which they attach themselves."

Unlike the theater people, the journalists and writers among
the émigrés spoke of themselves as "privileged people." They
did not compare themselves to the people in high Party positions or in leading positions in the economy which would
bring them into the world of special stores and food and
clothes, but they were far better off than ordinary citizens.
Membership in the Soviet Union of Writers was open to poets
and prose writers, translators and propaganda writers, a literary army of ten thousand people, all subject to the censorship
of the Ministry of Culture.

Konstantin S., a thirty-five-year-old journalist, considered
himself lucky because his last name was Russian. Though his
nationality as a Jew was stamped on his passport, his career
was not affected as it would have been if he had had to sign
his writings with a Jewish-sounding name. His articles and literary criticism appeared in *Yunost*, a popular journal. Though
he experienced anti-Semitism at the editorial offices of *Young
Guard*, a journal that belonged to the Central Committee of
the Komsomol, and expected it at the publishing houses connected with Russian nationalists and ideologists, he found the
four official Soviet publishing houses open to Jewish writers.
There were problems only when they seemed to dominate a
journal or a list of new titles. The propaganda of the nationalists who preached the expulsion of Jews from Russian literature
was impossible to ignore, but until he emigrated, Konstantin S.
lived in the "Pink Ghetto," the special apartments for writers
built by the Writers' Union in Moscow.

"These were cooperative apartments, and most of the tenants were Jews or half-Jews. There were playwrights and film
scenarists, along with the usual spectrum of good and bad

writers. The admitting committee for the Writers' Union had no artistic criteria. It was the quantity of published writing, not the quality, that accounted for acceptance in the union. If someone has written two bad novels that are published, it is enough. Artistic criteria are confused and unclear in a totalitarian society, and a very bad, anti-Semitic writer might be considered great."

The benefits available to members of the Writers' Union made membership very attractive. "I had a high salary," said Konstantin S. "I earned three hundred rubles a month and could usually pick up another two to six hundred rubles when my articles were sold. If a book came out, I might get two thousand rubles at once. More likely five hundred. I also had opportunities to give lectures and do television programs."

High on Konstantin's list of privileges was the right to go to a "first-class hospital where medicine was available and food was given to patients. The hospital would be associated with the Academy of Science, since I wrote for a journal that belonged to them." He also could look forward to vacations in the special homes for creative writers in the Crimea and the Caucasus and outside Leningrad and Moscow. "As a writer I had access to the same places and services as the Party workers on *Pravda* and *Izvestia*. I could get special books not available in bookstores, tickets to concerts and films before they were advertised for the general public. I had admission to the House of Journalists, which is a sign of belonging to an elite and also important because one of the best restaurants in Moscow is in the House of Journalists and I could invite my friends and let them enjoy the excellent service with me. I could even order a chicken or two pounds of meat and have it delivered to my house."

The most valued benefit from the Union of Writers was the possibility of taking trips abroad. Konstantin S. was able to arrange journeys to Belgium, Luxembourg, Sweden and Finland with the Union of Writers and then to Czechoslovakia and Yugoslavia with a theater group.

Konstantin S. described his privileges in such glowing terms that it was difficult to see why he had decided to leave for the uncertainties of life in the West. He was among those émigrés who wanted it to be clear that they had not left to improve their material life. "I decided to leave in 1975 for several reasons, not only because I'm Jewish. First of all it was because I'm a writer and I couldn't take any more of the censorship. Everything I wrote was either totally disfigured or left unpublished. In every writer there is a censorship from within, an internal censorship, and I always thought this should be enough, but I was censored at every step. Let's say I had an article published in the *Literaturnaya Gazeta*. This is a very good newspaper—cultured, intelligent, interesting. They published my articles three or four times a year, knowing that I was a liberal critic and that liberal readers would be interested in what I had to say. So the editor calls me to his office and says, 'This is an excellent article, but there are four Jewish names here.' And so I remind him that at least ten of the writers I mention are not Jewish. He suggests that we leave out 'two Jewish heroes' and save them for the next article. The next time, he does not need to say anything about Jews; it is just a complaint that there are four names in a row that he cannot include. He says, 'They already call us a *Zhid* newspaper.' 'They' are the Russian nationalists in Moscow, and he is afraid of them. So what can I do? I take out some names and bargain with him about the others. The next time I bring him an article there are other Jewish names and the whole thing starts all over again. Then there are the problems with political allusions. The editor asks, 'What are you hinting? What are you alluding to?' I say 'Nothing,' but he doesn't believe me. I was writing about a reform in poetry and said that poetic reforms and poetic revolutions end in nothing. They end as they began, with no changes. The editor was afraid I was alluding to the great October Socialist Revolution, and I had to convince him that it hadn't entered my mind."

The censorship was artistic as well as political and ideological. Swearwords were forbidden, even popular expressions. Foreign words were not permitted. Certain concepts could not be mentioned. It was not possible to use the words "abortion" or "contraception." Even "birth control" could not be mentioned. Konstantin S. did not believe it was possible to be a passive dissident and lacked the courage for open battles he knew he couldn't win. He decided to emigrate with his Russian wife and son to escape from the conflicts with himself as well as his struggles with the Ministry of Culture, the Central Party Committee and the network of censors who had to pass on every work to be published. "They might cross out one part at one step," said Konstantin, "another at the second step, and the last person to see it might then decide not to publish it at all."

Artists among the émigrés offer other versions of the endless struggle between creative and individualistic personalities and official policy. Moishe S., a painter and student of architecture from Odessa, saw himself and the art scene clearly.

"I wanted to be an artist from childhood on," he said. "I never had any other serious idea for a profession; but circumstances pushed me into the Architecture Institute. Even while studying architecture, I planned to be a painter, worked hard at drawing, always aware that it was frightening to do only painting. I was in school at the end of the thirties and there were still a lot of good teachers who'd been educated in Old Russia and France. Odessa had artistic traditions. There was a famous Southern Russian school of art that was close to the Impressionists.

"My parents warned me that things are difficult for artists, and it certainly turned out to be that way. Meanwhile I spent eight years working as an architect, finding there was no freedom for creativity at all in architecture. I thought that in painting, even when you were working for the state, you were mostly your own master. So I showed my paintings in exhibitions of watercolors and landscapes. I traveled a lot and drew a lot in the north.

"I should explain that the conditions of life for artists in Soviet Russia have nothing in common with the situation of the artist in America. In America you can be a good artist or a bad artist, a success or a failure, with no help or hindrance from anyone. In Russia, the government spends an enormous amount of money on propaganda and an army of artists take part in that effort. They are very often talented people, but never say what they think. They are the people who work purely on propaganda art in its most naked form. In addition there is the Union of Soviet Artists. It's very hard to get into the union.

"For someone like me from Odessa, it's necessary to get paintings into the regional shows first. From the regional shows a percentage is selected for the national exhibitions. In Kiev, meanwhile, there is an enormous jury of artists who follow the Party line and the chairmen of regional art unions, the bureaucrats of ministries, representatives of the Committee on Art, the Ministry of Education, the Ministry of Culture and the directors of museums in the major cities who are also Party workers. These people decide whether an artist should be permitted to send his paintings to Moscow. Mostly they confirm each other and emphasize the ideological messages they approve. Portraits must have the optimistic look, the courageous look. If the artist doesn't portray a worker as they think a worker should look, then the portrait will never make it through the competition no matter how good it is.

"Then there is a problem with subjects. Jewish themes are forbidden, also icons. Nudity is absolutely out. The slightest deviation from socialist realism is considered bourgeois and decadent. A false romanticism permitted fairy-tale subjects, but any sign of abstraction was persecuted.

"You couldn't find a fresh thought in the exhibitions. The Moscow Council was usually more intelligent and qualified than the one in Kiev, but they were all the same kind of people, following the same Party line. Then there were also the works of distinguished artists in the same exhibition as the newcomers', so that it was hard to find a place even in the huge exhibitions. In order to become a member of the Soviet Artists' Union you had to have your paintings exhibited in the national show two or three times.

"The liveliest and most artistic work seemed to come from Latvia, Estonia, Armenia and Georgia, where there was still some independence and daring left. The stuff from the Ukraine and Byelorussia and Moldavia are usually pure junk. The artists who get the most encouragement and support are those who paint Lenin sitting, Lenin standing, Lenin making peace, and there are many artists willing to do that for the big rewards. They painted Stalin and Khrushchev, and it is as if they painted over the faces on one and the same picture.

"Then there are the real artists who never lower themselves or degrade themselves, and they have studios of good work they do for themselves and sometimes manage to sell. They don't do well materially, never go abroad. They are not accepted in society, and when any of the ideological campaigns begin, they are the first to receive the blows."

Moishe S. remembered two talented young artists in Odessa who became so frustrated and indignant about their inability to exhibit their work officially that they hung up about two dozen of their pictures on the fence around a house under construction. "It's hard to understand the violent reaction to their innocent attempt to get some attention," said Moishe. "Somebody showed up immediately from the regional committee of the Party and the Komsomol to look into the hooliganism. They convened a meeting of the governing council of the Artists' Union. The young painters were ordered to take the pictures down. One lost his job. The other was threatened. Pictures could not be hung in a public place without official permission."

Young artists dragged out a pitiful existence. Old established artists had the benefit of agents from the Artistic Fund. The agents, according to Moishe, were often uneducated, but energetic and good at making deals. They traveled throughout the Soviet Union and made contacts with Party committees, plants, clubs and theaters that might need portraits or paintings, and they arranged orders and commissions for the artists in their union. "They knew how to get chairmen drunk, whom to bribe, how to make promises. The system worked because the people they dealt with were not interested in paintings but in the drinks and entertainments the agents offered. When the agents returned to their region, the governing council of the Artists' Union divided the assignments. It was not unusual for well-known artists to receive commissions which were carried out by groups of younger, more energetic painters who received nominal sums for their efforts. I was a member of the union. I know how it worked because I got my commissions through the agents that way."

The artists, art historians and museum workers among the émigrés described an official art scene so rigid and conservative that no one was ever told to paint portraits of Lenin or get fired but everyone knew that "moving forward up the staircase" required that one follow the unwritten rules. "You had a choice. You could get something good to chew on or go bang your head against a wall."

The older artists remembered when Impressionism had been considered a crime. Then the Soviet authorities recognized it and it became acceptable, but Cubism became outlawed. "Any free art always seems leftist to the authorities. We learned not to do things that seemed too far left, and if we did we were careful not to let anyone see what we had done."

Artists who paint without showing their work are no better off than writers who can't publish and playwrights who never see their work performed. The need to be visible occasionally overwhelms the wish to be safe from official punishment. Isaac V., an artist, geologist and occasional poet, painted for ten years without trying to exhibit his work. He didn't try to join the Leningrad Artists' Union because the conformism was too much for him. In 1967, however, he managed to organize three one-man shows. The first was at the Molecule Club, a youth group under the auspices of the Institute of Higher Molecular Structure, one of the larger chemical institutes in Leningrad. The pictures were hung in poor light, and only a few dozen people came. Most of them were surprised to find an unauthorized exhibit. The writer who mentioned it in a newspaper article was fired for having been there.

The second exhibition was arranged at the Writers' Union in Leningrad in January of 1968, coinciding with the movement for human rights that surfaced after the events in Czechoslovakia. Hundreds of people came to see the pictures and to hear Joseph Brodsky read his poems after his time of internal exile. Though Isaac V.'s paintings were often of icons and he described them as religious pictures, the KGB denounced what it called "a Zionist meeting at the Writers' Union."

The third exhibition was held at the Caravella Club under the auspices of the Research Institute of Electrical Machinery in Leningrad. Isaac was actually invited to hold a five-day show of his work that would include a public discussion. He was not aware that it was planned as a provocation by the Komsomol. Questions were prepared by selected members in the audience, and the discussion was arranged as a condemnation.

Isaac V. described the first major unofficial art exhibit that took place at the Gaza Palace of Culture in the workers' district of Leningrad, not far from the Kirov plant. The exhibition opened on December 22, 1974, in an atmosphere that he described as "a real war between us and the state." Showing the work of about fifty unknown artists became a political event. "Five to six thousand people waited outside during four cold and rainy days. Western newsmen came from Moscow, West Germany and the United States. The exhibition was held in the large semicircular foyer, about a hundred and twenty meters long. There were paintings on the walls and the window ledges, and many display boards were covered with pictures. Visitors were allowed in in groups of about a hundred and twenty. They entered the hall from one side and had to leave at the other in twenty minutes so another group could be let in. There was a whole regiment of police outside to control the line, and some artists swore they saw machine guns on the rooftop pointing down on us. Three trucks were lined up in front of the building. Two were empty and one was filled with policemen. Inside, the KGB men, their pockets bulging with tape recorders, were positioned an even distance apart. The artists stood in front of their paintings like guards on duty. One of the KGB agents stood directly in front of me for half an hour, staring at some place between my eyes and my feet, not saying a word, just to make me tense. At noon of the first day, the KGB officers asked us artists to help them push the visitors out when the time was up. Some of the artists were willing to link hands with the police and go across the foyer shoving people out. They were so naive politically that they didn't understand the meaning of the action. Some were so exhilarated by the strange excitement, the bizarre atmosphere at the exhibition that it took a bit of time before they realized they were involved in dirty business. I felt revulsion from the first minute.

"Then a strange team came to the exhibition to help the police and the KGB. They wore ordinary clothes and were made to look like students or young workers, but the way they smiled while they pushed the people out told me they were the same kind as those who beat up the journalists and artists during the Bulldozer Exhibition [the first unofficial exhibition, which ended in arrests and rioting] in Moscow. The professional way they had of handling a human body was evidence of KGB training. In Moscow they worked in pairs. One would strike a man on the back of his head with his palm while another pushed with his knee below the back to get the victim into the police car. The atmosphere of the exhibition was like a military action. It was not only against the artists but also against the line of people waiting to see the exhibition to show their solidarity with us. The days of the exhibition gave us the chance to protest against suppression of everything in the world without immediately being punished. That was why the people stood in line for so many hours. Only those who came by nine in the morning had a chance to get in by six in the evening. All those who came later would never get in. The police through the loudspeaker announced, 'There is nothing interesting in this exhibition. Go home. Why have you come here, citizens? There is nothing here to see.' Meanwhile people kept coming. There was no publicity. No ads. On the third day at 8:30 P.M., the black government cars arrived and the people in the special coats and special hats, the people with the special faces, the Party bosses came to see for themselves what was going on."

The artists during the day talked with the visitors. Many didn't understand the meaning of the pictures and asked what they were about. Meanwhile the government sent groups of provocateurs to insult the painters and mock them. "Just before closing on the fourth day," said Isaac V., "there was a contingent of workers and Party functionaries who'd been briefed for the visit." The ordinary visitors looked at the pictures and gradually dispersed through the foyer, but the people sent by the government didn't look at the pictures. They positioned themselves throughout the length of the hall and in unison, on command, began to shout. "They called us loafers and good-for-nothings. They said we ate bread we didn't earn, that we were living off their hard work. Some of the artists couldn't stand the insults and went home, but I decided to take them on. I told them I wasn't a loafer, that I was a geologist and painted on my own time in harsh field conditions. I told them I worked in the distant, unpopulated areas collecting stones, looking for the deposits of the metal they worked on, and that without people like me they'd have no raw materials to work with. What I said had an immediate effect. The provocateurs near me fell silent. The workers began to ask me serious questions about how long I worked and how it was in the north in winter. And when the workers realized that most artists did their creative work after a full day of regular toil, they were no longer hostile. They really wanted to understand how an artist lives, and when the provocateurs began shouting the workers told them to shut up."

Rita S., a Moscow artist who participated in one of the first unofficial exhibitions, said, "We waited to be arrested. My father is a lawyer and he was very upset and sure I'd go to prison. I had a friend in prison for nine years, so I knew it could happen." She too spoke of artists who had joined the union and accepted its controls. "Every design has to be approved, and you have to be very careful. If you don't do what they expect of you, then the Party refuses you an exhibition. So that's why artists find other ways to earn a living. They teach schoolchildren, do commercial art and paint as they please."

Rita made her living as an art director in a publishing house and as an illustrator of children's books but never saw herself as a "regular member of the art world." Her vision of herself was as someone "against" the regime, someone who would not compromise. In fact, however, her life was full of restrictions and compromises. Her sense of herself as a nonconformist was enhanced by her experiences with some liberal teachers who did not follow the Party line. Most of all she was sustained by a family that set itself apart by attending Passover *seders* and having secret celebrations on the Jewish New Year. Her parents knew Hebrew as well as Yiddish, and they taught their children Jewish history and Bible stories.

Isaac V. also had a father who knew Hebrew and Yiddish and who even held Hebrew classes in his apartment, but he was untouched by his father's loyalties and traditions. He had his own life as a geologist working in the far north and as a controversial, unofficial painter. He did not choose Jewish life, but everything he did forced him to remember that he was seen by others as a Jew.

It began with his decision to apply at the Leningrad Mining Institute when he graduated from high school in 1955. As a bright medal-winning student he would normally have been accepted at the University of Leningrad. That was totally closed to Jews, however, and the Mining Institute accepted Jewish students. He found himself among many "open Jews" with the "J" marked in their passports but also among a large number of hidden Jews who had Russian passports. Knowing that only one Jew was accepted in the freshman class in the mid-seventies, Isaac V. realized that he was lucky to have been there in the fifties when both students and faculty were proud of the liberal atmosphere that they created.

After graduation from the Institute, Isaac V. was unable to find work in Leningrad. He went off to a small town in Kazakhstan to work with the Agadyr Expedition doing a geological survey. For the next eleven years he spent six months in Leningrad and six months in a tent with a group of scientists in Agadyr. It was a protected life in spite of the hardships of the north. "I had many friends," he said. "It was a good scientific collective. I had people I could talk to and work with."

The disbanding of the Agadyr Expedition, however, brought an end to his isolation from Jewish problems. His description of himself as "a man under the cap" is a version of many similar stories of frustration. "It was in October of 1970 that the agents of the KGB came to me at work. It was all quite unexpected, and why they came was not at all clear to me. It was only later that the reasons became obvious. Four months had gone by since the so-called hijackers who were trying to get to Israel were arrested in Leningrad, and it was on their account that the KGB agents took me to the Big House for interrogation.

"The interrogation began with 'We know that you deal with gold mining in your work, and there has been a leak of information in that regard. Do you know anything about it?' This question was just a ploy to distract my attention. The next questions dealt with my alleged selling of my paintings to Western diplomats in Moscow. I knew all along that the apartments where I was selling paintings were bugged, so I wasn't surprised that the KGB knew about it. But after a whole day of interrogation they finally came to the real reason. There was an empty slot for me in the script of the hijackers' trial created by the KGB. It was pure accident that I didn't know any of the defendants. Some were close friends of my father's. There was another I could have met at my work, since we were both working on the mathematical statistics in geology, but our paths had not crossed.

"I didn't fit the script. They couldn't find me guilty of anything, but the fact that agents of the KGB came to fetch me at work generated all kinds of rumors. I began to be thought of as a dangerous person. When the organization I was working for was disbanded and the staff was transferred to the All-Union Institute of Geology, everyone was taken but me. I was the second man in research. I'd written the proposal of the work we were to do and formed a crew to do it, and now everyone was telling me to come back next week and again next week, and finally I was told that nothing was going to happen by a person who expressively pointed his finger at the ceiling so that I shouldn't think badly about him. It was a typical case of bureaucracy versus technocracy. They had orders from the KGB not to hire me. Among the complaints against me was that my father was giving Hebrew lessons and working on an anthology of Yiddish folk songs, none of which had anything to do with me.

"So I'd lost my job, and there were four or five places in Leningrad that could use me and they had all received instructions not to hire me. I was then under the cap. That's what they call KGB surveillance in the dissident's jargon. When it became clear to me that I couldn't find a job anywhere, I decided on a bold action. I went to the reception room of the KGB and demanded to speak to the officer who had interrogated me. He was a very skilled interrogator, a former spy. He could change the expression on his face as sweetly and easily as he could have exchanged one mask for another. He had made things very difficult for me psychologically because I had not thought of refusing to give any testimony and was just trying not to incriminate anyone. The other officer who came to pick me up from work did not make it any easier. He was the one who served as the mountain, the person who is so big that his size inspires fear.

"Berezhkov, the man I asked for, saw me alone, and I said what I had to say. I reminded him that he had said I was not to be prosecuted, that I was not guilty of anything. When he asked what I wanted of him, I told him I wanted him to make a phone call that would explain that I was innocent and could go back to work. It was then that he reminded me that I had not answered his questions about *samizdat,* and he gave me another chance to answer. I was clearly given to understand that if I wanted to get something from the KGB I would have to do a service for them in exchange."

Isaac V. pressed his case further. He went to a senior member of the KGB and repeated his grievance. "You could have summoned me by postcard or telephoned me, but you came after me in a car with three men, and though I'm not guilty I have lost my chance to work." He was promised that a telephone call would be made. He was assured that he was right "in the tone of a best friend who is only too glad to solve small misunderstandings of which he is not guilty. He saw me to the door, holding my elbow, and just as we were saying goodbye added, 'By the way, I saw your paintings. Very good. You should go on painting.' "

Nothing came of it all. Isaac V. was proud of having dared to confront the KGB. He took his case to the director of the organization that had rejected him. He behaved like a man who lived in a society in which one could complain and protest and was rebuked wherever he went. He was fighting for his right to a job as a junior scientific associate which paid no more than a hundred and twenty rubles per month. He ultimately accepted the rejections. Speaking of one of the directors who turned him down, he said, "Apart from my being Jewish and he a rabid anti-Semite, it was my feeling of freedom that bothered him. He knew me from the Agadyr Expedition. In geology you work closely with other people for months in isolation. It's impossible to conceal your nature."

Isaac V., by being himself, irritated many people. He had been under observation from the time he was in high school. The KGB had reports of him as an unorthodox adolescent. He had been an active member of a literary club at the Mining Institute which was disbanded by the KGB and the Leningrad Union of Writers in 1957 because the students had printed a collection of poems without permission. The KGB confiscated the poems even before they were bound, piled them in the courtyard of the Institute and burned them. Isaac V. attributed the panic of the authorities to the students' reaction to events in Hungary. The Soviet suppression of the Hungarian revolution had a profound effect upon the young. Many were arrested. At the Mining Institute they suffered only the loss of some poems and the dismantling of a literary group. "The authorities were suspicious of any independent activity. They saw any spontaneous action as a threat," he said. Meanwhile he gave up writing poetry and turned to drawing and painting as a way of expressing himself and his feelings of independence.

The men and women who hoped to find private spaces as musicians, artists, actors and writers came into head-on collision with the officials supervising "ideological work." Some discovered the problems early as students and members of Komsomol. Some tried to acquire some control by joining the Party. More avoided Party membership, seeing it as yet another infringement on the personal freedom they tried to assert. In this dilemma they were no different from other professionals.

Georgi S., who was born in Moscow in 1924, described himself as "a philosopher by education and in the work I did." He worked in the Institute of the History of Art and taught at the Industrial Arts Institute. He wrote art criticism for an art publishing house, mostly under a pseudonym. His involvement with the dissident movement forced him to become a kind of underground journalist. In 1956, however, after the 20th Party Congress, he joined the Party. "I had always wanted to be active," he said. "I thought the only way to influence events was by joining. I was critical of the Stalinist period, but I was still a Marxist and joining the Party wasn't against my conscience. I believed in the general ideals of communism but was critical of the way those ideals were realized. I decided to join in 1955, was a candidate first for a trial period and a member after that for twelve years."

By 1964, Georgi S. had changed his philosophical views. He had given up Marxism for existentialism. By 1968, the mood among intellectuals had changed completely. "No one with any self-respect would join the Party," he said. "It was hard to withdraw from it, however, because the person who leaves the Party finds himself outside society, an untouchable who can lose his job and be excluded from all opportunities. All writings by such a person would be banned. Works in progress would not be published if one left or were expelled from the

Party." He knew this from personal experience. He was expelled in April of 1968 for writing a letter in defense of Sinyavsky and Daniel that was signed by four members of the Writers' Union who were also Party members. That was the first of a series of actions deemed inappropriate for someone in the Party Bureau of his institute. Georgi S. had dared publicly to read a report on the violation of human rights in the Soviet Union. His official expulsion from the Party accused him of "slanderous actions against the Party, the Soviet people and revolutionary law." It did not take place, however, until he rejected all the efforts to persuade him to recant and admit to having been misled by foreign agents.

Georgi S. was an important member of a small group of dissidents involved in the human-rights movement. He was sufficiently well known to take risks without fear of arrest. He didn't want to emigrate. He hoped to live out his years as an underground writer. His experiences as a Party member were no different from those of an engineer who described the Party as "the road to power for some people and for others a place from which lightning can strike you."

Embarrassment about Party membership led a shop foreman from Leningrad to apologize for his parents' Party membership. "They were simple, uneducated people," he said. "They didn't know any better." Albert D., a journalist from Odessa, saw Party membership as a necessity of life, but something to be ashamed of. "When a person joins, he apologizes to his friends and says, 'You know I have to make my career. I have children to think about.' To be in the Party is to have made a dirty move. But it's known that you can't be promoted to a certain level if you don't join. If you want to be the head of a department you have to be a member to be considered reliable. But no one respects you for it."

It was generally agreed that the people born after 1940 joined the Party for special privileges and for opportunities to advance in their careers. Special pride was taken in managing without belonging. A television director from Leningrad said, "I said to myself, I'm not untalented. I'm capable and qualified.

Why do I need to join? I had no wish to submit to the Party heads. I did not want to depend upon anyone but myself." Ilya K., a Moscow engineer, boasted about getting clearance without joining. It was prestigious to be the exceptional technical person, the creative designer, the exception to the rule, to be able to say, "I could read and write secret information. I could visit plants that work for the military. I was trusted without Party membership." As the stories unfold, however, they tell of the loss of trust. Refusal to inform on fellow workers or denounce colleagues was the most frequent cause of difficulties with the Party. Such defections were still easier for nonmembers. There were higher standards and requirements for Party members. They had a harder time getting permission to emigrate. They were in danger not only of verbal denunciation but of severe beatings. Some did not survive the assaults.

The cynical and hostile comments about Party membership were sometimes carried over into descriptions of the legal profession, which enjoyed neither respect nor status because of its subservience to the Party. "My father was a lawyer," said Emanuel D., the engineer from Kharkov. "But the lawyer's role is only a formality. Everything written down concerning the laws differs sharply from what in fact happens. The dissidents are only trying to help Soviet authorities carry out their own laws. Unfortunately, the outcome of the judicial process and the sentence itself depend on a phone call from a Party committee. My father was a knowledgeable man irritated by the incredible Soviet hypocrisy. The things done in the name of the People's Court under the guise of legality were illegal, but lawyers could do nothing. My father saw his vocation as a kind of humiliation. He had a gigantic archive in which he recorded the court cases and all the terrible decisions. These were not sensational political trials, just financial trials, ordinary violations—scandalous perversions of administration of justice."

A twenty-two-year-old photographer from Vilnius spoke of his father's profession as a lawyer only in terms of the privileges his position made possible. "We lived well by Soviet standards," he said. "My father's students provided our family with food and clothing. There were army officers, police and KGB people among them and also directors of shops. My father would phone one of his students who worked as an attorney in a meat-supply store and order a turkey. He would come in the evening by car to deliver it and we would pay him. In return my father helped him pass his examination. It was very common. Most Soviet people live this way."

The young people among the émigrés knew all the ways of coping and described this sort of behavior without passing judgment or feeling outraged. The older émigrés were more likely to inveigh against the loss of idealism, the misery of living in a corrupt society.

Nikolay S., who was born in 1919, came to the Juridical Faculty in Moscow in 1936, when more than a third of the faculty and students were Jews. "It was a fabulous faculty," he said. "Many were professors from before the Revolution." A year after he began his studies, however, the entire faculty of the Civil Law Department and their students were arrested. Even old Bolsheviks and friends of Lenin were taken away. Nikolay S. was spared at the beginning of his studies and several times thereafter found himself the only Jew in institutes from which Jews were normally excluded. He was not accepted at the Faculty of International Law after graduation. He refused the study of trade law and was about to be sent off to Kazakhstan as an investigator when he was rescued by a high-placed friend at the Institute of Law at the Academy of Science. He was able to study international law at the Academy, learn the law of capitalist countries and ultimately defend his dissertation on "Boundaries in International Law."

Nikolay was able to do research at the Academy of Science and the Institute of International Relations and teach at several institutes until 1949, when he was expelled from all the institutions that had given him protection and a place to work. He considered himself lucky that he was not arrested for Zionism along with many of his friends. He was, however, unable to find work "at the most humble place and at the lowest salary." His wife, who was also a lawyer, supported him until he found a place for himself in the Institute of Legality in 1966. Here again he was the exception, the only Jew. In the years between 1949 and 1966 he was able only to do occasional lecturing in rural and provincial communities. He was freer than the lawyers who had something to lose. He had contacts with foreign journalists, with dissidents and human-rights activists.

In 1973, Nikolay S. began writing a book about the bribery, blackmail and corruption in Soviet life. "I was getting older," he said. "Time was running out." His need to speak his piece about a society that had educated him and then disillusioned him was stronger than his concern for his life and safety. Four years later he was an unwilling émigré, driven out of the Soviet Union. Offered a choice of arrest and a prison term or emigration, he chose what he thought would be a "grim future." He left with threats of retribution if he published his book in the West. "I felt as if my life had come to an end. I was fifty-eight years of age and knew I had no prospects."

Lia K., the wife of Nikolay, was the daughter of parents who were the first generation out of a Ukrainian village. Her mother had become a dentist and her father had graduated from the law school at the University of Kharkov. Lia K. spoke of her father with admiration and affection. He had combined a career of banking and law, had taught himself many languages. He had begun with only a *cheder* education but developed into a sophisticated and well-educated man. He had encouraged her in her wish to study law even when her interests were more romantic than practical. "I dreamed of becoming an investigator, of solving horrendous crimes, of finding murderers, and never thought of becoming a defense attorney."

Lia was only seventeen when she entered the Juridical Institute in 1937. It was a year of terror for the faculty and students in the Institute and also a traumatic year in the community in which she lived. "The parents of all my friends were arrested and disappeared. The houses emptied out before our eyes." Her father, the only bank official who was not a Party member, was the only one left after the arrests were made. After a while he was fired, but not imprisoned. In retrospect she marveled at the "ideological hypnosis that surrounded and enveloped us, that made it impossible for us to believe that people who were totally innocent could be arrested and destroyed." The events did not change her wish to be an investigator. In her third year at the Juridical Institute she went to the procurator's office for an apprenticeship. She went along with an experienced procurator on the searches of apartments, the confiscation of materials, and for the first time in a sheltered life she encountered the lives and sorrows of the poor.

"I went to the narrow streets where they had the workers' barracks," said Lia. "It was not the kind of workers' housing you see today. There was no electricity, no running water— no plumbing at all. Seven or eight people were packed into a small room. It was absolute poverty, the kind you couldn't imagine if you didn't see it with your own eyes. And we'd go into the rooms of people who worked in a factory and had taken some knitting wool or other small items. If they were caught such people could be tried and given twenty years. They had only the minimum of possessions. A bed, a table, a few dishes, one plate and one cup per person. Anything that was not assigned to them could be confiscated."

Lia K. never got over the shock of those discoveries. "I had grown up believing in the Soviet system, in the triumph of socialism, in the faith that workers were benefiting from the system. I could not bear to see people living in such poverty, knowing they would spend their whole lives under such conditions. It was on their behalf that I decided to become a defense attorney. It was a decision I never regretted during my entire life."

Her first job was as a legal adviser for a mine, and it included one day of work a week in the mine gathering coal. After her marriage to Nikolay S. in January 1942, she was taken into the Tashkent Collegium of Lawyers. There she was mobilized to work on the Tashkent Canal. Her enthusiasm and capacity for hard physical and mental work impressed the older lawyers. When the war was over she was welcomed into the Moscow Collegium of Lawyers and worked with them until she left the Soviet Union.

In the early days of her practice she took on the cases assigned to her by the Supreme Court. She particularly liked defending the economic criminals and the youthful offenders on trial for petty crimes. She prided herself on her ability to establish rapport with the offenders and tried to help people whom other lawyers condemned. The first case of a political nature was her defense of Bukovsky in February 1967. She defended his right to engage in a demonstration against the prosecution's contention that his slogans were anti-Soviet and a disruption of the civil order. The second case was a defense of Galinskov and Ginzburg, who were tried for compiling a booklet about the trial of Daniel and Sinyavsky. She acquired experience in handling demonstrations and political activities. Shortly after the arrest of Anatoly Shcharansky she was asked by his mother to defend him. Though advised by the director of the presidium to refuse, she could not bring herself to say no.

Lia K. went about her work as a defense attorney as if her clients had constitutional rights that could be defended and as if there were freedom of thought and expression in the courtroom. She got by with warnings and reprimands when others taking similar risks were disbarred. She seems to have avoided emotional appeals, preferring whenever possible to show that the charges should be dropped because no crime had been committed. The size of her practice was a measure of her success. She traveled to Leningrad, Kiev, Odessa, Tashkent and Uzbekistan to defend her clients in court. She had permission to visit labor camps and was able to travel without restriction within Soviet borders.

In 1970, however, in spite of the respect she claimed to have earned from her colleagues, she was expelled from the Moscow Collegium of Lawyers with no reason given. Her detailed de-

scription of the events before the expulsion reveals her willing-
ness and need to risk official disapproval. She believed in the
law and managed to keep that belief even after she had been
forced to leave the Soviet Union.

Lia K., lecturing at an American university, could speak dis-
passionately about the Soviet justice system. She said, "I
wanted to show the advantages and disadvantages of the Soviet
judicial system, to show how it operates. I don't like the idea
many Americans have that it operates inequitably. It has bad
laws and good laws, just like any other system of justice. The
Soviet legal system is not behind that of the French or English
courts. Though we may have fewer special services, we have
nothing to be ashamed of."

It is hard to reconcile Lia K.'s description of her profession
with that of Florina R. "The role of the defense lawyer is
very small," said Florina. "It's rare to get an acquittal in a
criminal case. The judge bases his actions on the supposition
that people are not arrested for nothing, not indicted without
reason. The defense lawyer can't prove anything. The only
thing you can do is try to get a lighter sentence."

Florina R. was the daughter of two lawyers. Eleven years
younger than Lia K., she too grew up in a family preoccupied
with legal questions. She was a good student, and her parents
were able to use their influence to get her accepted into the
University of Moscow at a time when few Jews were accepted. She graduated in 1953 but was not given a job assignment. "It was a time," she said, "when no organization would
hire a Jew. The majority of the Jewish students were given
free diplomas, which meant they could find their own jobs.
But again my mother took advantage of her position and
arranged a request for me as a jurist from a place which had
no need for a lawyer at that time. I worked therefore as a
junior editor in a publishing house while submitting my documents to the Moscow Collegium of Lawyers. I had good hopes
of being admitted. I had graduated well, and the children of
lawyers were usually given preference. I was one of three
Jewish girls applying, and we were all rejected. Six months

later they changed their minds and accepted us all. The father of one of the girls was very energetic and had important connections. Since it was impossible to accept his daughter without taking the rest of us, we were all admitted. I was taken on as a trainee working with an experienced defense lawyer. I spent the rest of my professional life working in the same legal-consultation office. I took all kinds of cases—civil, criminal and labor law. I turned nothing down."

In the mid-sixties, Florina R. defended dissidents in civil suits. When the wave of Jewish emigration began, young Jews came to her for legal advice. In her efforts to be of help to them she began to think of emigrating herself.

"Our family was in a very good situation by Soviet standards," she said. "I was a lawyer with a large practice. People sat in my waiting room for hours to get my advice, and the telephone in the apartment never stopped ringing. My husband had a Ph.D. and worked in a scientific-research institute, earning a good salary. We had one son, for whom we could provide everything. We had everything one could have in the Soviet Union. We had money, a car, a comfortable cooperative apartment we shared with my mother, without strange neighbors."

The conditions that Lia K. accepted as a fact of life were felt to be intolerable by Florina R. and her husband. Her husband, even in the time of Stalin, understood the regime and silently rejected it. She came under his influence and was also affected by the dissidents who came to her for help. "Our affluence only strengthened our decision to give everything up, to break away once and for all. We had this feeling that it is impossible to live when every step and thought are controlled by the government. It is impossible to live when you have to put a pillow on the phone, close the door and the windows if you want to talk seriously with your closest friends. We wanted to save our son from this life. We saw no future for him in Russia now that discrimination against Jews has become so strong. Our influence could not get him into the university. My influence was not what my mother's had been.

With the greatest of difficulty our son was accepted into the Civil Engineering Institute, where he was offered subjects in which he was not interested. And when he graduated, would he be able to find any work of interest to do? So we sold everything. We had savings and a car and we exchanged it all for our freedom."

Florina R. emigrated to save her son from the hardships of Soviet life. The son of Lia K. and Nikolay S. left the Soviet Union several years before his parents were forced to leave. The parents were surprised and upset by their son's decision. "We were very disturbed," his father said. "Despite his Jewish nationality, he was about to defend his dissertation and receive a candidate degree [Ph.D.] in history from the Institute of World Economy of the Institute of International Relations, a very prestigious body. He had the possibility of a good scientific career in the Soviet Union. He was the first among our close associates to leave." Nikolay S., who had risked his life to expose what he thought was a corrupt and decadent society, had not yet overcome his shock at having to leave it. He was not yet ready to admit that his son might be wiser and saner than he.

Lawyers, among the émigrés, have a hard time transferring their education to the United States or any Western country. They find not only very different systems but also very different objectives in the training of lawyers. Florina R. discovered that the legal system in the United States was based on common law and precedents rather than the application of definite standards fixed by law from which one cannot depart. Unlike the Soviet lawyer, who was trained to memorize the laws, she found American lawyers were judged by their ability to think logically and mediate conflicts between interests, rights and norms that have no counterpart in Soviet law.

The most visible difference is in the control of lawyers, who must belong to a collegium to practice. Private practice is forbidden. Clients who come for help pay fees that are set according to the length and complexity of the case. A percentage goes to the lawyer and the remainder goes to the collegium. A hardworking lawyer can earn 200 or 300 rubles a month. He may, in addition, receive gifts from satisfied clients that will not be reported and taxed. The lawyer who deviates from prescribed behavior can be expelled from his group and forced out of his profession. Lia K. described the fate of one of her colleagues who offered too emotional a defense of a dissident. "He was disbarred from the collegium of lawyers, lost his position as the head of the Consultation Center of Lawyers and his place as a member of the Presidium of the Moscow College of Lawyers. His position was aggravated by the fact that he was a member of the Party and also because reports of his defense were in the headline of a French newspaper. . . . After a long time of unemployment he found a place as a legal consultant in a small construction firm at a salary of a hundred rubles a month, where he remains to this day."

"Better to be a good doctor than a bad actor" is an old Russian saying. The seven physicians who were interviewed for this oral-history collection ranged in age between thirty-six and seventy-one. Their experiences while acquiring a medical education and delivering medical care reflect some of the changes in attitude toward their profession from the thirties to the seventies.

Raya B., the oldest of the doctors, came from a working-class family in Odessa. She was born in 1909, the youngest of three daughters. Her mother died of typhus during the famine of 1921. Her sisters managed to become teachers in spite of Revolution, poverty and life-threatening illnesses. "I really wanted to study," she said. "I had the capability, and education was free." She had studied at home with her sisters' help until she entered the fourth grade. After the seventh grade she went to a vocational school and then to work in a factory. She prepared for examinations for entrance into a medical institute at evening classes after a day's work on a production line and after four years was accepted into the medical institute in Odessa. She finished her medical education just when the Nazi invasion of Russia began and took her final examinations with German planes flying overhead dropping bombs. Many of her classmates went into the army immediately. She was caught in the siege of Odessa with a father dying of cancer. She managed with great difficulty to get him to the city of Penza, in central Russia, and cared for him until he died before she was sent as a surgeon to work in an army field hospital. Her husband had gone off to the front as soon as the fighting began. She had lost contact with her sisters and did not know if they had survived the bombings during the evacuations from Odessa.

Raya B. was sent first to the northern Caucasian front and then to East Prussia and after the victory over Germany to the Japanese front. She had earned a Red Star for her military service and suffered health problems the rest of her life incurred during the war.

She was a strong woman who had no reason to question her value to society. She had lived through the Revolution, had memories of the purges in the thirties when "the most honest, sincere, idealistic persons were considered to be enemies." She and her husband had taken risks to help friends who were in danger of arrest. She was a product of the values and disciplines of an older time—"the old mentality," it was called. She did not complain about a salary of 200 rubles per month after thirty years of practice. When asked if she did moonlighting, she answered, "I'm not that kind of person. I don't have that kind of character. Doctors have many possibilities if they want to, but I personally couldn't do that kind of thing." Raya B. was well aware that doctors went to visit patients at home for fees, that surgeons did private operations for an extra 150 rubles per operation and that even in conventional circumstances patients left little envelopes of money on the doctor's table. Such things went on though they were forbidden by law.

She accepted the need for "connections," however. It was important to know the right person to get into a hospital that had proper equipment, medicine, some comforts for patients. Even food and nursing care were not always available.

Raya B. noted that surgery had become a male province since her time of study. "The majority of the students in medical school were women when I was studying, but now men are preferred. There's a sharp change in the student body, and you can see it as soon as you enter a medical institute." She did not question the wisdom of the change. She knew how difficult it was for a woman to take care of her household and devote herself to research and study.

There was another change, however, that troubled her greatly. Growing up in Odessa, which she called "a Jewish city," in that unprecedented time of freedom for Jews just after the Revolution, she had not noticed that 70 percent of the students in her medical institute were Jews. Medicine was considered a Jewish profession at that time as well as a field for women. Even as late as 1950 there were reports of a medical institute with two boys in a class of a hundred and ninety-eight girls. In 1966, Raya B. attended the thirty-year reunion of her class at the medical institute. "Only then did we realize the extent to which Jews were admitted in our time. At that time you might have had trouble finding a single Jewish student in a medical institute. There were very few Jewish doctors in the clinics by the time I left."

The attack on Jewish doctors in 1953 had accomplished its purpose. Raya B. remembered that time as "extremely painful and unpleasant." Patients refused to be seen by Jewish doctors. "We went to work every day as if we were going to forced labor. We never knew what patient we might get at the clinic, what scandal might start, what distrust would be expressed. It took a long time for people to quiet down. It took a few years before the trust in Jewish doctors could be reestablished. It was a difficult time to be a Jewish doctor." By the time it was over, the famous old Jewish professors were no longer teaching. Parents were no longer urging their daughters and sons to become doctors. The stories of the next generations of doctors explained why.

Anna D. was ten years younger than Raya B. She grew up in a professional family in Moscow. Her father was a lawyer, a graduate of Moscow University. They lived in the Arbat, the neighborhood for professionals, and she and her brother went to a good school close to home in which they experienced few problems with anti-Semitism. "We never knew, among our friends, who was Jewish and who wasn't. The subject never came up and we were absolutely indifferent to it."

Anna D. went to a medical institute for five years, but the war broke out before she completed her examinations. She had already been accepted in graduate school to do a psychiatric residency, but everyone was sent out to work because of the war. She had graduated as a pediatrician and was sent to work in a small district clinic at a railroad junction outside Moscow.

The railroad went to Dombas, a major coal center, and the German planes began bombing the junction soon after she arrived. "I came as a young doctor to do pediatrics," she said, "but instead was taking care of wounded soldiers and civilians. There were all the young boys on the way to the front already wounded long before they reached their destination. No one knew what was going on. The war had only just begun. We didn't appreciate the full horror of it because we were sure it would end quickly.

"There was all this enthusiasm," she said. "The day that war was declared we met at the Komsomol meeting hall and everybody was asking to be sent to the front. It was all very sincere. And then we began to feel that we are Jews and the Germans are coming. There were only three of us, and everyone knew who we were. We heard people say, 'It won't be so terrible if the Germans come. If worse comes to worst we'll show them who the Jews are and they'll let us alone.' There was another doctor, the mother of the man I married. She was working there because her husband had been arrested and she had lost the right to live in Moscow. There was also a woman who was a pharmacist who'd been exiled from Leningrad."

The three Jewish women were not given permission to leave until the Germans were very close. Only then were they granted passes and the chance to set out on foot in the snow. A day's journey to the Ural Mountains took Anna D. two months. She would never forget the trek in the bitter cold without food, the struggles with rapists, the rides with soldiers in crowded freight cars. She barely survived the cold, the hunger and the dysentery.

She recovered in time to be drafted into the army and was sent to Estonia, which had just been occupied by the Soviet Union, to help with a typhus epidemic that had broken out in one of the camps. Anna D.'s first army medical experience was with a team of Estonian doctors responsible for eight hundred men hospitalized for typhus. The men slept on the ground in tents. They were in the middle of a forest. Barracks had not yet been built.

It was also her first experience as a Jewish doctor. The camp she thought was for soldiers preparing to go to the front was actually a concentration camp for Estonian government workers and former capitalists. It was run by the KGB, not the army. The Estonian doctors turned out to be mostly Jews who had been mobilized as military doctors. Anna D. admired their concern for individual patients. "They'd all been private doctors," she said, "and they treated the patients with more respect and kindness than I was used to. When nurses and orderlies became ill, the young doctors fed and carried the patients without concern for themselves."

This devotion seemed especially significant to her when the administrators from the Soviet army came to check conditions. "They didn't come anywhere near the patients or the doctors. They held their hands behind their backs and shouted commands at us from a distance. They had no interest in the patients. They were interested only in the figures and in lowering the mortality rate. They never spent more than ten minutes with us before getting into their cars and driving off. We followed their recommendations, in spite of the terrible impression they left with us. We sterilized clothes and instituted sanitary conditions. The instructions were correct. We followed them precisely, and gradually everything began to improve."

Anna D. was a doctor in the army for five years, most of the time in the Urals. She lived in tents, was transported from one camp to another in freight cars and waited impatiently for the war to end so she could continue her life. She said, "When I came to Moscow I expected to start graduate school. I had a document saying they would take me. I had wanted to study psychiatry all my life, and my war experiences confirmed my feelings about it. So I went to the dean of the institute, who was Jewish, and he couldn't say it outright, but said simply, 'You can apply, but you have absolutely no chance of getting in.' "

She didn't bother applying. It was already in the air that it had become impossible for Jews in Moscow to get into graduate schools and institutes. She had to get a job as quickly as possible because rationing was still in force and those who did not work received no ration cards. She found work in a psychiatric institute, whose administrators wanted to give her an internship but couldn't. They even created a special position for her but ultimately filled it with someone else. It was 1946. The war was over, but the Doctors' Plot scenario was already being organized.

Anna D. found work in a psychiatric institute where there were still older, Jewish doctors. "The atmosphere was warm and humane. Officially I was working at a normal salary, but in fact they were teaching me. I was the only one and was unofficially being trained as if I were a resident. Though it seemed a great misfortune that I couldn't get into graduate school in psychiatry, I had an equivalent experience and felt that things were working out for me after all."

By 1950, however, it had become even more difficult. Her father, who was a judge working on cases for government agencies, lost his post. Her mother, who worked as a secretary at the Serbsky Psychiatric Institute, was struck by a car and was unable to work. Meanwhile the older doctors who were her teachers and protectors were fired, and the children's division of the institute in which she worked was virtually destroyed. She remained in a temporary, marginal role, subject to all kinds of harassment.

"I kept going before this board, a kind of purge board whose function was to decide whom to get rid of. They turned my soul inside out. They left no stone unturned. My whole life, all my acquaintances, every possible detail had to be exposed. I was pregnant at that time, and that only made them torment me more. In the end they decided that I should be sent out of

Moscow to work in a regional clinic, but when it was time for me to leave I was kept on because everyone else was sent away and somebody had to do the work."

Anna D. remained at the institute for thirty years, a necessary but vulnerable person. She always had some protection from a person of power who needed her, but the harassment continued in some form until she left the country. One of her early defenders planned to use the case histories she was collecting for his dissertation. Another tried to get her to work as her agent and spy and made her life miserable when she refused.

"I had no rights whatsoever," she said. "I was never given a permanent position. I just took the places of other people when they went on vacation. I often worked in three different divisions, half-time in each. That was very hard to do with psychiatrically ill people. You had to know the patient. You had to talk to each one as an individual, and I would get new patients every two months."

The worst experiences were during the time of the Doctors' Plot when parents read in the newspapers that Jewish doctors were poisoners and murderers and came to the hospital to make sure their children were not seen by Jewish doctors. The nurses and orderlies refused to carry out their orders. "There was nothing you could do," said Anna D. "You just had to keep living from day to day. We were always threatened with losing our jobs. My friends were always on the lookout for some work I could do if that happened." When the storm passed, her situation improved, but it was never good.

Anna D., looking back on her career in pediatrics and psychiatry, took pride in the creative work she did in spite of the harassment. She had trained many young people who took legitimate internships at the institute. Her research with patients who exhibited marked aggressive fantasies was written about and praised. On the debit side of her account was thirty years of humiliation. She had no telephone in her office. She had to ask permission for everything she undertook to do. She was paid the lowest salary and refused overtime, which was given as a privilege to "trusted" people. She was never permitted to forget that she was a Jewish doctor. If that was not sufficient, she was also reminded that her brother, "a convinced and devoted communist, had been arrested and shot." His crime was that as a soldier he had been wounded and taken prisoner. When he escaped from the Germans, he was arrested as a traitor. It was on his account that his father was fired and his sister was unable to enter graduate school.

Alexei G., a successful orthopedic surgeon, is eleven years younger than Anna D., but old enough to have experienced medicine as a "Jewish profession." He also described it as a profession held back because it was so poorly paid and so heavily dominated by women. "Medicine," he said, "is basically a woman's field. According to official Soviet statistics there are 919,000 physicians, and seventy percent of them are women who have their own families and children to care for."

He saw "Soviet medicine supported on the shoulders of women who lacked the energy and time to do research, pay attention to recent discoveries and publications." He described the daily routine of a typical doctor as a man who had watched carefully from the vantage point of his more privileged position.

"She is the first to get up in her family, prepares breakfast for her husband and children. She runs out to do the shopping while stores are full and comes to work with heavy bags of food but only half-full. She has to stop at a milk store, a meat store, a vegetable market, and though she gives her utmost to her patients at the clinic, she also knows she must fill the bag before getting home, so she may run out for a few minutes during the day. After work you see the woman going home on the subway, bus or streetcar carrying bags that weigh from six to ten kilograms. I know many marvelous women physicians, marvelous surgeons, many who do great deeds with their hands, but they are the exceptions. The average level of women physicians is quite low, which is why Soviet medicine is so far behind."

He deplored the economics of medicine which makes the

official salary for a beginning doctor 120 rubles a month. Women, to add to their earnings, may work full time in a hospital and part time in a clinic. "Both jobs are done superficially. The examinations are superficial and so are the treatments, and after years of exhausting, backbreaking labor, doctors lose interest in their work and become accustomed to working at a low level." At the lowest level he saw the doctors at the outpatient clinics. A single doctor saw fifty patients a day and was responsible for a population of five thousand people.

Alexei had been the head of one of the leading departments in a clinic for traumatology and orthopedics in Moscow. He had also traveled all over the Soviet Union and had seen hospitals in hundreds of cities in the north of Russia, in the Caucasus and Central Asia. He had been to hospitals in cities such as Kostroma, Yaroslavl and Ivanovo. Like other physicians in his generation, he confirmed the fact that there were two distinct standards of medicine in the Soviet Union. There were perhaps ten institutions in the country which could compete with the best that America had to offer. There was excellent medical care available for the heads of government and for patients of affluence and connections. Ordinary people, however, get poor medical help, and there are no facilities for testing and diagnosis outside the major centers.

Alexei G. had taken part in official meetings of the Ministry of Health and knew that the cost of medical care was begrudged. "Nine billion rubles is not enough to treat the population of the Soviet Union." He was incensed by the official insistence that all medical care in the Soviet Union is free when in fact he knew that patients paid the middle- and lower-range hospital staff to get better care and that patients were expected to provide their own food. "You can see the long lines of grandmothers and mothers, wives and daughters carrying the food they bring from the stores and market."

Dr. Alexei G. had had an unusual medical career which left him with conflicting expectations and with an acute awareness of the inequalities and injustices around him. He had twenty-three years as a leading orthopedic surgeon. He was a member of the Learned Council which included only seventeen Moscow surgeons. Many students studied with him, and he had a large number of books, articles and inventions to his credit. He was also a writer of children's poetry and was accepted into the Writers' Union after he had published seven volumes of poems. As the director of a large clinic he earned 500 rubles, which he described as the maximum medical salary in the Soviet Union. With his wife adding another 200 rubles, they were affluent people. They had a Zhigoli car and a good cooperative apartment and could afford trips to Bulgaria and Yugoslavia. They had to leave their son as a hostage when they traveled, but it was still an enviable privilege.

Alexei prided himself on not taking advantage of his patients by asking them for money, but since he was well known and his services were in demand, it was not unusual for his patients to leave little envelopes on his desk which he did not refuse. He knew that younger, less experienced doctors took substantial and illegal fees from patients, but he also knew that provocateurs sometimes came with marked bills. The authorities would come in and find the marked money and the doctors would be arrested for bribery. He had no illusions about who he was and where he was. In 1976 he found himself feeling more fearful and distressed than at any previous time in his life. "The higher I went in my career, the more hemmed in I felt." He claimed that high earnings and comforts did not bring the satisfaction and security he needed. He boasted about his accomplishments and success and yet seemed alienated and unsure. Dr. Alexei G. raged against the deficiencies of the system that destroyed the dignity and efficacy of his profession. As the son of a surgeon who was the assistant director of the Surgery Institute in Moscow and dean of the Institute for Advanced Training of Physicians, he was brought up with values that no longer applied and expectations that could not be fulfilled.

Alexei's father had been able to look back and see how far he had come from the poor Jewish family into which he was born. He was in the first generation to get an education just after the Revolution. He was trained by Jewish doctors educated in Germany and France and adopted their style. Alexei's mother came from a noble Russian family. Her family rejected her after her marriage, and she had moved willingly into the Jewish milieu of her husband. Her name gave her son the Russian passport which made his professional life possible in a time when Jews had difficulty entering medical institutes and were totally excluded from the high positions in the ministries. Alexei knew that his Russian passport, his connections with people in high places and his personal talent and energy had opened doors that were closed to many other people in his generation.

The Russian passport, however, did not protect him entirely. Alexei G. was studying medicine during the years of the Doctors' Plot arrests, and he never forgot the terror. "The doctors who were arrested were all my father's friends. I'd visited them in their homes. Professor Feldman, whose name was first on the list of doctors who tried to poison Stalin, and Professor Vofsi, whose bier I carried at his funeral, were our good friends. We had photographs and letters from them that we had to destroy before the KGB came to search our apartment." His father was one of those who had a suitcase prepared with all the necessities for a long journey to prison. "There was not a night's sleep without the fear of the KGB agents coming in the middle of the night." His father narrowly escaped arrest several times. His colleagues were not so lucky. They disappeared. Their names were taken off the lists in the library. "We were forbidden to mention them, except to accuse them. What we were to accuse them of we didn't know."

It was known that Jewish students were likely to be sent to distant places after graduating from the medical institutes. "They were rarely sent closer than Yakutsk, more often to Kamchatka or Sakhalin," said Alexei G. When asked by the commission where they wished to go, they were expected to say, "I would like to serve wherever my motherland wants me to serve." He said what was expected of him but was sure that his Russian passport would save him from a journey to a distant place.

"I expected that my motherland would keep me in Moscow," said Alexei G. "I lost my bearings when I was told I was to be sent to the far north, to the Karelo-Finnish Republic, for three years." It was in 1953, when transportation and communication to the isolated areas were poor and conditions anywhere outside the large cities were harsh and primitive.

"I rented a small room in a peasant's house for which I paid a fourth of my salary of sixty rubles a month. I had no money for books or food. I looked for chances to do night duty to earn a few extra rubles. All the doctors lived like paupers. I couldn't have survived without the money and food packages my parents sent me."

It was not, however, as bad as he expected. He was able to fight for the right to stay in Petrozavodsk, the capital city, when the local medical administration tried to send him to a rural area. The hospital in the city had been founded by a Jewish physician, a man he found to be a marvelous surgeon and an excellent teacher even though he had no official recognition. He also found that the majority of the young doctors who had come from 1952 to 1956 were Jews from Moscow and Leningrad who had been sent away from the large cities. The level of medical care was relatively sophisticated, though hampered by the lack of medicine and equipment.

It was possible to get a good medical education in the north. Dr. Alexei G. organized a local hospital in an isolated village and served for a time as its only doctor. An unexpected advantage in living so far from official supervision was that he was free to listen to his large Telefunken receiver, a German war trophy that introduced him to BBC and the Voice of America. "My education was not only in politics but also in scientific achievement." The Soviet press was in the habit of censoring scientific and medical achievements. There was an ongoing problem about the use of foreign techniques and equipment. Alexei had learned to distrust government intervention as a student when Lysenko attacked the teachings of Mendel and claimed that communists by sheer willpower could change the structure of genes. He remembered the woman who taught genetics and embryology by reading editorials from *Pravda* aloud. His fascination with medical advances in the West was fired by the restrictions that made it difficult to get information and often impossible to obtain equipment.

In 1962, Dr. Alexei G. became director of the largest orthopedic clinic in Moscow. "It was in a very old hospital built during the Russo-Turkish War in 1875 for typhoid patients," he said. "There was no plumbing. No electrical equipment. I had two hundred patients, ten to twenty in a room. The beds were the old, narrow iron beds, and there was no elevator. The operating room was in another building, and patients had to be carried by student aides. Sometimes they were dropped. They had come in with one broken limb and another was broken in transit. There was a terrible shortage of beds, and when the streets were icy we would put patients on the floor and I had literally to walk over them when I came in in the morning. There was no place to instruct students. The beds were too close together for us to stand around them. And this was one of the important clinics in Moscow, not some place in the hinterlands."

He managed to transfer the clinic to a newer hospital, a modern hospital of seven-story buildings with eight to ten people in a room, but he described it as still fifty years behind similar facilities in the United States and Europe.

"Though our institute of orthopedics was one of the leading institutes in its field, we led a miserable existence. With the rarest exceptions we were forced to work with inferior equipment made in the Soviet Union and could not buy French, German or American materials, even for the sake of an experiment. Everything we produced had to be spoken of as the latest discovery of medical science. I researched many problems using my own funds if I could not get funding. I paid for parts in money or alcohol and once gave a workman a hundred and fifty rubles we had saved to buy my wife a winter coat. She sacrificed her coat so I could get my first model of an artificial joint."

Ultimately his passion for improving medical care and his

interest in what was happening in science beyond Soviet borders brought Alexei G. to grief and to the decision to emigrate. In 1975 he was denounced by his Party colleagues for favoring Western ideas and techniques and for depending upon Western rather than Soviet authors. He had left himself open for trouble in 1972 when one of the scientific workers in the Eye Disease Department applied for an exit visa. There was a meeting to chastise him, and Jewish professors were called to the rostrum to condemn him.

"I was officially Russian, but they called me up to say something about the traitor. The atmosphere was quite hysterical. Women were screaming, 'He betrayed the Motherland!' There were shouts of 'Traitor!' from all sides. And there I am, surrounded by several hundred colleagues. I don't know the man at all and basically sympathize with his desire to emigrate, but I couldn't say that because that would be the end of my work in the institute. I went up to the rostrum as if in some dense fog. I didn't know what to say, and I was overwhelmed by rage and embarrassment. I couldn't figure out how to get down without saying something bad about the person and the Jewish movement. I could see as I groped for words that the director was dissatisfied. I betrayed myself. They could see that I was not one of them, that I would not dance to their tune and scream with their screams. From that time on I was looked at in a very bad light."

The denunciation that led to his resignation from the institute involved an operation on the president of the Academy of Science performed secretly by an American surgeon who brought his own assistants and equipment. Alexei was not present at the operation, but some of his colleagues were and they described it to him. When his students heard of the operation they asked him about it, and he told them what he knew. He was accused of "inducing students to think along American scientific lines." After he resigned, he took a job as a consulting physician in the pay clinic at a salary of 130 rubles—the salary at which he had started twenty-three years before.

Dr. Yuri K., born in Moscow in 1930, had been Chief of Medicine in a hospital about 400 miles from Moscow until his emigration. He described a handful of "beautiful institutions for cardiac patients which can compete with American surgery and medical technology. They were available to top Party officials and those who could afford to pay. Ordinary people, however," he said, "have no access to those places."

Maxim K., who was born in Moscow in 1944, confirmed the observations of the older doctors but was removed from the "old mentality" that saw special status and honor in becoming a doctor. His father was a lawyer and his mother a chemical engineer. They were well aware of the difficulties that faced young Jews applying to scientific and medical institutes, and conceived of a strategy that might make their son an exception. "When I was fifteen," said Maxim, "my father told me that it would be good to quit school and take a job while finishing my high school studies at night. He had heard that it was easier to get into a university if one had worked for two years." His father had a friend in the Anatomy Department of the First Moscow Medical School who was willing to hire Maxim as a laboratory assistant in his department. In addition, his father hired tutors for him in Russian literature, chemistry, physics and a foreign language. The hope was that Maxim would be able to overwhelm his anti-Semitic interviewers with irresistible qualifications and that additional support from friends of his father's who were in important positions would gain him entrance into medical school at a time when it was very difficult for Jewish students.

Maxim at first had no interest in medicine, but his father's zeal in arranging his future led him to give it a try. Fortunately, his experiences in the Anatomy Department awakened his curiosity, and he was quite willing to study medicine for six years. He turned out to be an outstanding student. He won the first prize given by the Ministry of Public Health in pathology, published three articles and received a recommendation for the highest-quality residency.

The prize was given in a blind competition without the

names of the contestants, and it was withdrawn when it was found that the winner was a Jew. The recommendation for a residency in pathology was ignored. Maxim was obsessed with an ambition to do research in pathology and had shown proof of his talent. He was assigned, however, to an outpatient clinic where he would see fifty patients a day and have no chance to continue his study. He was as upset with his assignment as others might be with the news that they had been sent to Kamchatka or Novosibirsk.

He saw medical education less as a test of his ability than as a challenge to overcome obstacles not of his own creation. Overcoming barriers required the help of powerful people, who could joust in one's behalf with other powerful people. Getting an education was a journey through enemy territory for which one needed wit, strength and protectors.

An influential uncle with a Russian passport saved him from the outpatient clinic. If his style was less than ethical, it was seen as an appropriate response to the provocation. "My uncle was a very powerful person in building construction," said Maxim. "He had contracts for a few buildings for the Russian Ministry of Public Health. He took me with him to the Deputy Minister of Public Health responsible for building and introduced me as the son of a close friend who had just died and left him responsible for my future. He said that I was an outstanding student, recommended by the academicians, who had been cut down by the personnel department. The Minister was warned that his building would be finished a year later than expected unless he helped me. That's how it happened that a person from the provinces who had come to work in a scientific institute was unexpectedly sent to work at the outpatient clinic and I took her place at the institute. It was not a very good institute, but it was a place where research was possible."

Maxim did not complain about being singled out for mistreatment. He spoke as one who had been prepared for the kinds of problems that all Jews faced. "It's impossible to live without problems," he said. "I was no different from anyone else." He said that no one had ever beaten or insulted him directly because he let it be known that he would find some way to retaliate. He would nevertheless be offended by Russian acquaintances who claimed to like him because he was an untypical Jew. He insisted that he was indeed typical, just like the others.

Unlike older émigrés from Moscow who had Russian friends, Maxim found that he could not communicate with pure Russians. "I cannot explain why it is so, but I can't struggle with them. Some are very good people, and I tried to be friends, but something always stood in the way." Though some older Muscovites swore they could not distinguish between Russians and Jews if they were members of the intelligentsia, Maxim K. was convinced that he could recognize a Russian at five hundred meters. He also believed that the first question in any meeting between strangers would revolve around nationality. "Is he Russian, Ukrainian or Jewish? That is the first question to be answered."

Though Maxim did not come from a religious family, he knew that his grandfather had been a pious Jew in the Ukraine and also that he had been imprisoned for a few years because of his business before the Revolution. His father had worked as a district attorney until 1953 and had been a military attorney during World War II, but his family knew that he was very critical of the government and opposed to its policies. Maxim was conscious of himself as a Jew and an outsider from early childhood. "I read Russian newspapers from the time I was nine," he said. "I remember when they published the names of the people who were released from prison and rehabilitated. My parents explained things to me. I saw what was happening in 1968 when people of independent mind were prosecuted and removed from universities and jobs. I tried to do my work quietly as a scientist, but I knew what was going on around me."

Maxim's complaint was not about physical hardship but about the general lack of faith in communism and the inability to believe in the future. He said, "It's impossible to live without hope, without looking forward to something." He was not troubled with the concern about inequalities and corruption that enraged the generation before him which had a faith to lose. He was troubled by the lack of interest in work and in serious accomplishments. "Nobody wants to work. It doesn't matter how much they earn. They all want to do something for themselves during working hours, and I was all alone as the scientist trying to do experiments."

He was also untroubled by the fact that doctors accepted gifts in exchange for giving patients a little extra attention or better drugs. It was illegal, but so common it was considered normal rather than corrupt behavior. It was understood that a doctor's note for sick leave or disability was worth something to the patient. The amounts that doctors received in money and gifts tripled their salaries. Lawyers did the same. It was the only way to survive. A patient lying on the floor in a corridor knew that a 10-ruble note given to a nurse made a bed available much faster. In the Georgian cities where there was a tradition of open bribery, or "the giving of gifts," the rates were fixed so that patients knew what was expected of them. The doctors were paid only 100 rubles a month but received 10 to 20 rubles from each patient. Three hundred rubles was considered proper for an appendix operation. A thousand was expected for more serious surgery. There was a sliding scale of payment, so that a beginning surgeon might expect only 30 rubles for performing a procedure that would earn an ordinary M.D. 60 rubles and a well-known surgeon 100. The amounts of money that could be given to professionals with services to offer depended upon the ability of some people to earn money that they could not declare or spend too openly on luxury items.

Older doctors who mourned the loss of the old values and younger physicians who knew only the ways of their own time agreed that there was neither honor nor privilege in the profession of medicine. One of the women, describing the birth of her child, did not even mention a doctor. "Giving birth," she said, "gives you six days in a hospital with three bad meals a day. They teach you how to nurse and do exercise. It's always very dirty, and they don't allow you to bring any books because they say books may carry infection. No visitors are allowed. So there are ten bored women in a room waiting for their husbands to arrive outside with food, hair curlers and forbidden books. We'd lower a string from the window and the husband would tie on the package."

Abortion is the most common form of birth control. Women tell of having eighteen to twenty abortions in a lifetime. After three or four children, which would be unusual, a doctor might recommend an intrauterine device. The government would like to see a higher birthrate and is protective of unwed mothers, but insufficient housing and the lack of people who can take care of young children discourage women from raising families. The feeding of infants is also well organized, with special dairy kitchens for the infants of non-nursing mothers. Unmarried mothers who have to work and have neither husband nor mother to help are deterred from having more than one child in spite of government encouragement. (Women receive a two-month paid leave before giving birth and two months' paid leave after birth. Their jobs must be kept for them for a year, but they have no income after the second month.)

In every story of education and work one finds elements of anger and disappointment as well as a conviction that things are not as they should be. The small minority who do not complain about not having enough money are distressed by the lack of freedom to work as they wish, travel where they please, think, read and write without fear of punishment. They speak of it as "the ideological aspect," a factor in some form in every life.

Marsha L., a forty-year-old Latin teacher and musician, complained that "The most depressing aspect of teaching in the Soviet Union was due to the ideology, the hours spent with useless material, supporting what you don't believe in and distrusting your colleagues." She saw university instructors either as devoted supporters of the regime, as cynical people who knew how to get ahead or as frightened people who knew what they believed but would not dare to say it publicly. She thought of herself as belonging to the very few who dared to speak out.

Leonid K., a contemporary of hers, had graduated from the Department of Mathematics and Mechanics at the University of Moscow. He said, "They gave me a superb education, as good as I would have received at Harvard, Princeton or M.I.T. To be a mathematician, however, I had to study all the congresses of the Communist Party, know the heretics from Trotsky on the left to Bukharin on the right. When I was graduating I had to take two examinations. One was in mathematics. It was the kind of exam in which they can ask you anything from any field, and it was really a challenging opportunity to take this exam. The other was in what they call scientific communism. I had this problem. When I tried to prepare to take the examination I couldn't read the book. I just couldn't understand what they were talking about. I tried and tried and then gave up. When I came for the examination I knew I was talking nonsense. The professor from the Scientific Communism Department failed me and said I'd have to come back in a year to take the exam again."

Leonid K., however, was an outstanding student and was rescued by another professor, who argued that a student who had a straight A average while at the University was bound to know more about scientific communism than he seemed to in his exam. In the end he was given a B in Scientific Communism, which he didn't deserve. He was convinced that he would be able to get away with things as long as he proved himself as a mathematician.

Not everyone was so lucky. Irma Z., a well-trained chemist working in a "post-office box," one of the secret institutes that had no name or address, complained that she was never permitted to forget that she had only a "Fair" in Marxism, Leninism and Political Economy. It was part of her record, noted whenever she tried to change her job.

The "ideological aspect" turned up in tests of physical capability as well as in examinations in scientific communism. Victor C., a professional hockey player and teacher of physical education in Kiev, had problems with the "labor-defense program." Students were officially required to get 100 percent in labor defense to graduate from high school. It was a strenuous test of physical fitness that many students were incapable of passing. There was also no time set aside for the training that was necessary for them to pass the test. "We faked the exam for some," said Victor. "We found doctors who wrote medical excuses. It hurt me to do it, but if I didn't they wouldn't be able to graduate. It was better to close my eyes and give them the grade they needed."

There were men and women in all the professions who had been brought up in a stricter, less cynical time and had difficulty accepting the new mentality. They were teachers who were saddened by the prevalence of cheating and the open bribery of people at all levels. Researchers were caught in programs in which reports were routinely falsified to cover up errors. The obsessive scientific workers trying to lose themselves in projects that would help them escape the boredom of ordinary life knew they looked ludicrous in a relaxed, self-serving environment.

"The Geological Institute changed in 1965," said Tamara S. "The old professors left. The new generation had no interest in science. It was all naked place-seeking. They were just looking for opportunities to work in foreign countries or for certificates to use in special stores. They wanted a car or a cooperative apartment. I was doing my research, writing papers on my own time. I brought an article to the director of the Institute and all he could say was 'Why do you bother? You've written articles before. It's enough already.' " By 1975 the Institute was no longer doing scientific work. "We began to redo old books and old maps. The Institute was controlled by women who had husbands in high places. They were not the kind of people who'd be interested in ordinary geological expeditions. They saw science as a profitable entertainment, a chance to take trips to congresses in exotic places."

Every three years each scientific researcher was reevaluated. Tamara S. was always told she was doing well in her work and asked what new project she would like to undertake. When she asked for permission to use an electronic scan microscope that was gathering dust in the basement of the Institute, the director saw the request as a personal attack, a complaint about the lack of serious scientific work in the Institute.

The workers in art institutes, museums and archives grumbled about the boredom of their days as much as about the pitiful salaries. "One puts the paper from one side of the table to the other. You talk, smoke, kill time," said Zinaida T., an art historian. Eleanora S., a movie critic and museum worker, described the atmosphere at her museum. "A usual day at the museum is like this. We come to work. We have breakfast, and then we go to our desks. The women take out the brushes and lipsticks and mirrors and the pencils for the eyes and start making up their faces. That takes from nine-thirty to eleven. We had three rooms with desks, and they'd sit and talk and put on makeup and I'd always wonder how they could find so much that was new to talk about since six the night before. I was not like the other women. We all had the same education and lived in the same world, but I couldn't waste my days the way they did. I didn't make up my face. If I had work to do I did it. I wouldn't just talk for hours. I used the free time to read or to write my dissertation. So they would talk and I would write. They'd make fun of me, but I just couldn't chat with them in the corridor. I was writing articles. I wrote a whole book that way. How else could I have done it? I didn't get home till seven-thirty and then had to cook and wash clothes by hand. Another reason for not talking was that there was always one person at work who informed for the KGB. Why should I let them know what goes on in my head?"

The men and women who complained about the lack of standards in the workplace also explained that there was no anxiety about doing poor work for people who earned 60 to 80 rubles a month. Firing was rare except for dissident activity, for defending *refusniks* or for having a close relative who applied for an exit visa. It was necessary to have a job somewhere. There was no welfare system. There was disability security, but not enough to live on. Though workers in factories earned more than the idlers in some of the institutes, they too could not support a family on their earnings. Alla G., the mathematics teacher from Magnitogorsk, was the daughter of a factory worker. "When I was nineteen," she said, "I visited the metal factory where my father worked. I went as if I were a tourist on an excursion. I was taken around the factory as if it were an exhibition. I couldn't believe that my father had spent twenty-seven years in that place. His salary was not enough to feed four people. I did not get a dress of my own until I finished school in 1968. Until then I wore my mother's castoffs." Women and men confirmed the fact that good workers in factories earned no more than 180 rubles a month. It took the combined salaries of two people to feed a family of four.

Michael F., a thirty-five-year-old film maker from Moscow, learned about factory earnings as a worker rather than a visitor. His father was an army officer, and he decided to finish his education in evening school while doing manual labor during the day. He needed such experience for acceptance in the Institute of Cinematography.

His first experience outside his family jolted him out of his faith in the Soviet Union as a government of workers and peasants. "I was a Pioneer and a Komsomol member. I was oriented from earliest childhood to Soviet ideals. I went to work in the factory in Riga in a sincere way to learn about life. I was amazed to hear how the workers criticized the government, how dissatisfied they were with their lives and how poor they were. They showed me that there were two ways of life, the official one I had learned in school and from my father and that was confirmed in the newspaper, on television and in films, and the other which existed among simple people, who spoke out freely because they were at the bottom of life and could fall no lower."

The fear of remaining a factory worker or becoming one was behind the zeal for education, the struggle to find work in a profession that was stable and free of harassment and in a place not too far from civilization. The belief that the government provided jobs for all its citizens was not confirmed by the émigrés. After graduation from an institute there were three possibilities. There might be an opportunity to continue education in graduate school, an assignment for three years at a place of the government personnel department's choosing or a free diploma, which meant that the recipients had to do their own job hunting. Evening students and correspondence-course students were left to find their own jobs. The people who tried the hardest to move to a higher level of work often received the least help.

"When the government doesn't place you, you go from place to place asking for a job, begging, trying to find some connection. Lots of things are done only by connections. Some relative or friend, or friend of a friend has to call the right person. Only then does the situation open up."

Rhya K. graduated as a specialist in Russian literature in 1959, a relatively liberal year—but not for teachers with a "J" in their passports. "I had good marks and strong recommendations, but it was impossible to get into graduate school and even more impossible to find a job. I tried to find work in a publishing house, in a high school, in programs for foreign students, but couldn't get accepted anywhere. My name sounded Russian, and I didn't look Jewish at all, so they would agree to take me and say I'm perfect for the job and then when I'd fill out the questionnaire they would refuse me. They'd say there are many Arab students in the school and they would not want to offend them by hiring a Jewish teacher. In the end I had to go to my father for help. He was an old Party member. He was in prison in Stalin's time and had been rehabilitated. He got me a job in the evening school for workers, and that's where I stayed for many years. It was hard teaching because many students were rude and anti-Semitic. They'd think I'd be complimented when they'd tell me I was a good person, not at all like a Jew."

Maria P., a translator and interpreter in the same generation, had also been misled by the brief thaw that made it possible for her to get an education in the humanities. The education, however, did not include guarantees of work. "They say you have to work only in your field," she said bitterly. "But if you can't find a job, who cares? If you need money for food, who cares? You can just starve. They say you can work in a factory, but when you come for work they give you a job you can't do. You just can't do it. And what if you have a child to feed? It's nobody's business but your own."

Marton T., a mathematics student born in 1957, knew that Jews were afraid to leave a job because they might not find another in a time when it was official policy not to trust them, to speak of them as "the nation that betrays the state." Anti-Semitism was always there, a fact of life. It might become stronger or weaker, and it was experienced differently in different places, but the fifth point could not be forgotten. Emil A., an engineer in Siberia, thought it a problem only when one was between places. "The moment one got into an institute, one was safe. I could forget my Jewishness until it was time for promotion. Or if you were in a company that was liquidated, you'd see that interviews were being arranged for all the engineers but not for you. They would all be placed and you'd go around begging for work. In 1970, when the anti-Semitic restrictions began in the engineering fields, I couldn't find work anywhere."

Larisa P., a chief engineer doing what was normally a man's job, did not find it possible to forget her Jewishness. "I had lots of responsibilities. My husband did my work at home while I traveled a lot. I met the people in places of power. Meanwhile everything I did was colored in their eyes by my Jewishness. If I did something good or bad, if I made a mistake or accomplished something special, my Jewishness was mentioned."

To be reminded of Jewishness was always taken as a threat, a warning that one was vulnerable and under suspicion and should not expect to be treated equally with Russians. Some could take this calmly as a fact of life that could not be changed. Others denied that they suffered discrimination in one part of their interview and described the "normal" troubles in another. Leonid K., for example, said, "I had read and knew from other people about all sorts of harassment and anti-Semitism. Quite frankly, however, I never encountered that seriously." Later on he said, "There are very specific areas where you do encounter problems, but these are transient situations. It happens when you graduate from high school and try to enter a university and when you graduate and go looking for a job, and of course there are always nasty little kids in the street calling 'Jew.' But with all the restrictions and problems, I had gotten into Moscow University just after the death of Stalin and I ended up in a good job in research in spite of everything. So I didn't know that I was so Jewish. My hobby was astronomy, and when you are talking about the moon and the stars the Jewish question doesn't enter the discussion."

The harassment that was not serious for Leonid K. was taken by less intellectually gifted people as a threat to life and sanity. In a society in which connections and appropriate bribes were necessary for conducting normal affairs, the abnormal situation of Jews trying to cope with restrictions increased the tensions and the challenges.

Boris F., a computer analyst from Kharkov, was under thirty, but had developed his own way of coping. "You can get around things if you have contacts with a little power. It's very good to have somebody you know in City Hall. The best of all is to have somebody in the KGB militia. Then it's a green light all the way. The competitions for students are fierce. It's the only way to get through."

Marton T., the mathematics student from Moscow, was convinced that it was no longer possible to enter a good university on "smartness alone." Parents with strong connections outside and within the university were necessary. "If you have no connections, money can help you. If you have neither, you are lost."

The youngest émigrés, born after 1950, described their survival techniques without apology or embarrassment. They were born into a society where you had to "get," not buy, whatever you needed. They explained that food, clothes, education and housing were not equally available to all. "In English you say, 'Where do you buy?' In Russian we say, 'How do you get?' or 'What are they giving?' or 'What's being thrown on the market today?'" The twenty-year-olds knew that they needed a good friend in the department store if they wanted decent clothes. They knew that the call to the powerful person was more important than the grades they received. They were not surprised to hear that there were lists of children to be accepted into special schools available before the entrance exams were given. They were the children who had brought their teachers the foreign sweater, the tape recorder or the little envelope that made the difference.

The oldest of the émigrés, those who had lived through times harder than the youngest among them could imagine, were proud of their ability to survive terror, hunger and displacement. They would boast about their fortitude and shrewdness, and their children were not ashamed of them. It was among the men and women who grew up between the adaptable generations that there was much confusion about the qualities to be praised or disparaged.

It was not so hard in Georgia, where the private sector and the mentality to sustain it were never completely destroyed. The Georgians among the émigrés maintained that it was a disgrace to be poor in Tbilisi. Igor G., a student who was born and educated in that city, said, "Georgians are warm and generous people. They give ruble tips to taxi drivers and try to keep up with their neighbors. Young people dream of owning a pair of jeans that cost two hundred fifty rubles, and their parents think, if my neighbor can give his child such a gift, why can't I?"

In Moscow and Leningrad, however, there were many different and contradictory standards to contend with. Men and women who might win approval in Tbilisi were looked down upon as "Nothing but businessmen, good-for-nothings, bad people doing dirty things." The janitors who had low salaries but had the time to stand in line during the day to purchase winter boots, coats and food they would resell at high prices had many customers but few admirers. The cleaning women who worked in the closed dining rooms and buffets that were not seen by ordinary citizens had access to smoked salmon, salami, imported whisky and cigarettes which they made available at a price to some chosen clients. They were valued as resources but condemned as citizens.

They were seen to be particularly loathsome to those who prided themselves on their ability to live simply, who found the nourishment they required in their cultural circles, their research in esoteric subjects and their enjoyment of literature, philosophy, art and music. The women among them were proud of not standing in the "repulsive lines waiting for a piece of sausage." They would eat only what could be found with a minimum of effort and made much of the tomatoes and cucumbers that were plentiful in July, August and September. As for clothes, they would claim to be without envy of the symbols of status, the boots, the hat or the foreign sweater that were associated either with Party privileges or with black-market buying. "I could manage with a coat, two skirts and two blouses," said Nina S., a researcher at the Institute of Oriental Studies. "I could survive from one payment to the next, always counting every penny."

Among this self-chosen elite were those who saw themselves as the inheritors of the old European culture. They knew about forbidden books, had seen forbidden paintings and felt themselves to be the guardians of cultural values and standards. They were not concerned about equality as an ideal in society. They set themselves apart. They felt superior to their contemporaries who demeaned themselves in their efforts to earn an extra ruble. They took pride in being the kind of people who could not be bought with a foreign sweater or a box of chocolates.

Moishe S., a painter, spoke of people who had a great thirst for knowledge, "an unsatisfied hunger for art." He shared their curiosity about art in the West. He also deplored the state of

The Hermitage. "Most of the paintings are in storage rooms in the basement. There are enough paintings to fill fifteen separate museums in large cities that would give people a chance to see great things, to learn what art is. Instead they bring workers and peasants in herds. They rush them from one room to the next. The air is bad. There are fantastic Rembrandts and many good Impressionists, but you can hardly see the pictures. The workers and peasants don't know what they see."

Some of the men and women who tried to lose themselves in the study of literature and philosophy, humanists who claimed to be seekers of spiritual nourishment, were attracted by the Russian Orthodox Church. They were not like the Jews who had converted before the Revolution so that their children would be accepted as Russians, live in big cities and attend universities. They converted precisely because there was no advantage to be gained. All religions were in disrepute. It did not change the fifth point on their passports, which referred to nationality. It left them open to ridicule if their faces or names were particularly Jewish. The reasons given by Jewish converts included both defiance and despair. Some people managed without any religion. Some were able to get by with the faith in communism that was offered as a secular religion. But there were some who felt unmoored and deprived without some invisible means of support.

Rashel M. tried to explain her feelings of deprivation and her envy of those who had a capacity for faith. "There's no religion to sustain you in Russia. It's you and your disease and nothing in between. Nobody believes in anything. No future life. No second or third life. You just live and die and that's all. There's just your own conscience, your own willpower. I'm jealous of people who can pray, even though it's too late for me to try. I wish I could believe in something. It would be a lot easier to live. Really we live just as the animals do. We eat. We have children. But there's no inner life for us. We have tastes for some kind of poetry or music, but what's missing is something that comes from religion, something that turns people into human beings. But I know you have to have acquired it in childhood, not when you're a grown-up person and you've been your own judge and king, responsible only to yourself."

Conversion to the Russian Orthodox Church would begin with inner disquiet that developed along with the wish for some dramatic act of resistance. One had to be in the right circle, meet the right priest and be able to cope with the anti-Semitism that was inevitable. In this there was dramatic reversal from the conversions before the Revolution. It was then believed that it was easier for Jews to convert to Russian Orthodoxy than to marry Russians, who were likely to be prejudiced aristocrats or peasants. After the Revolution intermarriage between Jews and Russians or Ukrainians was not unusual, but conversion led nowhere. "It was only for the unbalanced, for the overemotional and the irrational Jews, a small minority who couldn't find a place for themselves anywhere," said a Jew from Odessa who preferred to be his own judge and king.

Eleanora S., a thirty-five-year-old museum worker from Leningrad, had other thoughts about the matter. She claimed to be religious in her own way. "I believe in my own God—not the God in the Bible, not the God that has a name." She was tempted by Russian Orthodoxy, but learned a humiliating lesson while visiting the monastery of Jordanville. A monk had accosted her husband and said, "What's someone with your face doing here?" He harangued him and everyone in the tour group with a virulent speech about how Jews had killed the Tsar and how American money was sent by Jews to Israel. "We couldn't get out of the place fast enough," said Eleanora. "It was a disgusting place and it was a mistake for us to have gone." She thought she might have done better if she had gone to a Catholic church. She had read somewhere that all great writers had been Catholics and that there was something humanizing in Catholic teaching. Though her passport marked her as Jewish, she knew nothing about Jewish teachings, nothing about Jewish faith or traditions. She knew only what she had picked up at random in her study of the history of Russian culture and literature. Everything she had gleaned there confirmed her wish to be Russian and her wish to escape the anti-Semitism that had embittered her parents' lives.

Olga D., a twenty-two-year-old nurse from Kiev, had her own view of the occasional Jewish conversions. She saw herself as a member of a generation for whom such a choice would be unthinkable but still tried to understand the phenomenon. "It's easier to find spiritual people who are Russian than spiritual people who are Jewish. If you go to a Russian church, even though the government doesn't like to see young people in a church any more than in a synagogue, you can speak to the priests. They explain things to you from the Russian Bible. If you go looking for a synagogue it is usually closed. You do not find a rabbi waiting to talk to you. The Chief Rabbi in Moscow is known to be an agent of the KGB just like the head of the Russian Orthodox Church, but the church is big and there are independent priests. It is hard to find a gentle person who would talk to you and comfort you."

Olga was the child of parents who were what she called "international" in their beliefs. "They wanted to belong with all the people in the world. They didn't want to separate themselves as Jews. People in their generation sometimes converted to Christianity because it was more 'international' than Judaism. My generation is not so 'international.' We know we will not be accepted by other people. We must find ourselves as Jews."

Her parents' generation included men and women who were sincere in their wish to belong to "all the people in the world" and also many who were secret Jews who outwardly served their government while secretly opposing its policies.

It is tempting but futile to speak of generations as if the generations were homogeneous in outlook and behavior. A generation was a group of people sharing knowledge that came from living through particular events, but there was no way of predicting how individuals would respond to the times that impinged upon their lives. Pressures that destroyed initiative in some people unleashed determination and creativity in others. Restraints and threats that created resignation and passivity in some produced desperate risk-taking in others.

When émigrés were asked who had status and respect in their country, their answers showed the range of possibilities.

Ballet dancers, actors and concert artists were high on the list. They were envied the talent that gave them an aura of freedom. Academicians and scientists were included among the people with prestige. Military people and Party leaders were mentioned and rejected as people not to be envied or emulated. Lyosha D., an engineer who measured people by their ability to resist the regime, had the most respect for Sakharov. The intelligentsia, however, were hard to pin down. They were united in their contempt for the shopkeepers and salespeople but had no heroes, no models in common.

Katya Z., a translator and editor of foreign scientific texts, took a practical view of the question. "My butcher was the most prestigious person I knew," she said, without irony. "He had real power, and you had to have connections to be in his favor. Among his customers were the president of an institute and the director of a factory. When the time came for his son or his nephew to seek admission or try for a first job, he could remind his best customers of the favors he had done them. The stipends he took were not without risks, and he could say, 'I've taken chances to do you favors for many years and now I have to beg a favor.' He would not be turned down. The president of the institute and the director of the factory do not have the time or patience to stand in line like ordinary people, and they want the little packages of meat to be saved for them. They also know that the butcher is taking risks on their account. If the government decides to catch him he can go to prison for taking illegal stipends."

The people who pay the butcher a little extra are likely to be the people who are receiving a little extra they can afford to part with. The ordinary workers, the teachers, engineers and office workers, envy and resent them even if they wouldn't trade places with them. Waiting in line, they vent their frustrations on one another. "If you ask the butcher for a piece of meat with less bone, he says, 'Meat doesn't come without bone,' and the line starts yelling, 'Who do you think you are? Take what you're given and get the hell out!' So you grab what is thrown at you."

Those who claimed that they didn't care about food and clothes were caught in the same system. "We spent seventy-five percent of our income on food," said Leonid K., the mathematician. "A lousy pair of shoes cost thirty-five rubles, which was above the normal price because we had to pay under the table. We went to Lithuania to buy some pressed-wood furniture and had to bribe heavily to get it. We would have preferred travel to buying things, but could not afford it. I was crazy about books, but couldn't afford to spend thirty rubles on the kind of book you could buy in America for six dollars."

Leonid earned 130 rubles a month, and his wife earned half of the normal teacher's salary by teaching in a workers' evening school. When they were unemployed after being refused exit visas he moved into the illegal world, writing doctoral papers for Georgians who were incapable of doing their own.

Eleanora S., the museum worker who wrote her dissertation while her colleagues gossiped and made up their faces, had her own reasons for dreading the lines in which she waited every day for bread, milk and vegetables. Though she felt herself to be Russian in culture and had no interest in Jews, her face sent forth another message. She heard daily the muttering around her. "Why don't you go to your motherland? Why are you taking space in this line? Go to Israel!" Worst of all were the hostile, sneering faces and the ugly murmur "A pity the Germans didn't kill them all in the war."

The "actual life" was like an intricate system of turning wheels. The men and women with a "J" for their fifth point could for a period of time find a place for themselves in the system and move with it. But there was always the danger that they might be blamed for anything that went wrong, that they would be seen as strangers and misfits who had to be removed so the wheels could keep turning. They were both the products of the system and its rejects. Some learned this early in life. Others tried as long as possible to deny the reality that was too painful to accept.

From Citizen to Emigré

 In 1972, WHEN I HAD my first contact with Soviet Jewish émigrés, 34,933 were able to leave Russia. All but 4 percent went to Israel. In 1979 there were 51,320 émigrés, with fewer than 40 percent choosing to settle in Israel. In 1983 the Soviet government granted only 1,307 visas. In November 1984, no visas were granted. Though there were 400,000 Jews trying to leave and 20,000 who had applied for visas and been refused, Soviet authorities publicly proclaimed that the Jewish-emigration question was solved and that almost all Soviet Jews who wanted to leave had gone.

Why has the Soviet Union stopped granting exit visas? In the agonizing search for reasons, there is a tendency to blame the émigrés who went to America. There have been reports that the Chief Rabbi of Moscow, authorized by the KGB, called the Chief Rabbi of Israel to express the displeasure of the Soviet government. The message he conveyed was that it was no offense to Russia if Jews left for their "historic motherland," but leaving for other countries—especially the United States—gave the impression that life in Russia was miserable. There were threats to halt emigration entirely in response to this insult to the nation.

There has been much confusion about the motives of those who choose to come to America rather than Israel. The Soviet

Union itself, however, is partly the cause of this phenomenon. With the permission for Jews to return to their "historic motherland" came a barrage of propaganda depicting Israel as a "fascist state" committed to violence, a country lacking industry, culture and any semblance of normal life. Zionism was portrayed as the embodiment of evil. It was no wonder that Soviet Jews, with no exposure to Jewish culture and no knowledge of Jewish history, were wary of going to a country about which they had heard only terrible things.

The first people to leave in the early 1970s were conscious of themselves as Zionists. They chose to go to Israel because they knew something about Jewish culture and commitment. Later émigrés, speaking of their decision to leave, would say, "We decided to go to Israel." When asked by an interviewer why they had changed their minds and come to America, there would be a moment of confusion until the interviewer understood that "going to Israel" simply meant leaving. For those who had no Zionist yearnings, no family there waiting for them, no images of what awaited them there, Israel was less a place than a metaphor for freedom. "I knew very little about America, but I knew nothing at all about Israel" was a recurrent theme.

"We knew not to believe the official propaganda," said one émigré, "but what *to* believe we had no idea." Having relatives abroad had been a liability to keep hidden. Meeting foreigners in the Soviet Union was discouraged. Mikhael M., an engineer born in Odessa in 1935, had American relatives he had ignored for almost thirty years. "In 1950 we destroyed everything in the house that was linked with America. I put American magazines into the stove with all the letters from my Uncle Jacob. You could be jailed if you were found with one of those magazines. It meant you were a propagandist of the American style of life and an enemy of the Russian people."

It was no small matter to decide to leave, to make the drastic decision from which one could not return to normal life. It was not illegal to ask for an exit visa, but it was a crime to teach or study Hebrew, to own Hebrew books or periodicals.

The waiting period after requesting a visa might be anything
from six months to three years, and some people are still waiting after ten or more years. The request incurred the loss of
jobs, housing and friends. It meant the beginning of a life as
an outlaw and an outcast. Jews who request an exit visa are
publicly denounced as traitors and criminals and treated ac-
cordingly.

Why do Soviet Jews decide to take such a momentous step?
Some émigrés say that they were born into skeptical, disbeliev-
ing families. Their mocking attitude toward everything official
was acquired from their parents. The indoctrination of Komsomol and camp left them only with "a feeling of the emptiness behind the words." In such families children learned early
to acquire a proper public face and to keep their private feelings to themselves. Eugenia S., a forty-year-old high school
German teacher in Moscow, came from such an "anti-Soviet"
family. Her alienation from Soviet ideology, however, did not
interfere with her deep affection for Russian culture. Her husband was a university lecturer in art history. They were academic people. They ignored, as much as possible, the "J" on
their passports. If their sixteen-year-old son had not threatened
to leave without them, they might have stayed until it was too
late and the opportunity was lost.

There were some independent spirits who felt alienated at
a tender age without the example of parents. Nina S. was only
thirteen when she shocked a conventional Komsomol friend
by telling him she wanted to get out of Russia. It was during
World War II, when loyalty and patriotism were taken for
granted. She did not yet have an internal passport marked "J"
to set her apart, but she had dreams of traveling everywhere
in the world. She thought of her Jewishness as "a problem of
blood, not culture or religion." In the late sixties she saw it as
more than a meaningless racial label. "For so many years they
keep telling you that you are a Jew and finally you get the
message. If you are already against the Soviet regime and their
policies toward minorities and especially Jews, you become an

aggressive super-Jew, always ready to defend yourself and your friends."

Most émigrés describe a gradual loss of faith, a series of passages through stages of disillusionment that made it possible to leave their country. "I wasn't born a dissident," said Lyosha D., a thirty-year-old engineer from Magnitogorsk. "I grew up with ordinary Soviet children and came from a loyal Soviet family. It was only when I began to know something about real life and started to think for myself that I found the need to resist. I couldn't support this regime, this power, this style of life. I couldn't do things that hurt people. To force me to do what goes against my nature restricts my freedom to be myself. I couldn't take part in the cannibalism that goes on there all the time."

Gennady P., a forty-nine-year-old journalist and editor, said his dissidence had begun while he was a university student majoring in philosophy. "I first had to give up my belief in Stalin and the world view in which communism is a secular religious faith. It's something we absorb early in life, and if we don't we have only this great emptiness inside. Soviet citizens who believe in Soviet ideology can lose their faith, but it's a slow, painful process. It takes years to become an adversary. We're formed without the massive flow of information that exists in an open society. We're shaped by carefully selected facts that are untrue but impossible to avoid."

The "carefully selected facts" often played an important role in awakening those who discovered that they were not true. Maxim K. was fourteen in 1958 when the American Exhibition was presented in Moscow. "That really opened our eyes," he said. He was very much impressed with what he saw and went back four times to confirm his feelings. "It was not the refrigerators and the automobiles that overwhelmed me," he said. "It was the idea that Russian propaganda was not to be believed. It was the idea that there was another world out there that was different and better than they said."

Rita S., a forty-year-old painter and illustrator from Moscow, said she was in the generation brought up in Stalin's culture. From the age of three in kindergarten she had been taught that she should be thankful for having the happiest childhood in the world. It only made her more bitter about the reality. "I had a terrible childhood," she said. "I didn't know the taste of butter, fruit or milk until I was five. I survived for a long time on onions. I was dragged from one city to another sick with typhus, dressed in rags. They told us from morning till night how lucky we were and that no one in the world was better off, and we could see with our own eyes that our standards were low, that we lived in a miserable way."

The process of disengagement, what one émigré spoke of as his "ideological divorce," began with the understanding that "something is wrong," that the news in the daily paper, the reports on radio and television were not to be believed. It was a process that could be checked before the drastic decision to leave was made, but it could not be reversed. Faith, like virginity, once lost was lost forever. Some men and women responded to the loss by withdrawing. An English teacher from Leningrad claimed that the only way to survive in the Soviet Union was "to build yourself a kind of tower in which to escape from the politics. You must not read the newspaper or watch television. You must not listen to the radio. Everything you would see or hear will disgust you, so you must live as if nothing that goes on concerned you. You just hide in your little tower behind your books, your Philharmonic, your Hermitage."

Those who were by nature activists could not hide. Once they began to be aware of the discrepancies between official truth and reality they began seeking information. Anastasia N., a fifty-three-year-old psychologist from Leningrad, saw no foreign newspapers in the fifties. She heard no foreign broadcasts and read no forbidden books. In the mid-sixties, however, there was an outpouring of *samizdat* literature. Itskov R., a sixty-three-year-old Orientalist from Leningrad, spoke of it as "a Soviet cottage industry." He said, "A person who knew English translated a book into Russian and prepared dozens of copies to sell on the black market. Such a book might cost thirty-five rubles and could be read by three hundred people before it fell apart." It was not considered a serious crime to read these books unless they were about Zionism or religion or were pornographic. To be caught selling a copy of *Playboy* was thought to be the most dangerous transaction. Those who acquired a copy were not likely to share it even with their best friends.

Lasar R., a forty-nine-year-old economist from Moscow with a good job and opportunities to publish and travel, claimed that his sense of himself and the world had been affected deeply by the books and articles he read through *samizdat*. During the seventies he read many works of fiction and poetry that were unknown or forbidden in the sixties. He said, "I can remember my friend calling me up to say, 'I can give you Orwell's *Nineteen Eighty-Four* for two nights.' He read it in the daytime and I had it at night." It was from his father, released from imprisonment when Lasar was a young man, that he had learned the pleasure one could find in literature and poetry. He thought nothing of traveling three hundred kilometers to buy a book by Pasternak. He memorized the poems quickly, and his head was filled with lines of Pasternak's poetry which he thought expressed his own basic credo. He took Pasternak's harassment very personally and when the poet died, took time off from his work to go to his funeral at Peredelkino.

In the sixties Lasar R. began to read about Jewish culture, which his father had not shared with him. The first Jewish history he picked up through *samizdat* was by Dubnow, and then he found copies of articles by Jabotinsky. He read about the Warsaw ghetto uprising for the first time. He began to acquire what he called "Jewish awareness," and the victory of Israel in 1967 was an enormous event in his life. He decided then to bring up his son as a person who knows he is Jewish and is proud of it.

Nina S., who had been curious about the outside world from the early years of adolescence, turned to *samizdat* for information about arrests and interrogations. She said, "We had no illusions after Khrushchev about the essence of Soviet power. A lot of people began to talk to each other. We didn't watch the propaganda on television. Instead we cultivated our little circles of friends. We traded news and rumors, mouth to mouth, and shared the stories of Soviet life that were hidden from the population." The little circles began helping the families of people who were arrested. They collected money and sent packages. Later they signed letters of protest against the closed trials of dissidents.

Some émigrés remember that they were once ashamed of their parents if they found them listening to Voice of America. Having been indoctrinated at school, they were torn between filial loyalty and patriotism. In the sixties these inhibitions grew thin. More and more people tuned in to foreign stations and discovered the fabrications that were fed to them in their own press. Rhya K., a forty-five-year-old teacher of Russian language and literature in Moscow, said that she listened to foreign broadcasts to pick up information about life in the Soviet Union. That was her main interest. She was not interested in Europe or America.

Foreign broadcasts were especially important as an antidote to the anti-Zionist campaign. Konstantin S. remembered hearing on Soviet radio that Israel had made its usual barbaric attack on Uganda, killing innocent Ugandan soldiers, without any mention of the fact that it was an attempt to rescue hostages. Joseph O., a Moscow music critic, never recovered from the Soviet description of what happened at Munich in 1972. He said the Soviet papers wrote that the intelligence agents of Israel had organized the killings of their athletes to gain sympathy for the Jewish cause. "I don't have the words to describe what I felt about this," he said. "Reading this in the newspaper was reason enough to make me want to leave and forget the Soviet Union for the rest of my life."

Some émigrés lived in isolation, nursing their private grievances without the support of close friends and without considering leaving. Zinaida T., a twenty-eight-year-old art historian from Moscow, described herself as "a private disaffected person," who felt unwanted and unhappy. "I was not a dissident. Dissidents have more honor and courage than I had. I just lost all faith that things could change for the better. To fight you have to believe that you can change something. I thought any change would be for the worse and that whatever happens, Jews will suffer."

Many of the men and women who took risks and involved themselves in protests admitted that they too had no hope of changing the Soviet Union. "We took chances to remain human beings," said Nina S. "We needed to say to ourselves and the authorities that we are still alive in spite of fifty years of Soviet rule. We still had some ideas about human rights and human dignity. We did not want to be like our parents, afraid of every knock on the door."

Acts of protest had a sacrificial quality. They were undertaken without hope by men and women who knew that the leaders of the Communist Party, like the tsars before them, had assumed the right to determine what kind of speech would be tolerated, what information should be available, what books could be published and read. No leader ever conceded the right to dissent from the infallible Party's policies. Dissenters also knew that they were out of step with the mass of Soviet citizens. Lasar R., the economist who read Orwell at night, had opportunities to travel throughout the Soviet Union. His work made it possible for him to talk to many people, and he was convinced that the majority, given a choice, would choose the government they had. This awareness only added to his feelings of isolation and alienation. He was troubled because his hatred for the regime kept growing and he felt contempt for himself as an accomplice in policies he deplored. He said, "I was the head of a department in a big institute, teaching and taking part in everything that was going on. And meanwhile I had the feeling that I wanted to spit on everything, break with everything, say once and for all what I really felt. In 1974 I felt I had to make a choice: either become a dissident or leave. To live so torn no longer seemed possible."

A physicist spoke of his guilt during the 1973 war in Israel.

"The arms used against Jews were produced in the Soviet Union by my students. I was on the wrong side." A poet who had spent three years in exile agonized about his inability to affect Soviet policies. He said, "When Czechoslovakia was occupied, it was occupied in my name. They wrote that all the Soviet people were behind it. This was offensive to me and I was supposed to be quiet."

The poet said he didn't want to be a dissident. He didn't send letters or make protests. He just kept on writing as he pleased and met anyone he wanted to meet. He had a name and reputation and imagined that he had freedom that didn't exist. He was not prepared for the summons to the prosecutor's office and the questions and threats that followed. He had no wish to leave Russia. He could not bear, however, to be misunderstood and mistreated. "It was the last drop," he said, "that made my cup overflow."

While some émigrés described their conscious efforts to respond to events and policies that disturbed them, others were caught unprepared and forced to confront realities they would have preferred to ignore.

A fifty-year-old artist and architect was designing museums of World War II. While doing his research, he came, for the first time, upon boxes of photographs and documents that revealed the details of Hitler's annihilation of the Jews. "Nowhere," he said, "not in one Soviet newspaper, not in a single Soviet book, had anything been written about that. I found documentary films made by the Germans, horrible films I would remember for the rest of my life. And through it all I kept asking myself, Why did Stalin hide this from us?"

He became obsessed with telling people what he had discovered and used his drawings and paintings to that end. His frustration grew when he found that the names of his pictures were changed in the catalogue of the exhibition so that his purpose would not be understood.

Masha B., an art historian, was working on a book about monuments to the Soviet dead of World War II when she discovered that photographs could not be used if they contained Jewish names. The authorities, she said, did not want to contradict the propaganda that portrayed Jews as cowardly people who had not defended the Motherland from the fascists. Any evidence to the contrary was suppressed. She found that the only places one could discover the names of Jewish soldiers who were killed were the old Moscow schools where the names of former students had been engraved. In some schools, 30 to 35 percent of the names were Jewish.

The suppression of information about Hitler's war against the Jews created a kind of morbid curiosity. Leo S. was an engineer, born in Kiev in 1935. He spent the war years in Kazakhstan, where his family was evacuated. Thirty years later, back in Kiev, he was fascinated by a strange-looking neighbor whose appearance reminded him of the war. "He was unusually tall," said Igor, "with broad shoulders and big hands and a disproportionately small face. His skin was the color of yellow parchment, like a papier-mâché mask. He had no teeth, and his lips were like a narrow strip across the bottom of his face." Leo would see him on Saturdays and Sundays taking his dog for a walk. The dog was a small Tibetan, and yet the man walked him as if he were restraining a large, fierce animal that might break loose at any moment. Leo kept asking about his neighbor and learned that he was an electrical engineer, seventy-two years old, teaching at the Kiev Institute of Automotive Engineering. That added to the mystery because most men of that age were retired pensioners.

Reading *Yunost*, a literary magazine that serialized Kuznetsov's novel *Babi Yar*, Leo S. found in a footnote that it was a documentary novel, based on actual lives. In particular it described his tall, small-faced neighbor, even giving his name. He had been one of the main executioners at Babi Yar. He had walked among the doomed prisoners with a huge German shepherd with the gait he later used for his tiny four-pound Tibetan. He was convicted after the war and spent ten years in prison—which explained why he had no pension. The issues of *Yunost* were taken out of the library when Kuznetsov defected to England, but any glimpse of the tall man and the small dog would remind Leo S. of Babi Yar.

Felix B., a conductor of the Central Children's Theater in

Moscow, described another road leading to self-consciousness. In 1974 he was entrusted with a visiting theater group from the State University of New York at Albany. It was one of the cultural-exchange programs that brought American and Soviet students together. He observed the energetic and relaxed Americans with astonishment at their free and informal behavior. "None of us," he said, "would dare to take a glass of water and sit down on the floor. It would seem like dangerous behavior that might reflect on our future."

At the final party before the Americans left, the Soviet actors performed for their guests and the Americans reciprocated. There was popular music, and the Albany students played the piano and their guitars. Suddenly there was a circle doing Israeli dances and singing Jewish songs. The Moscow theater people joined the circle without understanding what the songs were about. "The director of the theater," said Felix, "saw how the wind was blowing and began to pull our performers out of the circle. 'Don't you dare dance!' he screamed. The Americans watched in astonishment. A quarter of the American actors and musicians might have been Jewish, but the others were so offended by the director's behavior that they kept right on with their Jewish singing and dancing and were amused at the embarrassment of the officials. The officials began to turn off the lights. They sent our young people home, and they tried without success to force the Americans to leave the hall. It was a big event in my life. I wept when I came home because of this first contact, face to face, with the culture of which I'd been robbed. I had only a few fragments of memory of my grandmother, but that night I understood that it was still alive and I wanted it for myself."

There had been similar emotional responses in 1957 when a Jewish group from Israel came to participate in the World Youth Festival. The officials kept rescheduling their performances so that no one would be able to find them. They were relegated to some back street in Moscow, but the word spread like a forest fire. There were many witnesses to this "hunger for information about Israel." The police tried to interfere, but they couldn't stop the crowds from grabbing leaflets and pamphlets distributed by the Israelis.

Public encounters with American Jews and Israelis fed the imagination, but it was personal experiences with prejudice that led people to think of emigrating. "It's not till it strikes your head that you realize," said Albert D., a journalist whose early success came to a quick and unreasonable end. He had published in *Krokodil* and *Komsomolskaya*, in *Pravda* and the *Literaturnaya Gazeta*. He was thirty-five years old and thought his career was secure. "I was full of ideas and energy," he said, "and suddenly I was blacklisted for ridiculing a play of very low quality and poor taste. I didn't know the writer had become an official and couldn't be criticized. After ten years of writing for *Krokodil* I was called in and reprimanded as an inexperienced amateur. I was told I could not write documentary satire, which was what gave me a steady income, and they made me understand that my artistic future was over."

Journalists were particularly vulnerable. All of them complained about the censors who had disfigured their work or left it unpublished. Gennady P., who began his painful disengagement from Soviet ideology when he was a philosophy student, wrote for a newspaper that sent him to the agricultural and timber region in the north. He was already out of step with the propaganda which taught that the peasants of their own accord had requested collectivization. He went north willingly and accepted an assignment to write about the spring sowing campaign. Unfortunately, when he got to the *kholkoz* he found that there was no grain. "The earth was black," he said, "and everyone was walking around hungry." He went back to Moscow and told the editors and the regional Party Committee about the terrible situation. They agreed that it was tragic, but they insisted that he still write about the spring sowing and that he make no mention of the lack of grain.

He concluded from this experience that there were corrupt Party leaders who took advantage of others to advance their own careers, but he didn't generalize from his own experiences.

If he read in the newspaper that things were going well in other regions he didn't question the accuracy of the reports. He claimed that the people who work at writing the propaganda have no understanding of the scale of the brainwashing and they learn to believe what they read and write.

He managed for a while to fit into the system. He became a member of the Party and specialized in articles about the north country. He wrote about the romantic and dangerous life in the forest, and though he saw much poverty and hunger, he knew that he was not to write about it. He even convinced himself that he was witnessing a small pocket of disease in an otherwise wonderful society which would eventually be cured. In 1958, however, some of his observations slipped through his self-censorship. The article was denounced as an anti-Soviet piece, and he was fired and blacklisted.

Two years later he was back at work as the managing editor of a journal, but he was now a man without faith in his country. He had stopped believing in Marxism, and though he had no organized religion, he was no longer an atheist. He wouldn't go to the Moscow synagogue because he knew the rabbi was chosen by the KGB, but he went regularly to Israeli Embassy receptions for some evidence of another culture. The last blow to his Marxist illusions and communist faith came from the events in Czechoslovakia. He tried for a while to choose subjects that he could write about with honesty, but in 1968 gave up writing altogether. In 1973 he left the Party and applied for an exit visa.

The writers for popular magazines and television born after 1940 seemed to struggle less over ideology than the older journalists. A television director and sportswriter from Leningrad described himself as a person without political opinions. He had been interested only in producing entertaining programs for television. There had been efforts in the preceding ten years to create programs that would help people relax after a hard day's work. He began working during the thaw after Khrushchev came to power and had brought in a new light style. "I had no specific instructions to show this or that and felt no pressure from the State Security Department. I loved my job." He was one of many Jews working in television and not a member of the Party.

He had been bringing foreign entertainers to the Soviet Union as part of cultural-exchange programs and was on good terms with the American consulate, which paid for the performers. He welcomed jazz and country musicians. Jane Fonda had been his guest—not altogether successfully, since he wanted to hear about her work in films and she wanted only to talk about Vietnam, which didn't interest him at all. He was a lively, sociable person who avoided criticizing his own country and anyone else's. He had produced more than a thousand television programs; he had no complaints and no wish to leave Leningrad.

His troubles began with an interview of some famous Soviet hockey players that was published in a Leningrad newspaper. An article in *Soviet Sport* accused him of lying. The interview, which he described as very gentle, quoted the hockey players as saying that the coaches weren't doing a good job and that the players wanted some tactical changes. It ended optimistically with the hope that the mistakes would be corrected and that they would play better at the world championship. He had, however, made a grave error in expressing criticism which is not acceptable in the Soviet Union. His punishment was that he couldn't publish sports articles anymore. When he tried to argue, the officials said that there was no need to criticize. He was told that he should have asked what to write and gotten permission before he began. Hockey was a political sport, like soccer, and the government demanded total control.

That was only the beginning. The Regional Party in Leningrad discussed his case and passed a resolution that "Further utilization of this director is not advisable in the Department of Entertainment Programs in Leningrad Television owing to his mistake in *The Leningrad Worker*." Efforts were made to fire him, but there was insufficient cause. An accusation of provocation that placed the television organization under some kind of threat was retracted after he went to the Trade Union

Office and filed a complaint. "There was no sense to it and no logic," he said. "I could fight it because I knew the laws. I was not a political dissident and I had no contact with dissidents, so I could fight to prove I was right. It took a lot of strength. Meanwhile they gave me no work to do. For over a year I received my regular salary and my quarterly bonuses and I did nothing. I didn't even go in to work. I wasn't needed."

By the time they were ready to give him something to do, he was thinking of an exit visa. His parents were more ready to go than he was. His father listened to the Voice of America. He urged his parents to leave without him if they were so eager to go, but they were afraid for him and insisted that he leave with them.

Anti-Semitism is not mentioned in either of the foregoing stories, but other stories of unreasonable struggles with officialdom make it seem likely that it played some role. Yuli F., an older performer and moderator on Leningrad television, offered some clues to the official attitudes during the seventies. Yuli F. had been trained as a violinist and pushed by ambitious parents to make something of himself as a performer. Since he was born in 1927 in Byelorussia, he was conscious of his Jewishness as an important fact of his life. He attributed to it his drive for success and his need to work hard and be the best student. He also saw it as a barrier, a defect that was held against him when he went looking for work and even more of a problem when he was finally established in his career.

Yuli F. never made it as a violinist, but he became a popular figure on Leningrad television as the moderator of a music quiz program for high school students. He was responsible for choosing the jury of experts and inviting the students who came to his studio for the weekly competitions. In April of 1972 he received a call from the head of Soviet television. With great anger, he was asked, "What kind of faces are you showing on Soviet television?" When he asked what was meant by the question, he was told that all the participants on his program were Jewish. "The fact," he said, "was that one of the experts was a Georgian with a big nose and one was a pure

Russian guy who wore glasses, and they took all people with glasses to be Jewish." The director had seen the program during the finals of the competition, and the students were from the better schools in Leningrad, where they majored in physics, math or languages. They came from educated, middle-class families and had the faces associated with the intelligentsia, which the director thought were Jewish faces.

"The Soviet director wanted us to choose our kids by their faces and wanted us to reject students who looked Jewish. We were outraged," said Yuli.

The officials began videotaping the programs to be sure nothing untoward would get through. "We could speak out a little more when we were on live," said Yuli. "The excitement of the program came from the improvisation, even though we had to supply extensive scenarios for the improvisational programs. For example, if I asked a question about Shostakovich and his symphony written in Leningrad in 1942, they wanted possible answers and what my reaction would be to those answers. They were very cautious about the possible turns of a discussion and worried whether I would get into the hot region of contemporary art in the United States or France. They wanted to be absolutely sure we wouldn't wander into dangerous areas."

The dangerous areas were not always clearly marked. Yuli told of a controversy over Bob Dylan that defied reason. He asked some students about their preferences in contemporary music and they mentioned the Beatles, Simon and Garfunkel and Bob Dylan. He immediately received a little note from the editor of his program telling him that the answer had to be denounced because Bob Dylan was a bad person and a poor songwriter. He ignored the note. After the program he was told again to reprimand the student who had mentioned Bob Dylan. When he refused, she sent him an article from *Leningradskaya Pravda* which pointed out that Bob Dylan's real name was Zimmerman and that he contributed to Jewish causes and had given concerts in Israel.

The fuss over denouncing Bob Dylan came after the pressure to involve schools from the countryside rather than the city and the nagging to make his program less intellectual and more Russian. He left the program as a protest, and his colleagues left with him. It was the first and only time in the history of Soviet television that a group of experts quit together. Later, however, one of his colleagues returned and organized a new team of people willing to do as they were told.

Yuli F. had many stories to tell about his tangles with the nine levels of censorship. He had once been fined 150 rubles for speaking of the "great" French Revolution in connection with a program of Beethoven's music. Official policy decreed that "great" could be applied only to the Russian October Revolution.

Polina N., a physicist from Chelyabinsk, was a victim of her own youthful idealism. She had really believed in the constitution with its promises of equality for all, and she approved of the idea of socialism, of people working together and owning the property of the state. She had romantic ideas about the fight for justice and standing up for those hurt by the authorities. She was unprepared for rejection by Moscow University. She had the grades necessary for admission. It was another blow to be turned down by the Party when she tried to join. Her dreams of working as a scientist were achieved late in life after nine years of correspondence courses at the University of the Urals. When she finally found work as a physicist, she discovered that she was not able to experiment or to challenge existing opinions. All her efforts served only to earn her a reputation as a troublemaker. The open anti-Semitism in Kiev, where she lived, was the last straw. "I decided one day," she said, "that I cannot lead this life and cannot fight for another way of life that would be better. I knew I must leave."

Alexei G., a physician and a poet, said that he was too busy working as a surgeon to think about the world around him for many years. He did not try to publish his poems because he was sure he would be imprisoned for writing them. He had friends among writers, however, and in 1962 he found an apartment in a writers' cooperative. For the first time he learned about the Gulag Archipelago. He also met people who were close to dissidents. One had studied with Elena Bonner, Sakharov's wife. Another had come back from the camps. These acquaintances led him to think of emigration.

Thinking about leaving the Soviet Union, however, had little to do with the reality of trying to get an exit visa. Rhya K. said her vague wish to leave began with unpleasant encounters with anti-Semitism in the street. Then there were meetings with small circles of friends who expressed criticism of Soviet life and literature. She said, "In the beginning we didn't think of where to go. We knew only that we did not like our country. We didn't like the system and didn't know how we would survive in it." When her husband heard in 1971 that people were applying to leave, he decided to apply immediately. His wife, however, had misgivings in spite of her unhappiness. She had parents who were old and sick and needed her. She had friends and a job. She was not lacking a purpose in life.

Anastasia N., the fifty-three-year-old psychologist from Leningrad, said she had begun thinking about leaving in the early seventies. "But it was so unreal, so undefined and unimaginable. We thought of leaving and simultaneously planned our careers in the Soviet Union." Her son had an affidavit for Israel as early as 1972 and was ready to go, but she and her husband were uncertain about what to do. Her son had connections with people who were leaving. He had begun to study Jewish history and kept visiting his grandfather to ask questions about his ancestors. His wife was Russian, but he had "a well-developed Jewish consciousness."

Anastasia was aware of the dangers of remaining in the Soviet Union. "When the KGB began summoning people to its headquarters and following them in the street and making arrests without charges, I was afraid and wanted to leave very badly." She read a *samizdat* copy of *The Gulag Archipelago* with a lump in her throat, feeling as if she were choking. Her sister made up her mind to leave during the 1973 war in Israel. Listening to news about Israel, she came to the conclusion that Israel's fate had become the most important issue in her life.

"My sister was ready to say, 'To hell with Russia!' even if she did not plan to go to Israel. She was able finally to separate herself from her motherland. She lost all feeling for it and everything in Russia became unbearable and repulsive."

It took Anastasia a longer time than her sister, but she too was eventually ready to say, "I can't live here any longer." It was on her husband's account that she came to America. He knew English well and was afraid that he was too old to learn Hebrew.

Many émigrés had spent years in the first stages of alienation that culminated in their leaving without sharing their feelings or admitting them to themselves. "It was impossible for me to speak badly of my own country where I had lived all my life," said Lazer A., a seventy-year-old engineer from Minsk. He apologized for his countrymen, saying, "The Russian people are far from bad, but they are an intimidated people. After sixty years they have gotten used to the fact that it is forbidden to say anything and they have to do as they are told. It is forbidden to refuse. There are no pure human rights." A troubling experience in the waiting room of his dentist contributed to his decision to leave. A stranger struck up a conversation with him about some dissident. Another stranger, overhearing, ran out to call the KGB to say that two people were having an anti-Soviet conversation in the dentist's office. He said, "People are afraid that if they don't make the call to the KGB, then someone else will and they will be implicated. If you don't inform you are part of the crime."

In this fearful climate it was very important to have a small circle of trusted friends with whom it was possible to speak about controversial matters. Larisa P., the engineer from Kiev, found that her life changed when she acquired a circle of Jewish friends. They could talk about themselves as oppressed Jews, tell each other about who'd been insulted, rejected and excluded.

In forty years, Larisa had experienced a complete change of character. She was the daughter of a Chekist, a Komsomol member until the age of twenty-nine, who claimed that she had never felt Jewish in any way until the late sixties. Her father had the rank of major in 1937 when he was arrested and imprisoned for sixteen years. Her mother, however, was a secretary of the Party organization and had given her life to the regime. She explained her husband's arrest to her daughter by saying that it was a mistake, a chance injustice that had nothing to do with Party politics. His eventual amnesty and rehabilitation were accepted as proof of the error and his innocence. Larisa grew up as "the typical person of my generation who believed in purity, justice and the Party, who cried when Stalin died and laughed at Khrushchev. When Soviet troops put down the uprising in Hungary, we thought, Who are these Hungarians to question Soviet authority when the Soviet Union can settle any matter one-two-three?" She described herself as "a stupid, naive girl with no thoughts of my own. If it was written something was good, I shouted hurray with the others. If I was told to condemn something bad, I condemned without asking why."

There were thinking people at the university where she studied, but she did not know of their existence. She met a young man who was as naive and ignorant as she was. They married and went to Kolyma, in the north, as part of a Komsomol call-up. The labor camps were gone when she arrived in 1957, but there were still many members of the intelligentsia who had served their terms and stayed because they'd lost contact with their families and were afraid to "live among the wolves in the big cities."

Life was harsh in Kolyma, but Larisa was accustomed to living without comforts. She had been three when her father was taken to prison, and she and her mother and grandmother had lived in Kiev in a thirteen-square-meter room. Their quarters in Central Asia and Siberia during the war were even worse, and the student dormitories in Moscow were no alternative. She had good memories of her stint as a laboratory chemist in Kolyma and no complaints about living in a trailer with an icy floor. What mattered was the warm, human relationships, the freedom from gossip and squabbles and the pure friendships in a mixed circle that was so free of anti-Semitism that the Jews in it forgot they were Jewish. They also were all paid twice as much in the north as they would have received in Moscow and received high bonuses in addition. The people without families drank their earnings, but Larisa and her husband saved their money. They worked for thirty months without a vacation. When they got six months off they had a large sum to spend.

Life in Kolyma was no preparation for permanent settlement in Kiev. For the first time, Larisa found out how hard life was for Jews. She could not find a job without her father's help. She discovered that "anti-Semitism was not just something vile and stupid, unworthy of being taken seriously, but something profound and ineradicable." She heard every day at work that Jews were bad people but she was an exception. She found that she had to work ten times harder than any man doing the same job. "If I made a mistake, I paid for it ten times more than others. If I did something good, then I heard, 'Well, the Jews can do anything.' If I accomplished anything of value, it was not because I was skillful, experienced or conscientious but because I was a clever, pushy Jew. If I couldn't do something I set out to do, I heard 'Even she couldn't do it.' "

Larisa P. was an unusually energetic and determined woman, and she worked herself up to chief project engineer, the only woman in her organization at that high level. She said, "There was the expression 'to work like a house on fire,' and that's how I worked. The higher a person rises in a career, the more he learns about the policies. I burned for a long time and then burned myself out."

The concept of herself as a Jew formed gradually. "It began with this feeling of Why must I swallow this and remain silent? In spite of my position I couldn't talk back to anyone. I'd have to be out of my mind to quarrel with them. What could I prove? That I'm a good person? That all Jews are like me? It would have been senseless. Instead we gradually developed a circle of Jewish friends with whom we could talk as we had never talked before. When relations were broken with Israel in 1967, our non-Jewish friends drifted away from us."

In 1965 she went to watch the Israeli volleyball team. "I wanted to see how they looked. I thought of them as people from another planet. Then one of the players recognized from my face that I was Jewish and gave me a little pin. I had this moment of attraction to someone who didn't think me different or worse. It was so different from the looks I got from Ukrainians."

Later on, she met an Israeli guide at a poultry-farming exhibition and he took off the Star of David he wore around his neck and gave it to her. She made the mistake of showing it to one of her colleagues at work, and someone reported her to the Party bureau. When she was called in for questioning, she denied that she had been given anything, but was overwhelmed with indignation. She said, "I had such a feeling of anger. Why was it a crime to have this little star? People all around me wore crucifixes. Out of malice, I was ready to put on the Star of David and show the parasites who I was." She knew there was no point to it and relieved her feelings by talking to her Jewish friends. She acquired a new interest in anything that had to do with Jewish culture. She developed a feeling of warmth and sympathy for Israel without knowing anything about the country. She even learned that her father, who had given his life to the Soviet Union, knew about the State of Israel and was "a Zionist in his soul."

The invasion of Czechoslovakia made a great impression on Larisa P. and her husband. By then they were listening to Voice of America. She said, "We'd become profoundly critical of Soviet policies and understood what dictatorship meant. Our new Jewish friends helped us analyze things." They also served as role models. In 1972 she left her job before applying for an exit visa to Israel. Her wish to live as a Jew and her ability to take pride in Jewishness developed later. It was during the years of waiting as a *refusnik* that Larisa P. came to terms with herself as a Jew. She said that that was not unusual. She thought that as many as 70 percent of the Jews left without knowing what it meant to be a Jew beyond the fifth point on their passports.

What they could not miss, however, was the barrage of official anti-Semitic propaganda. Lazer A. shuddered at the memory of a pamphlet he had seen titled "Judaism Without Embellishment." Thirty years had gone by, but he still remembered the picture on the cover of a rabbi with his hands in a pool of blood and the caption "Beware of Zionism." Oleg S., an editor and journalist, said he was worn down by "the steady diet of news of Israel as some kind of hell full of bloodthirsty Zionists perpetrating daily murder of innocent Arab women and children. The ordinary abuse in any brawl is 'Go to Israel!'—as if the word 'Israel' were some bugaboo to blame for everything."

The people who remained in the same job in the same city for a long time found it easier to create some small sanctuary from direct contact with abuse. Any move brought reminders and confrontations with the realities of life. Irene A., the actress from Irkutsk in Siberia, said she had had no experience with anti-Semitism in her native city. "Jews in Siberia," she said, "are proud of themselves and very aggressive if insulted. No one ever touched me in my youth. No one called me *Zhidovka* until I came to Moscow." She could not cope with the petty brawling at the bakery and the post office. The first time she was called a "Sarah," she didn't know what was meant. When she realized she was being pointed out as a Jewess, she became very angry and began shouting so the whole bakery could hear. She didn't know that such a reaction was thought inappropriate in Moscow. "In Moscow," she said, "I learned that a Jew is a Jew and a Russian is a Russian; but I would not let an anti-Semite get away with anything without giving him a piece of my mind." Her husband and his relatives tried to calm her and urged her to pay no attention to the insults, but she could not control herself. She said, "I'd come home overwrought from every shopping trip. All I needed to hear was 'Go to Israel to do your shouting' and my nerves would boil over."

A thirty-five-year-old engineer from Kharkov was more philosophical. He was twenty years younger than Irene A. and had grown up with the idea that being Jewish was something shameful, an embarrassment from which there was no escape.

He claimed that he had never met anyone with a good Jewish sense of self. He accepted as a fact of life that many people in the Soviet Union are anti-Semitic. He said, "It's usually a simple, irrational anti-Semitism in people who have never met a Jew and don't know what one looks like. In the workplace, a petty boss thinks his anti-Semitism will further his own promotion and that he will gain something by being part of the anti-Zionist campaign. People spout phrases without knowing what they mean. They talk about Zionism and fascism without understanding. They've been trained from elementary school on." The torrent of Soviet propaganda after 1967 had raised his Jewish consciousness. He found out there was a country called Israel. Until then he had "tried to dissolve, to melt into the Russian people," whether they wanted him or not.

Albert D., another engineer who came from Odessa, was pained not by the mindless anti-Semitism of ignorant people but by the barbs of sophisticated Russians who liked to be with Jews. "My Russian friends enjoyed being with Jews because the conversation was livelier and there was less drunkenness, but if I said something troublesome I would hear, 'Now, don't evoke the anti-Semite in me,' to warn me that it was there and there were limits to our friendship."

Many émigrés remembered teachers who were not aware of the pain they caused with the phrase "He is a Jew but a nice person." The teachers were not forgiven for not stopping the children who taunted the Jewish students. It was customary to tell the Jewish children to ignore the teasing. Every family had its version of Larisa P.'s story of her daughter asking, "Is it true that we are Jews?" When told that it was true, she asked, "Can't you do something so we aren't Jews?" The young girl had been sitting at a desk with a boy who was being teased as a Jew, and she had joined in the teasing until he said, "Why are you saying that? You're one too."

Children's teasing served as warning of what was to come. There were memories of beatings which set up habits of defensiveness that lasted a lifetime. The real blows came from the rejections from institutions of higher learning. Anastasia N., working as a psychologist, knew of the demoralization and depression among outstanding students who were unjustly failed in oral exams because they were Jews. She said, "The admission committees received lists of high school graduates with marks near their names to show who was to be failed. Everything was decided beforehand, and nothing could be done. There was an occasional battle against an unfair decision and a Jew was admitted, but it was an exception to the rule."

The exceptions would eventually have to face the next series of trials in their effort to find jobs in the fields for which they trained. An art historian said, "My husband and I counted up that the two of us had twenty-one different job offers in which an interviewer wanted to hire us only to have Personnel reject us as Jews. I had seven such refusals. My husband had fourteen."

Misha H., a sixty-five-year-old musician, described his twenty-five-year struggle with the Ministry of Culture. He began his career as a violinist in the Bolshoi Theater in 1929, at the age of nineteen. Four years later he was the assistant concertmaster and fifteen years after that was the conductor of the Bolshoi. "In 1951," he said, "I was called before the troika which included the director of the institute, the head of the Communist Party and the director of the trade union. They asked me how my work was going, and I said that I was playing and conducting and teaching at the Conservatory in Moscow. Everything was fine. They said they were glad to hear it and then said that there was to be a meeting about the situation of Jewish people in the U.S.S.R. Foreign enemies were saying that there was anti-Semitism and they wanted me to make a speech that it was a lie. I said I couldn't do that. I myself had no complaint, but I could not speak for the Jewish people as a whole."

Misha H. knew Jewish violinists had been moved back for no reason and replaced by people who were less competent. He knew that the professional committee responsible for judging musicians was often ignored by the Party leaders, who made changes in secret and gave no explanations. He did not think that he would be dismissed as a person who was unsuitable for work at the Bolshoi Theater, where he had worked successfully for twenty-two years. He was, however, fired on March 23, 1951, and never permitted to work with a professional orchestra again.

Misha H. was a stubborn man. He made a marginal living first as a proofreader in a composers' organization, then as a choir director in a suburban high school. He conducted orchestras of students that won prizes at national festivals. In 1957 Shostakovich wrote to the Minister of Culture in his behalf and he was offered one more chance for a new life as a professional conductor. The authorities were willing to forget about the speech he had refused to give if he was willing to act as "a good citizen." The last opportunity to return to the podium as a professional conductor seemed even less acceptable than the ones before. "In simple words," said Misha H., "they wanted me to be a spy, to report on musicians and performers, to serve as a guard when we traveled at home and abroad."

He said no for the last time in 1962, and though it was dangerous even to think of it then, he began thinking of emigration. When it became possible, he was ready to leave.

Georgi S. described himself as a person who wanted to be active and take part in events. He joined the Party in 1956 after the 20th Party Congress. He was then a thirty-two-year-old philosopher and art critic at the Institute of Art History. Georgi S. was critical of Soviet history and the Stalinist period, but he was a Marxist, a believer in the general ideals of communism.

His loss of faith began in the sixties with the arrest of Yuri Daniel and Andrei Sinyavsky, who were charged with illegally publishing "anti-Soviet" works abroad, under pseudonyms. The protests awakened hundreds of scientists, writers and scholars who had no personal involvement with the men being tried. Georgi S., however, was caught up in the events because his wife was a close friend of Yuri Daniel's. She was summoned for interrogation by the KGB, and it was at this time that he made a decision that would change his life. "According to the current norms of Soviet life we should have abandoned the arrested writer and his family. We should have broken off all relations with them and pretended either that we did not know them or that we blamed them for their troubles," said Georgi S. He believed that his "previous moral and spiritual development" made it impossible to abandon his friends and that this was a radical departure from normal behavior.

When the trial was held, Georgi S. and his wife went to the courthouse. They were in the crowd of people waiting out in the February cold all day along with foreign correspondents and KGB agents. On the second day of the trial, they became involved in a scuffle between a KGB agent and an elderly correspondent. When his wife went to the police for help, she found the police were also KGB agents, and Georgi found himself being interrogated as if he were a criminal. Led through dark alleys, he felt threatened by the possibility of a beating, and though the worst did not happen, he emerged from the experience with "the distinct feeling that I had been face to face with fascism, a taste of what it must have been like in Germany in the thirties."

That feeling grew stronger when Yuri Daniel was sentenced and sent to a concentration camp in Mordovia. When Daniel's wife was given permission to visit him, Georgi S.'s wife, her best friend, went with her. The women returned with descriptions of a Soviet camp. Georgi thought it was the first time that members of the Moscow intelligentsia had seen a concentration camp with their own eyes.

Larissa Bogoraz, Yuri Daniel's wife, wrote a twenty-page letter describing the camp, and Georgi S. was involved in sending copies to the most respected writers, scholars and members of the Supreme Soviet, a total of about three hundred people. A handful of people did the typing. The letters were mailed at night in different boxes throughout the city to avoid suspicion." I remember walking around the whole night," he said, "putting two or three envelopes in each box. It was my first dissident action."

There were many similar actions in the years that followed. There were demonstrations in Pushkin Square, and Georgi also went to Mordovia to see the camp himself. He became acquainted with most of the dissidents in Moscow. He said, "It was a small, tight-knit group. It was not a political movement, not a defined program, not part of any party. It was part of a concern for human beings. When you saw that they arrested your friend or someone else's friend, when you saw repression all around you, you had a choice. Either you could pay no attention, or you could protest."

Georgi S. imagined he had choices that most Soviet citizens did not think were available to them. Albert D., a forty-year-old engineer from Odessa, spoke for the majority when he said, "The Soviet system survives because people can't protest. They are carefully watched and informed upon. The system is also not productive enough to leave time and energy for thinking, for longing for improvements and for protesting."

Georgi S., as a philosopher, had time for thinking. He worked in an unusually liberal institute with liberal Party members in an atmosphere that permitted dreams of more general freedom than existed. He could take risks with the knowledge that he was surrounded by colleagues and friends who could come to his defense. Though born to Jewish parents in a Yiddish-speaking family, Georgi S. had divorced himself from Jewish loyalties and Jewish protests. Instead he allied himself with the human-rights movement concerned with the welfare of Crimean Tatars, Latvian Catholics, Baptists and religious and national groups that were not trying to emigrate. He was opposed to emigration on principle, sharing the feelings of Isaac V., the geologist and artist, who said, "If you can manage to remain a decent person, living in Russia can be an act of great social significance."

Georgi S. saw himself as a unique individual who behaved more honorably than most Soviet citizens. He gradually lost his faith in Marxism. "My departure from it," he said, "was not an emotional decision but a serious act of reflection. I decided it was a false ideology." He would have withdrawn from the Party when it became clear that anyone with self-respect was no longer joining it, but he found that that was difficult. "A person who leaves the Party," he said, "finds himself outside society, a kind of untouchable." Georgi S. and many of his friends remained in the Party long after they were opposed to its policies.

Georgi S., Party member and former Marxist, began writing and distributing *samizdat*. He drafted a letter in defense of Daniel and Sinyavsky and obtained signatures from members of the Union of Writers, including four people in his institute. The Central Committee accused him of "slanderous action," but his colleagues and friends defended him, asserting that citizens had the right to express their opinions freely about unjust verdicts. The conflict took on another character after the trial of Aleksandr Ginzburg, who was accused of publishing the details of the Daniel-Sinyavsky trial in Paris.

"Again there was a trial," said Georgi, "and the people waiting in the cold, but this time many more than before." He said that a thousand people signed letters that he and a friend of his wrote. He gathered the signatures of eighty-one respected scholars and sent the letter to members of the Supreme Court. A letter was also sent to the International Meeting of the Communist Party in Budapest, appealing to world opinion. He and twelve others signed the letter. When his behavior was investigated, he read a report that lasted more than an hour on the violations of human rights in the Soviet Union. He talked about the conditions in the camps, about the Crimean Tatars, the trial of Sinyavsky and Daniel. He was given opportunities to retract his statements to save his place in the Party and the institute, but he would not. He and an unnamed friend were expelled from the Party in April 1968. They lost their jobs. Their published work was banned and the work that was forthcoming was rejected.

Georgi S. planned to spend the rest of his life as an underground journalist, writing unofficially. He didn't think he could change the Soviet system, but he thought he might have some influence and that he could maintain his individuality and integrity. He learned, however, that this was not possible. "I had to do everything secretly. Not even my friends could know about the articles I was writing. If you tell your friend, he'll tell his wife and she'll tell her best friend, so I could tell no one. My wife and I were in a difficult psychological position. We became very isolated, not only from society but from people close to us. I was not afraid of being arrested, because I was well known and there would be lots of publicity, but I didn't want to be prevented from writing."

Georgi S.'s efforts to remain himself ended in his acceptance of reality. "When you are involved in dissident activity, you become more and more daring," he said. "Then the day comes when you are confronted with the choice of emigrating or going to jail." Once he made the choice, he had only three months to get permission to leave. "They took revenge for our dissident activity by giving us only a week in which to get out."

His quick departure was not unusual. Though Jews who were begging to leave were refused and kept waiting for years, dissidents who wished to remain were quickly sent packing. His wife, Lia K., a defense attorney in the Collegium of Lawyers from 1944 to 1977, was forced to resign from the Collegium in 1977 and given six days to leave. "We begged for a few extra days, but the plane tickets were ordered for us," she said. "Six months' pension owed to us was hurried up. Jewish activists bought the suitcases and packed and sorted our things. We could not have left without their help. Our books had to be evaluated before we could take them out. We had to pay three thousand rubles for permission, also duty for the dishes and a lamp. We could not take books that had been autographed, and the authorities even took back the henna soap I needed for my hair. To the last minute they threatened that they would take revenge on me if I dared to write a memoir or publish any books abroad."

Georgi S., the philosopher and journalist, and Lia K., defender of dissidents, were both in their fifties. They were in the generation that was shaken by the invasion of Czechoslovakia in 1968. They were both from Jewish families but without ties to Jewish culture. In different professions they resisted a regime they had believed in and supported until it rejected them.

The stories told by émigrés under thirty offer a different perspective. The young, usually living with their parents, took risks and made demands that their elders would not dream of. They were the ones who gathered in Pushkin Square for poetry readings in defiance of the authorities. They danced and sang in front of the synagogue on Arkhipova Street. Marc T., grandson of an army general and the son of a military engineer, was fifteen in 1971. He was a student in the English school, taking a required course in military education taught by a retired army officer. When the officer gave the usual speech about U.S.S.R. aid to Arabs to smash Israel, Marc T. and some of his friends, including Russians, got up and walked out. At about the same time, a Lithuanian Jewish student wrote the KGB that he didn't recognize the Soviet Union as his homeland and asked to be deported. His younger brother, already in trouble because he had let his hair grow long, went to Riga with a wreath and a Yiddish inscription to place where Jews were killed during the Hitler occupation. Placing such a wreath was considered to be a revolutionary act against the state.

The young rarely spoke of having a faith in the Soviet Union to give up. Instead they seemed cynical or lost, alienated and without a focus for their feelings. Inna F., a twenty-six-year-old artist, described the search for stability and purpose that led to her emigration. She grew up in Leningrad. Her father was a Jewish musician, her mother a Russian dressmaker. She was conscious of the fact that her parents came from two different, incompatible cultures and didn't blame her father when they were divorced. Her mother remarried, and Inna grew up in a communal apartment with a drunken stepfather and a mother who worked all the time to make enough money for food.

"I grew up as a street child," Inna said. "I didn't like school,

and I hated the Pioneer meetings and the social activities."
Inna began swimming at an early age, and the coach at the
pool began to train her for the swimming team. She also began sketching at the age of six. Swimming and drawing ap-
pealed to her because they were solitary occupations. At the
age of fifteen, Inna ran away from home.

She'd met some artists, and they let her sleep in their communal apartment. She was among drunkards, drug addicts and
prostitutes, a varied group of people, many of whom had
served prison terms. "I liked living with them because of the
nonconformism of it all," she said. "That was very important
to me." She said there were many communal apartments where
all the people were alcoholics. The prostitutes worked as models in the Academy to keep the police away.

"I came out of it all right," said Inna. "I was able to recede
into myself and not take part in what was going on. They
were all my good friends, but I did not do what they were doing. I was training for the swimming team the whole time I
lived in the commune." She met her first educated people at
the pool where diplomats came to swim. "It was the first time
I understood the idea of 'abroad' and sensed that there was another world out there somewhere."

When it was time to choose between a special school for
athletes and the art institute, she chose the art institute. "I
dropped sports," she said, "because the athletes in the Soviet
Union are so dense I couldn't imagine spending all my time
with them." Getting into the Academy of Arts, however, was
very difficult. "Talent," said Inna, "was the smallest part of it.
You had to have connections and money for bribes and maybe
sleep with someone to get in." She met a man in the sculpture
department, twenty years her senior. She lived with him and
studied at the Academy. Her mother was upset and very unhappy with the arrangement. "I was not like the others," she
said. "They'd get drunk and think it was so wonderful. In the
morning they'd recover from their hangovers and start drinking again. Then they'd go out and do some cheap work for
the money."

Looking for more congenial company, Inna met some people in the dissident movement. She took part in the underground art exhibitions. She collected signatures on petitions to free prisoners and was picked up and taken to a psychiatric hospital. Once on record as a difficult person, Inna was picked up on all holidays, when Leningrad was to be protected from "dangerous elements." She said, "The woman in a white coat would come to the door with a policeman, the building superintendent and someone from the KGB. They might come several times before they found me at home. They'd go around to the neighbors to ask if anyone knew where I was. When they found me, they'd say I had to come with them because they wanted to talk to me. If I refused they'd accuse me of resisting the police, so I'd have to get into the car and let them take me to the hospital." They usually didn't give her any medication. Only once was she given a drug, amenozine, which made her feel calm and lazy. They put her in a ward with both the healthy and the insane. She said, "It was awful at night with the insane ones throwing themselves on you and screaming. Bedlam. If someone was killed, no one would know."

One day she met a friend who said he was leaving the country for good. "I couldn't see how that was possible," she said, "but if it was, I knew that would be my way out of a miserable life, suspended between heaven and hell."

Inna said she had been surrounded by Russians for so long that she had forgotten she was half-Jewish. It didn't occur to her to try to get an invitation from Israel, which was what Jews would do. Instead, she and four of her friends staged a hunger strike. They wrote to Ovir, the agency that granted exit visas, contacted Andrei Sakharov and Yuri Orlov and were mentioned on BBC. They hid from the doctors who came to take them to the mental hospital.

"My mother was so frightened," said Inna, "I was really sorry for her. She'd gone hungry during the war and couldn't understand what we were doing. She's a very Soviet kind of person and was in trouble with her relatives about my behavior. When the five of us went back to Ovir, the emigration office, we looked terrible, really emaciated and in rags and tatters, and the director of Ovir just said, 'You can starve if you want. You have the right to die but not to leave.' So we understood nothing would come of it."

It was during the light-headed days of fasting that Inna went to church and decided that she didn't like it. She tried services at a mosque but said she found no peace there either. Since a lot of her dissident friends were Jewish and going to synagogue, they took her along. "And suddenly," she said, "I found my place. The Jews opened some essence in me." She began to study Hebrew and became seriously interested in Judaism. She met the young man she would marry at the synagogue on the twenty-third day of her hunger strike. When she stopped fasting and regained her strength, they were married. They were denied emigration for a few years, but they kept trying and finally were permitted to leave.

The young people who left without regret or nostalgia and the older ones who left before they had psychologically separated themselves from the country they called their motherland were brought together by the process of emigration. Most experienced it as an extended period of harassment, set up to discourage the crucial request from which one could not retreat. Rita S., a Moscow artist, said, "We talked for two years. Yes and no and maybe. We thought maybe we had a chance to get out and give our children a normal life in a normal society, but my sister, who is a lawyer, kept saying, 'Are you crazy? We'll never see each other again. Are you crazy?'"

Maxim K., who had been fascinated by the American exhibition in Moscow when he was fourteen, was an angry forty-year-old physician, troubled by the inequalities in the Soviet Union. "It bothered me," he said, "to see a special village for Russian diplomats with goods available that no ordinary Russian ever saw." He was furious as a doctor, collecting blood for a blood bank, to find that "blood is taken from all citizens as an obligation, but Party leaders are excused."

Michael F., a film director from Riga who had once believed that he lived in a society of "comrades and brothers," mourned the general loss of faith. "The main goal in life is to get a new apartment," he said. "To have a car is the highest ambition. It's no longer shameful to make money the goal in life. A man's capabilities in the Soviet Union are not used in his work; they're used in cheating the government. All this is going on while Soviet children are being taught that they live in a pure and idealistic society."

The decision to apply for a visa was most often made in a fit of despair. It was seen as a sign of defeat, an admission that there was no hope that life would improve. This was especially true for those who came to it at an agonizingly slow pace, uncertain to the last moment about the wisdom of their decision. The most thoughtful people were the most afraid of uprooting themselves. They could imagine the disorientation and loss of identity that lay ahead of them. Ultimately they chose between the fear of remaining and the fear of leaving.

Zina K., the textile engineer from Leningrad, said, "We decided on emigration not because we wanted a better life. On the contrary, I thought of it almost as of death. I thought maybe forty years is long enough for a person to live. My father was shot at the age of forty in 1937. My husband's father was killed in the war at forty. So how were we any better? It was awfully difficult to decide to emigrate, but life had become absolutely impossible. It was impossible to breathe and also impossible to tear oneself away, pull up one's roots and leave friends and family forever." When she told her mother she planned to go to America, her mother said, "I was imprisoned in Potsmy and Kolyma and all I need now is America." Her daughter answered, "If you don't want to go, then I won't go. You can just watch me perish here."

Galina K., a thirty-five-year-old English teacher from Leningrad, had a less desperate view. "We thought just once in our lives that we must undertake an action that was risky and dangerous. If we must suffer we would suffer, but it would be exciting. For the first time we would try to interfere with our lives in which everything had always been determined for us by others."

The first problem was to get an invitation from Israel. This was easy for those who were part of a Jewish circle, but for the others it was necessary to find knowledgeable people who knew how to make the arrangements. Then there was the request for an exit visa, which required references, documents and certificates that were difficult to acquire. "I first had to return my Party card," said Itskov R., "but no one would take it. I had to explain my reasons for leaving, and then the militia came to our apartment house to tell the neighbors that we were American spies who wanted to leave the country. Some believed the story and didn't understand why we weren't sent to Siberia. Then we were given the forms to fill out. I had to get references from the director of my Institute and the Party chief and so went back every day, four or five times, before they would see me. As soon as they saw me, I was fired."

Moishe S., the artist from Odessa, dreaded bringing his application to leave to the Union of Artists. "I saw the smiles," he said, "and at that moment I became a stranger to the people I'd worked with for years. Within three days I was expelled from the union. People stood up and called me a traitor and a bastard and then later apologized and said they had no choice. For seven months I sat in my studio and drew what God put into my head while I waited for permission to leave."

Those who refused to denounce their colleagues who were leaving were denounced as subversives and became outcasts themselves. Many émigrés left their jobs before applying for an exit visa to protect their colleagues and superiors and to save themselves the anguish of listening to the orchestrated denunciations. Leya Y., an engineer from Leningrad, said she feared she would not be able to cope with the harassment. She said, "They would scream that you got your education from Russia, that so much money had been spent on you and now you were a traitor going to Israel, selling out your country after all it did for you." When looking for a job after being fired for requesting an exit visa, she found workers would refuse to work with a Jewish person. She eventually found a small factory with a director who could be persuaded to hire her. "I brought him a little gift," she said. "My father taught me how to arrange such things."

There were all kinds of fathers to contend with. One told his son, "You do not have my approval in your decision to emigrate, but you have my understanding." Leonid K. said his father, whom he loved, tried to scare him before he applied. When he told his father he planned to leave, his father said, "You have just committed suicide and have only to wait for the funeral." The approval of parents was, however, required by the visa department. Lazer A., the engineer from Minsk, gave his daughter his approval before she left with her family in 1977, but then found sanctions directed against him. "I lost my job," he said. "I was told that I had failed to raise my daughter in a communist spirit and it was my fault that she had changed her homeland to Israel, the terrible country that causes so much trouble in the world. There were meetings. I was publicly denounced. People who had respected me avoided me. Even my good friends hid from me."

Strategies to minimize the problems that followed the request for an exit visa became more sophisticated as would-be émigrés witnessed the humiliation of their friends. Julia V., a forty-year-old physicist, left the work that required secret clearance after the Czech invasion and waited five years before applying for an exit visa. Before applying, she left her work at a scientific institute and found work as a part-time translator for the Institute of World History.

Polina N., another physicist who was a professor at Chelyabinsk Polytechnical Institute, was concerned about the fate of her graduate students if she left before they were able to defend their degrees. She waited long enough to see that they would not be hurt by her departure. She left Chelyabinsk and went looking for an unskilled job before applying for a visa in a city from which it was easy to leave. It was known that there were different policies in different cities. It was, for example, easy to get an exit visa in Vilnius in 1979. There were no lines. In Riga, however, it was necessary to give up one's apartment to get the visa. Where one was to live while waiting for permission was no one's concern. It was impossible to stay in a hotel without a passport. If the request for an exit visa was refused in Riga, the passport would be returned, but not the apartment or the job that had been lost. In Vilnius, on the other hand, it was possible to keep one's job and remain in one's apartment till the day of departure.

Polina N. and her husband and son settled in the provincial town of Gomel. She took a job as a janitor in a kindergarten. "The way I arranged it," she said, "was that there is a book in which your work record is kept. When it gets too thick they add a supplement. So I just withheld the supplement which showed my work as a physicist. They accepted me, which was important because I could then send my son to the kindergarten." She did her work as a janitor very well and then also fought for the right of a cleaning person to eat in the dining room at a table with the teachers. She was dismayed to find that the cleaning people were expected to eat their lunch in the toilet or the laundry. When she left after four months, the people who hired her were reprimanded and told that a physicist with an advanced degree and many published works was not permitted to do manual labor. In the months of waiting that were still ahead of her, she found she could support herself as a seamstress with less indignity. The concern was that she not be refused an exit visa. In the city of Chelyabinsk, where she was well known, it was likely that they would punish her, make her an example that would deter others from applying.

Asking for an exit visa was like playing a game of roulette. Some were winners. They received the visa without harassment and kept their jobs and apartments. Their only worries were family concerns. There were elderly parents who refused to leave but did not want to part from their children. There were also sick and old parents who insisted on leaving though they lacked the strength for the ordeal. Then there were émigrés who waited only two months for permission that took others a year, two years or longer to receive.

The long-term *refusniks*, those who were refused for six years and even longer, were prime examples of the folly of trying to leave. Izabella K., a doctor who struggled too long with obdurate authorities, spoke of the "refusal situation." She said, "We are all different people with different professions, different convictions and different styles of life. We have in common only that we want to leave, and this unifies us in spite of our different character and mentalities. It is horrible to live without knowing the time limit for refusal. If it's five years, even ten years, you can plan your life. But they said they will never tell how long we have to wait."

This uncertainty was easier for the young to accept. Marton T., a mathematics student in Moscow, was refused in 1977 and expelled from the university in his third year. He knew he was subject to the draft and decided to hide out so the army couldn't find him. He left the crowded room he shared with his parents and stayed with friends for over a year. "It was the happiest year of my life," he said. "I studied English and mathematics by myself. I just lived and didn't think of the future, didn't worry about being arrested. I just wasn't afraid. I just forgot I could be caught and thrown into prison. My friends didn't turn away from me. They were real friends. My parents, however, had a hard time. They did all the worrying for me."

Leonid K. was involved in dissident activities but was not given permission to leave when he applied for an exit visa. His wife, a teacher of Russian literature, did not apply, so that she could keep her job during the years that her husband was jobless. Every morning he was awakened by the local policeman who came to tell him he had to find work, and every morning he would agree to take any job offered to him. He was arrested for parasitism and offered a job as a night watchman. He accepted it, but when he came to the place and they saw in his workbook that he had a Ph.D., they said he was too educated for the job.

When the educational tax was introduced, Leonid K. wrote a documented report of emigration with estimates of how much the Soviet Union could collect by selling educated Jews. When the report with his name on it was published in England, he was arrested again. "The arrests weren't serious," he said. "I was never beaten, just dragged off to the police and kept for a few days." His friends came to visit him. His daring behavior made him a hero.

Leonid K., with the help of an American student in Moscow, sent letters to colleagues abroad. He wrote to Senator Jacob Javits of New York and Senator Abraham Ribicoff of Connecticut. One letter reached Professor Paul Samuelson of M.I.T. in Cambridge, Massachusetts, a Nobel Prize winner, who contacted the president of the Soviet Academy of Science and said he would not accept any visitors for scientific exchange until Dr. Leonid K. was allowed to leave. Leonid said, "The letter was mailed from Cambridge, Massachusetts, on December 18. Twelve days later I found a postcard in my mailbox telling me to bring my documents to the visa office. This meant I was going to get permission to leave."

Six years of waiting had brought Izabella K. to a state of despair and frustration that could be relieved only by some unprecedented action. "I had the feeling of being doomed forever," she said. "I was no longer afraid of anything. I could not just sit in my flat indefinitely with the feeling of my life cut at the root." Many *refusniks* were depressed because all semblance of normality was lost, but Dr. Izabella K. was depressed because a facade of normal life was preserved for her. "We went to the cinema," she said. "We met with foreigners. But we couldn't shake the feeling of depression. Most people didn't work, didn't know when the refusal ordeal would end. We couldn't plan the next ordinary things. To have children? To provide for them?"

Izabella K. organized a women's demonstration that was reported on the BBC and American stations on March 8, 1978. There was another on June 1 and yet another on June 9 to coincide with International Children's Day. She described the naive and poignant struggles of eighteen women and children battling with police and the KGB. They gathered at the flat of a family that had been refused for six years and sent a letter to the KGB explaining their grievances and stating their demands.

They affixed their signatures so that they would accept responsibility for their actions.

Their plan had two alternatives. The first possibility was that they walk together to Red Square with banners proclaiming their protest against the Soviet Union's emigration policies. The other was to demonstrate from the windows of the apartment.

"Eleven women and seven children came to the apartment during the day, planning to stay the night and go to the square in the morning," Izabella said. "We spent the night feeding the children, singing songs, acting as natural as we could, packed into the three small rooms."

When they woke up early the next morning, the huge eleven-story house was surrounded by KGB autos, patrol cars, motorcycles, Black Marias and crowds of people. "We saw through the peephole that the landing was full of people. We couldn't open the door because they were leaning on it," said Izabella. The women spent the morning preparing their posters, painting their slogans on the rolls of white wallpaper they brought with them. On dozens of meters they wrote, "Visas for Israel," alternating with "Motherland for Our Children" and Stars of David. At three o'clock, when they had promised to be in the square, they held the posters out the window. They shouted from the eleventh floor without loudspeakers, but the KGB had men on the roof with boathooks to tear the posters out of their hands. "People came running out of the foreigners' hostel and the Plekhanov Institute across the street. The children were crying," said Izabella. "We were in a terrible state of exaltation for about twenty minutes, trying to get posters out the window faster than they could knock them down, shouting for an end to brutality and freedom to leave."

When the demonstration was over, the women found themselves locked in with their crying children with the hallway packed with men who would not let them open their door. "By seven o'clock it was unbearable and I decided to try to push my way out. I held my daughter, who was the smallest of the children, thinking they'd take pity, but they nearly stifled her in the pushing." The men rushed into the apartment and pulled the women from the windows, where they shouted for help. "We were like furies," she said. "We told them the whole world would know about their stupidity and sadism, that they were acting against logic and common sense to keep us from going home; but they refused." The women then threatened a hunger strike. "We had no reserves of food. I said that I was a doctor and would display the state of the children's health from the windows every hour and the whole world would know."

The order to let them go came as an anticlimax. "We were too exhausted to think clearly. We should have demanded that someone with the power to make decisions in our behalf come talk with us, but all we could think of was that we should not go in the cars they offered because we were afraid of being beaten." The husbands were waiting for their wives and children. They walked to the subway station in silence, with KGB cars ahead of them and behind them. At the station, the women went their separate ways. When they reached their homes, they found them cordoned off so that foreign correspondents couldn't get in. They managed anyway to give interviews and answer questions. The effects of the demonstration did not disappear. Under the windows where the posters were displayed there were large black letters the next morning that spelled out "The Jews into Coffins." The family that had been refused took out their prayer books and stood on both sides of the inscription and said *kaddish*. A photograph was taken and sent to Israel, but the demonstration received no coverage there.

Dr. Izabella K. participated in five demonstrations. She said that the first was a success, reported in foreign papers with headlines and comments. The second had less effect. The third, with the children, received some attention in the West but none in Israel. The fourth passed unnoticed. The fifth included the prominent *refusnik* Ida Nudel and took place opposite the KGB building. It was in 1978. Only eight people were involved. The correspondents no longer bothered to come. "The KGB was ready for violence, and the victims had been chosen. Ida was tried in court along with Vladimir Slepak, Shcharansky and Orlov. They were show trials to intimidate *refusniks* and other Jews."

Marton T., the Moscow student, found that the demonstrations and show trials that intimidated some people only raised the determination of others. He described a "very peaceful Jewish demonstration in Moscow. They went to the Supreme Court, sat inside and then went in a line to the Kremlin. The only way you could tell it was a protest was that the people put yellow stars on their clothes. But the police came along and tried to pull the stars off. They kept shouting, 'Take the dirty stars off!' They don't want Jews to have their own culture, but it flourishes in spite of them."

His friends went to synagogue and read everything they could find about Jewish history. They read and contributed to a new magazine titled *Jews in the Soviet Union*, which they passed along and discussed. Some of his friends were the children or grandchildren of observant Jews. Others were new Jews, created by a hostile environment.

Dr. Izabella K., the frustrated leader of demonstrations, was one of the newcomers. "When we applied for an exit visa," she said, "we decided that we must be Jews. We hadn't been Jews before in spite of the 'J' on our passports. For six years we were striving to feel ourselves citizens of Israel even though we lived in Moscow." She did not think of it as a state in which real people lived and worked but as a fantasy of perfection, the place where she would be understood, loved and protected, the heaven in which all her problems would be solved.

"Going to Israel" meant leaving the Soviet Union. Israel, however, for most Soviet citizens, was an unknown and frightening place. The Soviet Union was the first country to recognize Israel in 1948, and there had been some hope that Israel would be part of the Soviet bloc. For a while there was no mention of the new state at all, and then in 1952, at the time of the Doctors' Plot, relations with Israel were broken off. From that time on, Soviet citizens heard only that Israel, the

Jewish state, was a fascist country, an oppressor of non-Jews and nonreligious people. Letters from Israel from new Soviet immigrants describing the struggle with culture shock and problems with language, climate and work often confirmed the rumors and fears. There were legitimate fears about violence and war that the Zionists among the émigrés could handle but that were overwhelming for émigrés who had no strong convictions or loyalties to sustain them.

Marriage partners preparing to emigrate were rarely at the same stage of psychological separation from Soviet life or the same place in their newly acquired Jewish consciousness. The normal struggles between children and parents were exacerbated by the decision to emigrate and the question of settling in Israel or trying to go to the United States or Europe. The decisions had to be made without objective information about any of the places. "We knew nothing about America," said Zina K., "and nothing about Israel." People who thought they were more Russian than Jewish, who spoke only Russian and observed no Jewish traditions, were surprised at the depth of their feelings when Israel was attacked and when Jews were publicly persecuted. Nonetheless, when faced with the prospect of living in the country that had suddenly become so important to them, they often backed off.

Feelings of ambivalence, even guilt, would follow them to America. "I was terribly tired of any kind of ideology," said Zina K. "The ideological pressure to go to Israel made us decide to come to America. I thought we would be deceiving the government of Israel if we went there. They were inviting and expecting Jews, and we were really Russian intellectuals whose Jewish identity had been determined only by persecution and repression. It seemed realistic to think that after adjusting in the United States we could move to Israel. The most important thing was to be on the other side of the Iron Curtain."

Rita S., an artist from Moscow, had grown up in a Zionist family with dreams of settling in Jerusalem, where there was a street named for her grandfather. The letters she received from friends who went to Israel tried to discourage her. "The arguments divided the family," she said, "and we came to America, a wonderful country that has nothing to do with me. I still plan to go to Israel. I want my children to go there."

There was no way of predicting how families would be divided on the question of settling in Israel. In some families the pressure to go to Israel came from grandparents who had relatives and friends there. In others it came from one parent who was "the strong nationalist" in the family. Most often the pressure came from young people. "Why not Israel?" said Efim S. "Isn't it our true native country?" His mother was disturbed by her son's Zionism. He had been meeting secretly with other young Jews. Some of his friends had disappeared into the army or jail. Some had been beaten for wanting to go to Israel. "We are Russian," his mother said. "Russia gave us our language, our culture, even our Jewishness."

The decision about where to go was always made under pressure and in ignorance. The fear of not getting out at all could not be shaken until the plane left the ground or the train pulled out of the station at Chop, the last border to be crossed. There were cases in which passengers were returned from the airport because of a sudden lawsuit or a claim that money had been borrowed and not returned. The customs officers were rude and rough and had to be bribed at every step. Lazer A. spoke bitterly of his "final hours of being torn out of the Soviet Union." He said, "They treated us as if we were animals. They were inhuman and disrespectful. There was a law that nothing worth more than two hundred fifty rubles could be taken. All heirlooms had to be left at the border. Each family was allowed seven hundred fifty kilos in a special crate. Every time you moved you had to bribe someone with fifty rubles. The contents were scattered, broken, stolen."

Moishe S., the painter from Odessa, described his encounter with Soviet customs officials at Chop as "an absolute pogrom." He said, "We were part of a long line of émigrés standing on the platform waiting with our luggage, and not until the departure siren went off did the customs people arrive, cheerful and drunk, to check our luggage. We had to put the suitcases

on the conveyer and they began rummaging through everything. The things we had spent weeks packing so carefully
were flying all around. They took what they wanted and
dumped the suitcases in a heap for us to repack while the train
signals were going off. Finally we stuffed things into the suitcases and struggled to the train."

The journey was so tense and confusing that many émigrés
arrived in Vienna too exhausted to feel an exhilarating sense
of freedom. "They were dragging us from one place to another," said one émigré. "My son's wallet was stolen with the
luggage certificates and all the money we had. And suddenly
they began telling us about this country, Israel, and what the
young man from the Jewish Agency tells us sounds so alien and
frightening. We were in a terrible hotel run by a very unpleasant woman. Four of us were crowded in a small room.
We squeezed together in a narrow corridor and watched a
film about Israel, and all I could think of was that it was a new
ghetto. I thought of what happened to the Jews in Poland and
I was filled with this sadness for Jews wandering from place
to place. We hesitated and tried to make up our minds, but I
felt I didn't have the strength to live with the fear of bombs
and the hatred of Arabs." She was over seventy, and she had
had her share of anxiety. She and her son went on to Rome,
where her son found work as a translator and English teacher
and tried to earn back the money he had lost.

In Vienna and in Rome, émigrés were given official forms
to fill out in which simple answers were expected to simple
questions. Thoughtful people had problems with the questions
and the answers. In the Soviet Union they did not dare to
argue with official policy, but once beyond the border of their
country they tried to assert themselves. In Rome, Mark D., a
twenty-four-year-old researcher in Russian literature, said, "I
was told to write that I had left because of anti-Semitism and
because I wanted to be a Jew in America, but I said I had left
because I hated Soviet power and couldn't fight it while I was
there." In Moscow, Rhya K., a forty-two-year-old teacher of
Russian literature, had no choices when she applied to leave.

"The only way I could apply was to write that I want to go to my own country, my true motherland." After she applied she began to look into her Jewish heritage, and she tried to acquire some information about the "true motherland" that was supposed to be hers. In Vienna and again in Rome she struggled with the reality. "I was born in the room in which my mother was married in a communal apartment that had belonged to my grandparents before the Revolution. I spoke only Russian and knew practically nothing about Israel." Her husband was a computer scientist and mathematician who had decided that Israel was the place for them. He said, "I had not been a Zionist at any time of my life, but I still believed that if I am so persistently called a Jew then I must be one." At the last minute, however, he changed his mind. "I was turned away by two or three pounds of Russian newspapers published in Israel. *Tribuna* and *Nasha Strand* were just like Soviet publications. My wife said she saw no sense in going so far to meet up with the same kind of people we had in Russia. Though I knew there had to be other kinds of people, I couldn't argue with her."

Galina K. was one of many émigrés who were very grateful for the help they had received from the American Joint Distribution Committee, the Hebrew Immigrant Aid Society and NYANA (the New York Association for New Americans). Emigrés were provided with a place to sleep in Vienna and given money for maintenance and were also supported during their stay in Italy while they waited for permission to come to the United States. She was distressed by the behavior of fellow émigrés who seemed unworthy of the help they were given. "They took it all for granted," she said. "They'd come to the Joint and demand more than they were given. It was a disgrace. They gave no thought to the people who sacrificed their lives so they could leave."

In Vienna, Soviet émigrés faced for the first time the real consequences of their decision. They had to make choices for which they were not prepared. They were also, for the first time, encountering fellow Soviet Jews from other cities, other circles and levels of life. Anastasia N. remembered the euphoria, the "feeling of having thrown down a heavy burden from my shoulders . . . of having managed to jump from a trap," even though she had not been in physical danger. Georgi S., the unwilling émigré, described himself as "a man in a strange condition," unable to relate to his new surroundings. Even when he got to Rome he spent his days in his room writing the articles he had begun in Moscow. "I was in no mood to be a tourist," he said. His wife, however, begged and pleaded with him until he agreed to go to Venice with her. That too was a shock. He said, "I almost fainted when I arrived at the Grand Canal. My soul opened up. The depression lifted. I had been so sorry to leave the Soviet Union. I had lots of friends who would never leave. It took me a long time to get over losing them."

Julia V., a physicist, was able to speak Hebrew to the Jewish Agency representative who met her when she arrived in Vienna. She would not go on to Israel, however, when she discovered that it was not possible for a single woman to get a private room. "I had shared a bathroom in Moscow with twenty-four people," she said, "and lived with my mother in half a room shared with another woman. I hated the very word 'neighbor.' I had acquired my own apartment a short time before I left and could not bear to lose this privacy I treasured so much." She went on to Rome. She met an Italian who lent her his typewriter, and she sent job applications and résumés to all the colleagues she had ever met or heard of. When she arrived in the United States in 1975, she went directly to Catholic University in Washington, D.C., where she had a postdoctoral position doing the same work she had been trained for in Moscow.

Julia V. was single, independent and self-reliant. She was a well-trained physicist and a competent English translator. She knew why she left the Soviet Union and had no nostalgia for the life she had left behind. Her ability to find work in her profession even before she arrived in the United States set her apart from other émigrés who were less qualified and fortunate. Her need to discover her purpose and identity in America, however, would remain a challenge that could not be evaded or escaped. Her work and her English made it easier to begin. She could never, however, enjoy the illusion that her problems would be solved if she spoke English and did the work for which she had been trained.

America

 MANY SOVIET ÉMIGRÉS spoke of immigration as a kind of sickness from which they were not sure they would recover. They experienced America as a "powerful psychological shock" that left them nervous and disoriented. If they were interviewed within a year after arrival, the panic and confusion showed in their stories, sometimes disguised by a facade of coolness that broke down in the course of the interview. If they told their stories after they had learned English, found work and made friends, the details of their gradual recovery would emerge. The process was slow and was different for each individual, but there were stages and patterns that seemed common to the large majority.

Most of the émigrés describe passing through a period of mourning for the people and places they would never see again. They also grieve for the loss of confidence and competence, for the reflexes that have to be retrained to fit into a new environment. Most of all, there is anxiety about creating a new life.

In Boston, in the mid nineteen-seventies, I met Soviet émigrés at the Hebrew College, where they studied English. I wandered through the corridors listening to the classes. "Show . . . me . . . the . . . town. . . . Where . . . is . . . bakery? . . . I . . . want . . . to . . . go . . . to . . . post office." Adults learned "up" from "down," "right" from "left," "back" from "front," like little children or stroke victims. A genial teacher corrected their word order, added missing articles and drilled them in numbers.

After class, the émigrés introduced themselves to me as teachers, doctors, dentists and engineers. Many found English harder to learn than they had expected and expressed their fear of not being able to work in their professions without it. Some spoke as if they had no identity beyond that conferred by their certificates and diplomas, as if they would be lost forever if they could not do the work for which they were trained.

Rhya K., the teacher of Russian language and literature in Moscow, spent her first year in America in a basement apartment in Boston, afraid to go out. "My English was so poor I couldn't even ask directions." Her life centered upon her daughter. "First I waited for her to come home from school and then we both waited for my husband to come from work. We didn't know a soul in the city. All we had was our family life."

She spent most of her time in bed, reading "sad, sad books," the Russian literature she could not read in Moscow. "I was in a very bad mood for that whole year," she said. "I felt I had made a great mistake. In Moscow I had friends, a job, some purpose in life. In Boston I sat alone in the dark, thinking only of the past and the people I would never see again."

Other educated émigrés who had escaped from the most unpleasant facts of their society by immersing themselves in their work in the Soviet Union told of finally reading the books that forced them to confront the disagreeable facts from which they had turned away. Many were depressed by the discovery that the society they had fled was even worse than they had thought. They were also troubled to find that they were the products of the totalitarian system they had opposed and were not prepared for life in a free society.

Rita S., the Moscow artist, remembered her first year as the time when she saw everything as "black or white, with no gradations. We were inflexible and rigid and always going to the extremes. We were constantly asking ourselves if we were pro-Soviet or anti-Soviet, if the Russian way was better or the American. We brought our Soviet conservatism with us and also the aggressiveness. We didn't trust kindness. We had never experienced it from strangers."

Rita S., however, maintained that she emerged from the first phase of her American education as a very different person. "First," she said, "I learned about my dear Soviet country. While I was there I had only bits of information. Everybody is afraid to talk. Anyone may be an informer. You trust no one. And yet you know only that life and think it normal." She said she did not comprehend the abnormality of Soviet life until she spent time in America. When she tried to explain what she had learned to her sister, who had remained in Moscow, she found it impossible. "Step by step and little by little, I had become another kind of person, a stranger to my sister. The new information I acquired had changed me."

The changes, however, could be neither forced nor predicted. "There are many things I understand in my mind," said Leonid K., "but not in my stomach or my liver." Moishe S., the painter from Odessa, tried to explain his uneasiness by saying, "A Soviet person is not used to freedom. He's geared up to resisting pressure and violence. Without pressure and violence he feels as if he has landed in some airless space."

Soviet life, he said, had made him wary and belligerent. He had been warned that he would be eaten alive by the human wolves that prowled in America. In his own society he could recognize his friends and his enemies. In America it was hard to be sure.

When I first met Soviet émigrés in Vienna in 1972, I sensed their anxiety in the way they scrutinized every gesture of those who welcomed them. They were looking for some clues about what the future held for them. They had no experience with social workers and volunteer workers and often responded to all strangers as if they were Soviet bureaucrats who must be distrusted and resisted.

I could also see that they were uneasy with each other. The

Israelis and Americans who helped them in transit ignored the barriers of status, class and geography that normally separated them. Jews from Moscow, Kiev, Kharkov, Leningrad, Odessa, Cznernovtsy and Tbilisi waited in the same lines, slept in the same hostel and were fed in the same dining halls. The most educated and the least came off the same *Chopin Express* together.

In Boston, a musician from Moscow confessed how terrified he had been when he arrived at Schonau. It was not the barbed wire, the police or the dogs that caused him anguish but finding himself among people from "lower levels of life." He and his wife feared that they had ended up in some kind of slave-labor camp. To be among poorer or less educated people evoked memories of the evacuations during World War II and stories they had heard of exile and imprisonment. Too young to remember the war years, they knew enough about them to be frightened.

Like other educated Soviet émigrés who considered themselves members of the intelligentsia, the musician and his wife claimed to have no contacts outside their small group of peers. Many educated émigrés expressed their surprise at meeting "strange Jews" with different accents, faces and manners. Georgi S., the dissident philosopher, complained bitterly about his first encounters with Jews from Odessa. "They were completely different from us," he said, as if that alone made them unacceptable. He found it demeaning to go to English classes with them in Rome. "One more time with these people," he said, "and I thought I would die." Another Soviet writer thought he saw evidence of racism in the special staircase for Russians at the HIAS (Hebrew Immigrant Aid Society) building in Rome because it separated émigrés from other tenants, who could use the elevator. Signs in Russian that said "Don't spit . . . Don't throw papers on the floor . . . Don't eat in class" humiliated many.

A sixty-year-old lawyer and journalist, upset by what he thought was insulting and degrading treatment of Soviet immigrants in Rome, said, "An individual from a proletarian country expects to be treated with respect as an individual when he comes to a place of freedom, but this does not happen." His recollections differed sharply from those of other émigrés who were effusive in their praise for the help they received. "I will never forget what they did for me," said Irina G., a biology teacher from Odessa. Sergei S. felt that he was taken care of at every step. "It was the first time in my life that I encountered an organization where I could come with my grievances and be given attention." Dr. Alexei G. was impressed by the efficiency and generosity of the Jewish agencies and thought the effort "one of the great achievements of the twentieth century."

In Vienna, in Rome and finally in America, Soviet émigrés were forced to reconcile their expectations and fantasies of the West with the realities available to them. The range of their responses to the people helping them reflected the psychological state they were in. Leonid K. was one of many who argued with Jewish Agency workers in Vienna, demanding assurance that he would find work in his profession in Israel and refusing to come without some promise. In Rome the musicians angled for auditions. Scientists and academics spent their days sending *curricula vitae* to educational institutions all over the world. Professional and lay workers were not prepared for such demanding and determined refugees. They expected gratitude and compliance, not complaints and demands. There was grumbling about the difficult Russians, who in turn deplored the heartlessness and indifference of caseworkers.

Polina N. was shocked in Rome by the caseworker who gathered all the men and women with Ph.D.s together and said, "I guarantee that none of you will get a job in your field. So understand that now." Polina went to the director of HIAS to protest. "I begged them not to do that to people. Why couldn't she just have warned us that it might be difficult? Why couldn't she have told us we'd have to try very hard? Couldn't she just wish us luck even if we didn't have much chance?" She thought that kind of discouragement was both unkind and wrong. "Four of us were physicists," she said.

"Three already had job offers from America." She was one who later found a job in an American university, teaching the same subjects and continuing the research she had begun in Chelyabinsk.

Polina N. was one of the fortunate émigrés who said they found everything they had hoped for in America. "I wasn't expecting better economic conditions," she said. "I was just looking for another spiritual life, not in religious terms but in terms of freedom." She had left her mother weeping and told her that she had no choice. She said, "I reminded her that she had taken risks to save her children during World War II and now it was necessary for me to save mine."

Her life had turned out better than expected. Her husband, who had been a choral director, was studying to be a synagogue cantor. She was able to support her family, and there was even hope that her eighty-one-year-old mother might join the family in New York.

Ella B., a graduate of the Music Institute in Lvov, found her first interview with a social worker at NYANA a devastating experience. "She asked what I could do," she said, "and I told her I'd worked in a music school and a cultural center. Then she asked what else I could do and I had to admit that I couldn't do anything else. So she said, 'What do you expect to find here? What are you going to do?' She spoke as if I would have to walk the streets or learn to sew or wash windows to earn a living. I'd been in America for only a week. I was in a state of shock."

Three years later, Ella B. was in social-work school training to become a caseworker. The fear of being helpless and jobless had passed. She wanted to be of help to other newcomers, to use her understanding of the anger and confusion that they experienced. Dora M. was another who felt a strong obligation to repay her debt to society. She would have preferred to keep her distance from other émigrés and enjoy the new American friends she had made. She nevertheless worked as a volunteer, teaching English to Soviet grandmothers. "I've proved that it's never too late to learn," she said. "If we could adjust to the bad

life in Russia, then we can adjust to the good life in America."
She thought her "grannies" looked younger than they did
when she began teaching them two and a half years ago and
hoped she did too.

The stories émigrés tell about their first months in America
show how difficult it is to give and receive help, especially
when the transactions are between people of different cultures.
"We were quite bitter about the treatment we received at the
beginning," said Leonid K. "Our caseworker was a civilized
man, and he would call and invite us for a chat. The price of
the nice little chat was forty minutes on the subway and forty-
five cents one way for my wife, my daughter and me. It would
have been worth it if he did something for us, but he was only
checking on us. He had no idea of what we needed or how to
help us."

Leonid's real complaint, however, was addressed to society
in general. "We didn't have one friend," he said. "We didn't
have a single relative or an acquaintance to share a word with.
We were the so-called Soviet Jews, and we saw cars speeding
by with bumper stickers that said 'Save Soviet Jewry.' Okay.
Everybody was willing to save Soviet Jewry, but nobody was
willing to save us. There was no one to explain what a check is
and how you cash it. No one took us into a supermarket and
told us how to shop, to explain what was cheap and what was
expensive, what was nutritious and what was worthless. We
didn't know the most ordinary things, and there was no one to
ask. My colleagues at work were decent people, but had no
interest in me. My wife and I wandered the streets of the
town, a pleasant, clean Jewish suburb, watching a world that
seemed closed to us. We were like the frozen children in the
Christmas tale, looking into windows, seeing tables and candles
of nice Jewish people eating and drinking without asking us in."

The "nice Jewish people" who were concerned with saving
Soviet Jewry were no better prepared for the Soviet émigrés
who came to the United States than the émigrés were prepared
for what they called "another planet." The caseworkers in
family agencies were concerned with Americanization, with

getting their clients to English classes, with providing vocational guidance and temporary help with housing. They were not interested in the accomplishments or struggles of their clients in the Soviet Union but in how quickly they could support themselves. They drew upon their experiences with German refugees and Holocaust survivors after World War II. Newcomers were then expected to do manual labor in factories or to work as clerks or waiters for the privilege of living in America.

Soviet émigrés, like other immigrants, were expected to shed their language and loyalties, to take whatever jobs could be found for them. It was always assumed that what America had to offer was better than the life from which they had fled. Newcomers were urged to look forward, not backward. "They must cast off the European skin, never to resume it," said John Quincy Adams in 1819, and there were still vestiges of that expectation in the 1980s. Neither the lay nor the professional people working with Russian resettlement were ready for talented and educated men and women who came with diplomas, certificates, published and unpublished dissertations and other proofs of accomplishment that they thought would assure them a secure future.

"We are the best immigrants ever to have come to America," said a former member of the Moscow Symphony to one of the Jewish leaders in his community. "We have important contributions to make. We have nothing in common with the illiterate, backward *shtetl* Jews who came at the turn of the century." He was unaware that his contempt for Yiddish-speaking *shtetl* Jews would disturb his listener or that most of the affluent, university-educated Jews he met were the children or grandchildren of *shtetl* Jews.

The memories and stories about the immigrants who came before World War I created problems for the Soviet Jewish émigrés of the 1970s, especially for those young enough to think they were the first Russian Jews to come to America. They were not amused by the welcoming committees who came to greet them carrying bunches of bananas, sure that they had never seen a banana before.

More serious problems were created by the American images of pious Soviet Jews unable to observe Jewish traditions, of *refusnik*s starving themselves to get attention and innocent prisoners just released from Soviet jails. American Jews were not expecting sophisticated intellectuals who brought their libraries of Russian books with them and sometimes icons as well. Instead of impoverished refugees, grateful for a roof over their heads and a full refrigerator, they were meeting strong personalities who were prepared to defend their identity as Russians and ready to continue the struggle for status and self-respect that had led them to emigrate in the first place.

Not only were such émigrés unwilling and unable to "cast off their European skin," but they were convinced of the superiority of Russian and European culture. Some writers, musicians and scholars among them came with expectations that they would be treated as honored guests bringing valuable skills to a "materialistic" and culturally "primitive" country.

The poet among them was the sharpest critic of what he saw as the "phoniness" of American intellectuals. He deplored the conformism of Americans, finding it "even greater than in the Soviet Union in some respects. The conformism there is forced with a gun," he said. "Here the high level of conformism is achieved without any gun."

The poet had spent eight months in Lubyanka Prison, three years under arrest in a small village in Siberia and another four years without permission to set foot in Moscow. Because of his reputation as a rebel, he had had difficulty getting admitted into the Literary Institute and had worked in a factory, as a laborer on a railway and as an unpaid worker in a *kolkhoz*. When I asked him what he hoped to do in America, he said that he was a Russian poet and planned to keep writing poems. His daughter, who spoke English, said he planned no American adjustment. When I persisted and asked what he hoped to find in America, the poet and his sixteen-year-old daughter thumbed through their Russian-English dictionary searching for the precise word. After some discussion between them they said they had found it. It was "dignity."

Five years later, interviewed in Russian, he was still adamant about his right to refuse to change. "If I had to change myself so much, I might just as well have stayed where I was. The kind of person I was in Russia is the same kind of person that I am here." His problems, he said, "were spiritual, not material." He was still emotionally tied to the country that had forced him to leave and to its people, who seemed more real to him because they "lived at the edge" and were forced by suffering to think seriously about life. He felt no affection for his American city. "The only place I want to be is Moscow. If I am not there it doesn't matter to me where I am." An extreme case of the inability to adjust, he even saw an advantage in not learning English. "I think it simplified my life," he said, "actually made it easier. If I knew English well enough to express everything I want to say as sharply as I want to say it, my relationships would be even worse. This lack of English actually played a role of a shock absorber."

The émigrés in his city in America were excited, at first, to be in the same community as a famous Russian poet. His poems had given them words for their discontent in Moscow and for their nostalgia and confusion in America. After a time, however, they would speak of him with more embarrassment than pride. Some mocked his inability to adjust and spoke of him as an unreasonable and unpleasable man. His search for spirituality in the Russian Orthodox Church was seen as proof of his inflexibility.

At the other end of the spectrum were Soviet émigrés who came eager for Americanization and grateful for everything. Irina G., a forty-year-old biology and chemistry teacher from Odessa, had been a loyal Soviet citizen until she decided to emigrate. Once in America, she was loyal to her new country. It was not in her nature to be in opposition or to condone criticism. She would not permit criticism of the United States in her presence, just as it had not been possible for her to accept criticism of Soviet policy. "I love the United States very much," she said. "Even my husband cannot say a bad word about America in front of me. If someone says something, I say, 'Please do me a favor. You are talking to the wrong person.' I will not hear any complaints about this great good country."

Between the extremes, there were endless and painful struggles to give up Soviet habits and judgments and to accommodate to American realities. Emigrés who could not speak English had a period of grace in which they could imagine that the lack of language was the only cause of their unhappiness. It could be blamed for their inability to find work in their professions, their problems with making friends and most of all their difficulties understanding America and Americans. Those who arrived with fluency in English were immediately faced with the cultural differences that would leave them disoriented for years.

Vladimir B., a forty-three-year-old engineer from Moscow, could be pointed out as an unusually successful émigré. He came with fluency in English and an engineering specialty that was in demand. He immediately found a good job and bought a house that he renovated with his own hands, a car and tickets to the major cultural events in his city. "I was very happy the first two years," he said. "I thought I was adjusted and had no problems. Now, after four years, I see that I am not. The longer I stay, the more I see that it will take years. If you change your country you can never really belong, never really be happy."

He was saddened by his inability to replace the friends he had lost. He needed a new network of relationships with Americans to soften his feelings of strangeness. He had hoped to make friends with his colleagues at work, but that had not happened. They were not curious about him, not interested in his opinions and experiences. Like other educated Soviet émigrés, he had assumed that Americans studied Soviet literature and culture as avidly as he had studied about life in the West. It was a shock to find that Russian studies were not popular in America and that educated Americans were not embarrassed to admit that they knew very little about the Soviet Union.

Vladimir B. was troubled by the knowledge that Americans

did not know that only a small minority in the Soviet Union thought of America as the leading democratic country and that the majority knew only the propaganda that presented it as an aggressor, an imperialist country which supports fascists and dictators. He attended lectures at Harvard University and was overwhelmed by what he heard. "I became too angry to speak," he said. "The lecturers don't know what they are talking about. They don't understand the Soviet system at all. They don't see it as the malignant cancer it is." Like most of his fellow émigrés, he insisted that the Soviets understand only force and see flexibility as weakness that can be taken advantage of, even though they respect America as a highly developed country with superior technology.

Moishe S., the painter from Odessa, said he had acquired his impressions of America from Soviet propaganda and from reading Dreiser, Upton Sinclair, Faulkner and Hemingway. He expected "a strong, tough country, quick on the draw and invincible." He said, "I was very surprised by its softness, even its weakness. It hurt me to see it because I like the country so much, and I'm sorry that it seems so lost, so lacking in discipline and order."

In spite of all their differences, émigrés shared this fear of American "weakness." A fifty-year-old cultural anthropologist from Moscow expressed her concern about America's unaggressive stance toward the Soviet Union by comparing it to "a civilized person giving a philosophy lesson to a hooligan holding a knife." Emigrés were conscious of their "Soviet mentality" but unable to free themselves of the aggressive responses they had been taught. Leonid K. could not understand why protestors against Vietnam were not jailed and executed. Other émigrés thought all murderers should be "shot on the spot."

Some émigrés were aware that Americans were as incapable of imagining the mind-set of a Soviet citizen as they were incapable of understanding Americans. "It's impossible for a normal Western person to believe the cruelty, the horror, the arbitrariness of Soviet power," said Lasar R. "No matter how

Solzhenitsyn tries to explain it, no matter how much bitterness Maksimov poured into his *Rhinoceros*, no matter how I try to explain to my American friends, it's useless." Efim S., a young law student who was concerned about "the different ways of thinking" that separated Soviet émigrés from Americans, echoed Lasar R.'s words. "I'm asked if it is as bad as the papers say," he said. "People are sure it is all exaggerated, and I have to tell them it is a thousand times worse than they can imagine. Western reporters can't comprehend what is happening to us there. They can't see the destruction of human nature, the depersonalization, the careful weeding out of everything good and moral."

Efim S. could not cope with American liberalism. He associated only with other Russians. He didn't believe in détente or in peaceful coexistence. "There must be no deals with the devil," he said in typical Soviet style. The language used to repudiate Soviet society was often similar to that which had been used in the Soviet Union to teach fear of America as an inhuman, corrupt and decadent society.

After a few years in America, émigrés were usually able to separate the American reality from the propaganda which they had absorbed. Those who had rejected all the official pronouncements, however, had created private fantasies of America as a paradise where all their dreams would be fulfilled, where all obstacles would vanish and where all the privileges they longed for would be granted. Adjusting to America was easier for those who expected the worst.

"The problem," said Michael F., "was that America was so far away, we just didn't know much about it." As a film director in Moscow, he had had access to more information than most Soviet citizens. He had seen films set in New York, Washington, D.C., Chicago and San Francisco. He knew about slums and strikes, about drug addicts and prostitution. He had come with the image of America as "a stone jungle," a replica of Manhattan from coast to coast. He was delighted to discover small towns, forests, beaches. "I knew nothing about the beauty of the country, nothing about cultural life."

Konstantin S., who had expected "everything to be wonderful in America," received his first shock in the bus from Kennedy Airport, driving through the ruins of the South Bronx. "We were horrified by the broken houses and the filth." His wife never would get used to the dirty streets of New York. He was more concerned with his ambition to continue his work as a writer and teacher and became fascinated by the city in spite of its overflowing garbage pails. A grant from the American Council for Emigrés in the Professions led to an invitation for Konstantin S. and his wife to be Scholars in Residence at Queens College. They would gradually discover that America was different from what they expected, but worth exploring.

Emigrés who said they knew exactly why they left the Soviet Union seemed to find it easier to admit that they knew very little about America. They could say, "I did not expect to find . . ." without adding a lecture on the superiority of Russian culture, education, snow removal, friendship and spirituality. Those who had left with uncertainty about their motives for leaving were more prone to inveigh against the imperfections of America, especially when compared with their idealized and nostalgic memory of Russia. The most strident criticism, however, would be of American institutions that remind Soviet émigrés of the patterns and institutions they left behind them.

"I hate to go to the Housing Authority," said Dora M. "I feel as if I were in Russia. The same style. Nobody cares. Why do they walk as if paralyzed? Why do they work so slowly? It's unbelievable." More serious were the responses to the discovery that it was difficult for writers to publish their work even without official censorship and problems with anti-Semitism. World-class musicians would have opportunities to perform, but the second- and third-rate would struggle in America as they had struggled in the Soviet Union. Artists who had thought themselves avant-garde among Soviet realists brought work that looked old-fashioned and provincial in America.

Joseph O., a thirty-four-year-old music critic, examined the advantages and disadvantages of American life and came to the conclusion that all countries in the world had problems. He decided that life in a democratic country was "the least bad" and said, "I prefer to live with the problems of the United States rather than those of the Soviet Union."

One by one the émigrés would create their balance sheets, their lists of gains and losses, their changing perceptions of what was normal and abnormal, desirable and repulsive, which culminated for most of them in the ability to say, "I have found what I needed in America . . . and it was worth the pain of emigration."

For Maya G., the elderly actress and singer, the telephone became the symbol of American freedom. "I cannot tell you what happiness it is to say what I please on the phone. I was always so afraid of saying something that would cause me trouble. When I hung up the phone in Moscow I would think, Oh, my God, what did I say? Maybe I shouldn't have said that. And did I say it in the right way?" She looked back on all the years in which she had raised her hand "not because I wanted to but because I was afraid that my neighbor would see that I had not raised it. You cannot know what a joy it is not to have to worry about such things. I love this country . . . and especially that I can walk in the street and speak Yiddish and nobody looks at me with nasty eyes."

At dinner with Nina S. and some other Russian émigrés, I discovered that even after three years in Boston, an unexpected knock on the door could still produce the old reflex of fear. The knock I scarcely heard stopped the conversation abruptly. I could feel a ripple of anxiety circle the table and then the embarrassment as the door opened and a neighbor came in with a gift of apples. "It is not the KGB," said one of the guests. "This is Boston."

Nina was exhilarated by the opportunity to fashion a new life. She said, "I do many things I never did before. I teach, which I could not do in the Soviet Union, where I was not trusted to do ideological work. I speak English. I drive a car and own a house. I want to write and publish. Everything I wrote and published in the Soviet Union has been destroyed. My name cannot be found there in any catalogue or index. I start over with the hope that I can do it."

She had once thought she might find a better life in a European country, but by the time of her interview she had come to terms with America and had given up her fantasies of better or different places.

Leonid K., the mathematician, emerged from his first year of culture shock and disappointment ready to argue with his fellow émigrés who looked down on the quality of intellectual life in America. He was ready to do battle with those who thought the Moscow intelligentsia was something special and that it was impossible to find people of equal caliber in the United States unless they came from Moscow or Leningrad.

"If I may put it in strong terms," he said, "this is bullshit. There are interesting people here and there were interesting people there. The American intelligentsia is no worse than that of Moscow. It's just different." He found that Americans worked harder and were less likely to stay up all night talking about intellectual issues. "If I did no work at all in Moscow, no one would know," said Leonid. "Here I'm under pressure all the time to accomplish something useful. I come home dead tired by Friday. I have no need to sit around talking about what everyone can read in the newspaper or watch on television. I'm no longer the privileged person who has access to something forbidden to the rest of the population. Everything is available to everyone. No one has special privileges."

Georgi S., the philosopher and dissident who left the Soviet Union against his will, says that he no longer regrets his emigration. "When I knew we had to leave," he said, "I had a feeling of total darkness, complete hopelessness. I knew that I wouldn't be able to continue my writing, which was my life. And then one sleepless night I began to think of positive things I could do, of books I might publish and lectures I could give. Now that I'm here I see that my dreams have not been fulfilled, but I'm satisfied with what I have done and think I'll be able to do more writing and lecturing. Of course we haven't achieved prosperity, but that isn't disillusioning. There I had no job and no hope of ever getting one. Here I have the chance to work, to lecture, to develop as a human being."

When Georgi compared himself with his friends who had remained in the Soviet Union, he decided that immigration was a rejuvenating experience. "Our friends who stayed feel like old men," he said. "Nothing changes. There is nothing to hope for." He found that knowledge of America was very important for an intellectual. "It widens your imagination and your understanding. No reading can replace the experience of being here."

Georgi attributed his rapid intellectual adjustment to the fact that he had lived "outside society" for six years as a dissident in the Soviet Union. "I lived by different norms," he said. "I was already accustomed to freedom and didn't have to undergo the terrifying change from the Soviet to the Western way of life."

Rhya K. spoke of her struggle with this change when she first began teaching in an American university. "It was an incredible thing for me," she said. "I was teaching about the Soviet press and for the first time in my life said what I wanted to say. It was very difficult because I felt this controlling system in my head, my inner censor telling me I can't say this and I mustn't say that. But step by step I became free with the material and could discuss what the students wanted to discuss and nobody controlled me."

A Moscow teacher of Russian art history spoke of his escape from his "self-censorship" in another context. He thought he had permanently suppressed all vestiges of his Jewish upbringing in an Orthodox family in the Ukraine. While lecturing in an American university he found himself, for the first time in his adult life, speaking of "God," using the word not as a meaningless expression associated with ignorant people, but as he had known it as a child, praying at the side of his grandfather.

The intellectuals among the émigrés described their Americanization as a slow process that was often painful. Words, concepts and beliefs that they had taken for granted had to be reexamined and reevaluated. Many were unable to imagine other ways of seeing the world and other ways of relating to people than their own. Leonid K., who had fought for the right to be an independent individual in the Soviet Union, admitted that he had nevertheless been "born totalitarian" and educated in a system that discouraged freedom of thought and tolerance for others. It was possible to yearn for freedom without understanding what freedom meant in America.

The need to differentiate between different classes and to defend their place in society often seemed stronger than the longing for freedom. Marsha L., a forty-year-old pianist from Leningrad, tried to explain the differences between émigrés while establishing her own reasons for emigrating. "This emigration," she said, "represents all the strata of Jewish population in the Soviet Union. Some people came in search of freedom. Some came to escape persecution. There are also people who came to live better, to make money and have an easier life. I don't condemn them. I just don't have anything in common with them."

Emigrés who said they came for "spiritual" reasons rather than material comfort set themselves apart and were often quick to condemn those who had left for what they saw as ignoble reasons. The idea of coming to America to have a more comfortable life was considered shameful.

"My reasons for emigration had nothing to do with material things," said Boris F., a computer analyst from Kharkov. "It's true that there were five of us living in two rooms, but that meant nothing to us because everyone lived like that. You have to understand that it's very difficult to change your language, your culture and your habits. A reasonable person doesn't give up his friends and relatives for the sake of a bigger apartment and the chance to eat strawberries in January."

Boris F. came to America as a Jew, grateful for the chance to "become one with my people," and also grateful for "this Jewishness" which had helped him leave the Soviet Union. He was aware that he could have assimilated totally except for this unknown heritage which he had chosen to respect and to try to understand. It had helped him separate himself from the culture in which he was raised and connected him instead to a culture that was two or three thousand years old. It had also helped him separate himself from his father, who still believed in the Soviet ideals. "He had looked for new ideas, new ideals and symbols," said Boris, "but all he had found was emptiness and suspicion." He wanted something better for his son. It pleased him to be able to send him to a Jewish school in Chicago. He hoped he would acquire a positive Jewish identity and the dignity of belonging to an ancient people. He also wanted him to enjoy American freedom.

Almost all the émigrés had difficulty responding to American freedom. They had no preparation for it and were also unable to explain what was possible to the friends and relatives they had left behind.

A graduate student at Brandeis University who had emigrated without his parents told of a letter he had received from his father in Moscow. "My father," he said, "was very worried about me because I left New York University and came to Brandeis, where I was offered a scholarship. He scolded me for becoming a criminal so quickly and for daring to leave New York without permission. I tried to explain that I didn't need permission, that I could live anywhere I pleased, but he wouldn't believe me. He wrote, 'You can tell me anything you want, but you can't tell me that people just live anywhere they please without government permission. No country could permit such chaos.' "

Soviet citizens who had never had the freedom to live where they pleased sometimes needed to do a lot of traveling and moving about to prove to themselves that it was really possible. There were more choices than they had imagined possible. Books and films, cars and clothes, newspapers that contradicted each other, religions and cults, political parties with no official pronouncements to follow, no way of knowing what to believe.

There were émigrés who were less flexible and less open to

new opportunities who felt emotionally incapable of making choices and were frightened by a society without authorities who made the decisions over all aspects of life. Dora M., a seventy-year-old English teacher, spoke for many of the older émigrés when she complained about American freedom. "That is why you have crime and unpleasantness from which you will perish," she said adamantly. "Every person must know his duty, what he can do and cannot do and most of all what he should do. It cannot be 'I want this and don't want that. I will go where I please and do what I like.' It's just craziness to have so much liberation."

Irene A., the fifty-six-year-old actress who came because her husband and son decided to leave, spoke for those who had more personal complaints. "America doesn't suit me," she said. "I have no bad words for America. It's a wonderful country. It is not to blame that it is not for me. I blame my husband for my unhappiness." She admitted that she lived as she had never lived before and that her suburb was "a corner of paradise." All the beauty and comfort was no consolation, however, for the fact that she didn't have a soul to talk to. "In Moscow I had friends and relatives. I knew the language. I could listen to the radio and watch television. I'm a city person. I like noise. I like to be among crowds of people. If I were younger I might change my habits and character, but it's too late at my age."

It was not a matter of age alone. Some Soviet émigrés were afraid of living in suburbs, which they associated with exile. Whether they had lived in Moscow or Leningrad or only wished to, they felt safer and more at home in a metropolis. "I hate the dead streets of Detroit," said Eleanora S., a thirty-three-year-old museum worker from Leningrad. She found only two lively streets with crowds of people after six o'clock, and those were the streets where Russians lived. Rita S., a forty-two-year-old artist from Moscow, complained about the quiet and the isolation of her Boston suburb. It took her a long time to reconcile herself to a private house all for herself and her family. "I like apartments," she said. "I like to hear cars running under my window and the noise of crowded places. I can't bear to sit in this noiseless house watching the stupid television."

Lia K., who had led a stormy life in Moscow as a defense lawyer for dissidents and was forced to leave the Soviet Union, preferred to be in a quiet suburb of Washington, D.C. "I adore it," she said. "It has always been my dream to live in a small house with not too many people around, with no neighbors above or below me. This is what I always wanted."

Adjustment in America depended upon what émigrés wanted and expected and upon their experiences in the Soviet Union even more than upon what America had to offer. Lasar R., the fifty-year-old economist and writer, had decided to emigrate in spite of what appeared to be a successful life. "We were well off in the last ten years," he said. "And my parents said, 'Why must you leave when everything is so good for you?'" He and his wife had come to feel that the material things they had acquired had no meaning. As an economist he felt he was participating in immoral activity and that he would have no self-respect if he did not leave when it was possible. He was also still haunted by his difficult childhood. His father was arrested in 1938, when he was seven, and rehabilitated when he was twenty-three. His experiences as the son of "an enemy of the people" were so unpleasant that no amount of success could compensate for his feelings of anxiety and deprivation.

Lasar R. said, "My wife and I knew that we must be prepared to work at anything under any conditions if we emigrate. We would have to get rid of our pride, our arrogance, our feelings of self-importance. The book I was about to publish would be lost. I would have to separate myself from my friends and associates." He quit his job to save his colleagues the embarrassment of firing him. He gave his friends permission to denounce him publicly without concern for his feelings. He came to America without any doubt that he had done the right thing and yet was also very much aware of himself as a person with "a Soviet mentality." He spoke of it as the prism through which he observed America and Americans.

His readiness to give up his pride and his status was not

shared by many émigrés who had not been successful in their professions. Emigrés who had been unable to do the work for which they had trained or who had had years of joblessness while waiting for emigration were less willing to work at anything. They expected in America to find the opportunity that had been denied to them and had also often lost their tolerance for accommodation. They could not focus on freedom, beyond the particular freedom they had been denied.

The narrow vision of the youngest of the émigrés showed how limited in understanding even the rebels could be. Lev S., a twenty-two-year-old student from Leningrad, could not understand the value of freedom of speech. "So we didn't have freedom of speech," he said. "So what? It didn't bother me. I had a few friends I could talk honestly to. What more did I need? I'd never make a loud speech on a streetcar or a bus. But why should I? What would be the sense of it? The people I spent my free time with were the ones who mattered to me. I had no interest in the others."

Mark D., the twenty-four-year-old researcher in Russian literature, described himself as "a Moscow hippie," one of "the hairy ones" who had dreamed of being a flower child in America. He was one of the young searchers who knew about the hashish culture of the Moslems in the Soviet Union, of the drug use by convicts and the alcoholism of most of the hippies. He remembered the celebration of International Children's Day in 1971 when he was sixteen and one of the thousands of Russian hippies. He was among the hundreds who were arrested and sent to a mental hospital. Later he looked for spiritual nourishment among Hasidic Jews, but was put off by all their rules. "Their religion is dead," he said. "It's nothing but following a book of rules."

America was a terrible disappointment to Mark. "There is no freedom in America," he said bitterly. "I was sure I could be totally free in America, but nobody is. There's freedom to buy and sell, but everybody has to work his skin off to live." He gave up his dream of freedom the very first day that he came and went to work just like everyone else.

The first struggles over issues of freedom were likely to be within émigré families. Soviet émigrés who had raised their children in the close quarters of a communal apartment were accustomed to holding a tight rein. Parents in the Soviet Union chose their children's friends and schools and decided what they would study and what work they would do.

Rita S. thought that childhood should be a time of intellectual nourishment, not freedom. She worried about her children being led astray by eleven-year-olds who sat around eating popcorn and watching television, by twelve-year-old girls who dreamed of boyfriends and by children and adults of all ages who talked only about the things they wanted to buy, where to find them and how much they cost.

Konstantin S. wanted his fifteen-year-old son to become Americanized as quickly as possible, but feared that he had acquired American concepts of freedom too soon. "We make him study hard," he said, "and he thinks that should be his business. He thinks it's his life and that it is up to him to decide to get good grades or bad grades. I think he has grown used to democracy faster than his parents. He knows more about his rights than about his duties."

Lawyers among the émigrés spoke of criminals they had defended. Teachers told of assaults by Russian students. A museum architect described an official museum of crime in Moscow in which the implements of thieves and murderers are displayed. Many Soviet émigrés were convinced, however, that criminal behavior was the consequence of an excess of freedom. Robbery, rape and murder were not reported in Soviet newspapers, and the pictures and stories found in American newspapers terrified émigrés who were already anxious and fearful of being among the victims. Though they had been fearful of the police in the Soviet Union, they wished for more police protection in America.

Soviet equation of freedom with disorder and violence was not easily shed. There was also confusion among Soviet women about "women's liberation" in America. Zina K., the design engineer from "the generation without fathers," grew up among women working beyond the limits of their strength. She had yearned all her life for less pressure and for the opportunity to be emotionally dependent upon a man who was stronger and more capable than she was. She was one of many successful professional women who envisaged liberation as a chance to wear beautiful clothes, look feminine and be less responsible than a Soviet engineer could dare to be.

Women who considered themselves members of the intelligentsia were not expected to show any interest in clothes. Something of their feelings about the meaning of dress was expressed by the émigré who couldn't understand why Americans said "Thank you" if an article of clothing they wore was admired. "I puzzled over that for a long time," she said. "In the Soviet Union it was not to your merit to have a beautiful thing to wear. Either you came upon it accidentally by luck or you got it through connections. Either way, it was not a sign of good taste, so you would not say 'Thank you' if you were praised for your clothes."

Many émigrés spoke of their confusion about what they called "the everyday etiquette" or "the conversational style of Americans." Some were suspicious of what they saw as "meaningless politeness" and friendliness that was no promise of friendship. Most, however, were grateful for the respite from rudeness and for the casual generosity of strangers. "I could not believe all those friendly smiles," said Itskov R., the Orientalist from Leningrad. "I was so accustomed to the tired, angry Soviet faces. We have lived in Boston and Amherst. We have gone all the way to Monterey, California, and not once in five years have I heard an insult. Nobody offended us. I never heard the word 'kike' or 'nigger.' In Leningrad I was often told, 'Go to Israel!' On the walls I saw every derogatory word there was for 'Jew.' "

Inna F. could not understand why Americans were so nice to each other. "I can't believe the kindness I see here," she said. "People are like packs of wolves in the Soviet Union. I've seen relatives claw at each other like dogs. And here everyone tries to be helpful. I've really come into my own. I've been helped so much by people who hardly know me that I want to help others." She admitted that she was depressed at first because of not knowing English, but added that it was getting easier every day. "I never forget even for a minute what I came for and why I'm here."

Rhya K. was grateful for American tolerance for foreign accents and said she liked being able to talk to a policeman without being frightened. "I can't get over the way people trust me. No one asks to see my documents. No one says You are a foreigner and cannot have a job. No one forbids me to take an apartment." It took her a long time to believe that Jews were Americans and not a separate nationality in America, and she was also surprised to find people of different nationalities and colors living and working side by side without doing one another harm. Like most of the émigrés, she had not expected to find a welfare system in America. "In the Soviet Union we knew only that it is the end of you if you lose your job. We never heard that there was Social Security in America."

The older émigrés were astonished to find social activities planned for senior citizens. Pensioners in the Soviet Union said that they were not welcome in the clubs that had been open to them while they were working and they felt cut off from life when they were retired. Family life and a few intense friendships were therefore of great importance to them. Having had no alternatives, they expected none in America. Maya G. was overwhelmed by the welcome she received in a Jewish community center. "It was from the goodness in their hearts," she said with emotion. "I had done nothing for them. I just walked in one Friday night without knowing where I was or what was going on. There were tables covered with white cloths. There were candles and flowers, and they welcomed me in as if I were an invited guest."

Emigrés were surprised by the openness of American hospitality, especially in the Jewish communities. Many explained that invitations from strangers had not been part of their experience. "In Leningrad I would never invite people I didn't

know into my home," said Eleanora S. "After a year or two
of meeting them outside or among mutual friends I might
consider it. I would first have to be sure that they are my kind
of people and that I could share my feelings with them."

Among the émigrés who admitted that they had known
nothing about American life were many who were surprised
by the roles played by black Americans. The images they
came with were from novels and old films, and they had not
expected to find black children attending school, black neighbors driving cars, working in shops and banks, running for
political office. Some expressed their fear of blacks in the inner
cities, and others were confused by the discovery that "a black
person on welfare in the United States was better fed and
housed than many Russian workers."

Gradually émigrés learned that the vocabulary they had
learned in the Soviet Union had a different meaning in the
United States. For example, they were accustomed to hear the
word "business" as a synonym for "corruption." They heard
the word "private" as a synonym for "illegal." When they
spoke of themselves as "humanitarians," they meant people
who were interested in art and literature and had no talent for
science or mathematics. If they described someone as an "internationalist" they might mean that he was not an anti-Semite
and believed in equal opportunity for all nationalities in the
Soviet Union.

The most unexpected and far-reaching discovery, however,
was that Soviet émigrés could accelerate their Americanization
by rediscovering their Jewish heritage and finding a place for
themselves in the Jewish communities that welcomed and supported them. This was not possible for people like Esther S.
who saw a religious service as something "artificial and un-
necessary, an insincere game that people played." It would
change the lives, however, of those who shared the experience
of Galina K.

"We were never dedicated Jews, and I never thought I was
emigrating to become Jewish," said Galina K. "I made the
discovery only after I came. The only thing I could think of

in Leningrad was to save my son, to give him some hope for a future. Here I want to give him a good Jewish education. I want him to have a Bar Mitzvah. I want him to be a Jewish American." She said her parents had tried to pass on some Jewish traditions, but she had resisted all their efforts. "I was so stupid," she said. "I thought, Why do I need that? I have American literature and English literature. I have music and art. I had this and that. And I had no idea of who I was."

The Judaization of Galina K. began when her son was given a scholarship to a Jewish camp and she witnessed enthusiasm for Jewish observance that she had never seen. Then she began going to services on Friday nights. A Jewish music festival in New York made her weep. "This huge hall," she said, "was filled with Jewish people enjoying themselves. There was wonderful dancing, and I thought I'd never seen such proud, beautiful people. I began crying and couldn't stop, and I knew this was why I had emigrated, for this feeling that I didn't know I could have."

Another woman spoke of herself as "good earth in which to plant Jewishness." She went to synagogue for the first time in Rome in 1978. "It was so exciting to see how interesting it was. It just seemed incredible to me to find something that I had been told was long over and dead alive and thriving." When she came to New York, she began going to synagogue every Saturday morning "to see real Jews, to meet people and listen to a rabbi." She said that she had never spoken seriously about being Jewish in Russia. In America it had become an important part of her life.

Rhya K. said that she had tried to be Jewish in Moscow but had not really felt "completely Jewish" until she came to America. Ilya K., a forty-year-old Moscow engineer, admitted that he had become a religious man in America. He said, "I don't think it started from zero, but I was not educated in Jewishness and still don't know very much, but I'm a religious person all the same." He didn't pretend to love all the rules, didn't observe the dietary laws and worked on the Sabbath. "I don't go to synagogue every week to show everybody that I'm a good Jew. I keep most of it inside myself. It may be that in my heart I was always secretly religious. I go to synagogue a few times a year when I need to. I'm very thankful to be in Cincinnati with thirty thousand Jews and at least thirty synagogues. In all of Moscow there was only one."

The identity struggles that had not been resolved in the Soviet Union were faced in America. Reveka K., however, the seventy-two-year-old Yiddish actress, saw no possible choice and said, "I am first of all Jewish. I am a Russian Jew. It is there that I was born and became what I am. It would be ridiculous to say that I'm an American." Irene A. did not agree. She had been "a proud Jew in Irkutsk" and had fought the anti-Semites in a Moscow bakery, but once in America she swore that she did not feel Jewish. "Nobody tells me I'm Jewish," she said. "I have no one to fight with. I was frightened there all the time because of my Jewishness. Here I live calmly. Nobody bothers me. I am a Russian woman."

Without fear and pressure, Jewish identity diminished for some and took root for others. There was no way of predicting how men and women would behave. Many remained atheists and nonbelievers but, like Maya G., "came to love the Jewish people and have strong national pride."

There were also émigrés who felt no special bond to Jews in the Soviet Union and claimed no attachment to them in America. "Why do people ask, 'What are you?' and 'Who are you?'" said a forty-year-old English translator. "Why must you put me in a category? Jew? Christian? I am a human being. Why can't I be accepted as a human being?" She was a convert to Russian Orthodoxy in spite of the "J" on the fifth line of her passport. She could not understand why her father, a writer and teacher still in the Soviet Union, was so outraged by her conversion to Christianity and why American Jews were so intolerant of her search for a spiritual life.

A forty-two-year-old physicist from Odessa defended his decision to take no part in American Jewish life by declaring his disappointment in American Jews. He had expected them to be different from their Soviet counterparts, "more independent and courageous" but he found them "kind of strange and insecure," still having problems as a minority and having difficulties with their families. He decided therefore to keep his distance from what he considered to be "Jewish instability" and to remain a Russian, preserving Russian culture in America.

A less critical mother refused the offer of free Hebrew lessons for her son by saying, "Why would he need Hebrew lessons? He is already studying the violin and shows talent." She was sure that he would find his spiritual nourishment in music and that he had nothing to gain from Jewish instruction.

Yuli F., a fifty-two-year-old musicologist, the son of a Zionist and the grandson of a pious and learned Jew, tried to explain his reluctance to be Jewish in America. "I was an atheist and an internationalist. I grew up with the idea that all nations would melt together and that we'd see the end of nationalism and join in one big happy family under the red banner of socialism that would cover the world. I accepted this emotionally without understanding my feelings. I studied. I knew the theories. A catechism of phrases had been hammered into my soul. It was a religion rather than an intellectual perception of society. Socialism meant the brotherhood of all peoples, the giving up of privacy, of personal and family needs, for the good of society. I believed that we were chosen to build the perfect society. It was a messianic feeling." To choose to be Jewish in that climate was to repudiate the hopes and dreams for a better future for all. A kind of conversion would have to take place before a believer in socialism would be able to take Judaism seriously. Jewish messianism would have to displace socialism, just as socialism had replaced Judaism in another generation.

The idea of conversion was taken seriously and literally by young Soviet Jews who were caught up in the Jewish renaissance of the late sixties. They were young enough to be cynical about the perfect socialist society, and the searchers among them went looking for something to believe in. Efim S., son of two academic parents with strong attachments to Russian culture, was among them.

He was seventeen when he came to the United States. Without his parents' permission or advice, he found his way to a Hasidic center and arranged to be circumcised. He studied Hebrew, had a Bar Mitzvah and immersed himself in traditional Jewish life. He said that he was drawn to the Hasidic center because of his upbringing in an atheistic and antireligious environment. "I decided," he said, "that religion, which I had been taught was repulsive, must in fact be good. I also liked being among people who believed in what they were doing and who lived according to their beliefs. I liked the discipline. Maybe it was because of my totalitarian upbringing, but I liked living a totally spiritual life. It pleased me to embrace all the rules and not leave anything out. I liked the idea of the God who chose us, the God of the whole world."

Efim S. had left the Hasidic center by the time of his interview. He was a student in law school by then. He did not wish to speak of his reasons for leaving. The center seemed to have provided him with safe passage into both Jewish and American life. It had met his need for faith and structure at a crucial time of his development. Once he felt secure, he could live without the tight discipline it provided. Its lessons and models were his to keep for life. He came to pray on occasion, but no longer called himself a Hasid.

Five years after his arrival, Efim S. spent a lot of his time thinking about the misunderstandings and "different ways of thinking" that made American and Soviet Jews uncomfortable with each other. "American Jews don't understand what we are all about," he said sadly. "We don't want to accept what they are all about. They think we are the same people only speaking a different language. I see it as a tragedy." His sensitivity to the differences showed how much he had learned in a short time, but he could not know that he was responding to the first steps of a long process and that it was too soon to think of it as a "tragedy."

Igor G., another student, saw no point in agonizing over differences. He was distressed by Soviet émigrés who clung to each other. "It's stupid to live in Brighton Beach and speak

Russian as if you were still in Odessa. I won't do that. It's wrong to live here and not be part of American life. I read *The New York Times* and the *New York Post*. I came here to be American, not to think of Russia." Igor, who came from Tbilisi, was interviewed only a few months after his arrival in New York, before he had time to think about the adjustments he would have to make. He had learned English in Tbilisi and was eager to be free in New York.

Konstantin S., who had often thought he would be more at home in a European country, had only good things to say about America. "I like Americans tremendously," he said. "I like the stores, the streets, the whole nation and its people. From the Hasidim to the Anglo-Saxons, from the blacks to the Puerto Ricans." When he was interviewed in 1979, two years after his arrival in New York, he spoke no English. He had been spending his time writing a book about the Russian Jewish intelligentsia. He insisted, however, that he did not feel like a stranger in America. "I feel like a real American, more American than many people who have been here since their birth."

His enthusiasm seemed unrooted in reality. "I've stopped identifying myself as a Jew since I came to the United States," he said, untroubled by the fact that his mother spoke Yiddish and spent her time at a Jewish religious center. None of his contacts with Orthodox Jews disturbed his conviction that "feeling Jewish is only due to anti-Semitism." Without the pressure of official anti-Semites, he felt free "to be an individual, the individual I was born on God's earth."

Konstantin S. in 1979 was convinced that the Jewish problem in the Soviet Union would be resolved by emigration. "The number of Jews allowed to leave is getting bigger and bigger," he said. But the next year saw the beginning of the end of the exodus. In 1984 the doors were virtually closed. Soviet citizens asking for exit visas had no more hope of getting them than they had had in the fifties.

Americans visiting *refusniks* in Soviet cities bring back reports of continued persecution and intimidation of Soviet Jews. They tell of arrests and jail sentences for the crime of teaching Hebrew, and of the difficulties of young Jews who want to attend institutions of higher education. They also tell of meeting Jews who are observing Jewish traditions, studying Jewish history and Hebrew, circumcising their sons and arranging Jewish marriages. Children are still singing the Hebrew songs that were forbidden in the late sixties and seventies. They are not rebellious adolescents defying their parents and government, but seven- and eight-year-olds who learned the words from their parents, who are trying to keep the Jewish renaissance alive within their families.

In Boston, where I still listen for Russian voices and accents, the Soviet émigré population has grown from the forty families I knew of in 1973 to about thirty-five hundred people. One can hear Russian spoken in the street and the supermarket. Russian Jewish émigrés can be found working as hairdressers, dressmakers and shoemakers as well as scientists, musicians, teachers, doctors and computer scientists. Their children attend public, private and Jewish schools.

Though there are signs of what is thought to be a Russian Jewish community, it would be more accurate to speak of a Russian Jewish constituency. The community activities in which they participate are not of their own organizing. They are arranged by Jewish institutions which are trying to reach out to Soviet émigrés. The émigrés are not joiners. They remain cautious about choosing their friends and associates. Friendships begun in Moscow or Leningrad are maintained. Emigrés keep their distance from their compatriots who were not in their circle in the Soviet Union.

Special invitations to lectures, to films or to concerts of Jewish or Russian music, however, bring Soviet Jewish émigrés together. A handful of outgoing men and women have become intermediaries between the organized Jewish community and the émigrés. They are the translators and teachers who were quicker to find a foothold in the new environment than the majority. Though they lack experience in the ways of the organized Jewish community, they are able to offer help to individuals and small groups.

Americans who have direct contact with émigrés who are colleagues, neighbors or relatives see changes and adjustments, signs of assimilation. Emigrés, however, value their privacy and keep their thoughts to themselves. Invitations to participate in seminars or open discussions are usually turned down. Russian students in American classrooms may be outspoken, but their parents often claim to "need more time" before they will be ready to speak out.

A departure from the usual behavior took place in June 1983 when a television program called *Frontline:* "The Russians Are Here" brought forth a storm of protest from émigrés who saw the program as "a malicious caricature" and an insult. Their letters to newspapers carried more than a hundred and fifty signatures. Emigrés came in person to the television station to express their outrage about the "half-truths." They were outraged by the choice of only individuals who had had negative experiences and who lacked gratitude and the ability to cope with American life. They were most distressed about any suggestion that Soviet émigrés would wish to return to the Soviet Union. They were sure that the study of statistics compiled by Jewish organizations would tell of successes and adjustments, stories that were less sensational but closer to the truth.

The most dramatic example of the changes among Soviet émigrés was exhibited in a mass wedding ceremony held at Temple Mishkan Tefilah in May 1982. Sixty brides and grooms, ten rabbis and three cantors stood under a thousand square feet of flower-decked canopy built for the occasion. A thousand guests were witnesses. The food, wine, wedding rings and rented wedding clothes were the gifts of local merchants. The guests paid for the privilege of attending with contributions to the agencies that served Soviet émigrés.

Among the couples being married according to Jewish laws were grandparents who had had civil marriages in Kiev, Kharkov and Moscow in the 1930s, young couples who had had

civil marriages in Boston in 1980 and representatives of all the
generations between. The event was an extraordinary mixture
of *shtetl* sentimentality and suburban Jewish affluence. It had
elements of a protest meeting and a political rally, with senators,
congressmen and local politicians attending. All the Jewish
national organizations were represented, and even Menachem
Begin sent his good wishes.

It was a rare moment of Jewish solidarity, a celebration of
the meaning as well as the reality of freedom for Soviet Jews
who had yearned for freedom without knowing what it was
and for American Jews who had taken it for granted as their
birthright. Russians wept for the people they left behind,
Americans for their connections to the legacy shared that
night. What was a conventional wedding for American Jews
was a radical event in the lives of Soviet émigrés. "We are
making history," said an émigré I had not met before.

The sense of "making history" was not limited to that night.
The social workers and volunteers involved in resettling Soviet
Jewish émigrés also spoke of "participating in history." Their
Soviet clients have been replaced by Iranians, Rumanians and
Indo-Chinese immigrants, but they speak emotionally about
their "Russian education." Some see their own Jewish community with a new perspective because they have seen it
through Russian Jewish eyes as well as their own. Young social workers admit that working with Soviet émigrés changed
their lives. "Trying to help them forced me to think of myself
as a Jew," said one woman. "I took my job because I had majored in Russian. I had not expected to become so much involved with my Jewish history and background."

In 1985 emigration has stopped, but efforts to reach Soviet
Jews continue. Emigrés in Israel and the United States, and
refusniks in the Soviet Union, make it difficult to forget or
ignore their special legacy, the history they lived through and
made.

A Note to the Reader

The William E. Wiener Oral History Library of the American Jewish Committee was established in 1969 to record significant aspects of the American Jewish experience in the 20th century. Its collection of 1,700 taped interviews is a unique memory bank and a storehouse of history and data that are available to scholars and researchers. The 176 oral memoirs of Soviet Jewish émigrés were taped between 1978 and 1980. These memoirs take their place alongside the collection of two hundred and fifty oral memoirs of Holocaust survivors. Both of these projects were made possible by major grants from the National Endowment for the Humanities and constitute a significant record of the two mass migrations of Jews to America since the end of World War II.

MILTON E. KRENTS
Director

Index

NOTE: *Pseudonyms are indexed alphabetically by* first *name.*

abortion, 188, 227
Abram A. (professor), 65–71,
    147–48, 164; imprisonment of,
    50, 71, 80; rehabilitation, 111–
    112, 127–28
Academy of Arts, 119, 273
Academy of Science, 119, 145,
    174, 186, 222, 281; Institute
    of Law, 202
actors, 20, 175, 181–85, 240
Adams, John Quincy, 298
Afghanistan, 116
Agadyr Expedition, 196, 198
Akademgorodok, Siberia, 166–
    167
Akhandinsk, 152
Akhmatova, Anna, 160
Albert D. (engineer/journalist),
    44, 136, 144, 200, 253, 265, 269
alcoholism, 273, 312
Aleichem, Sholom, 107, 183
Alexander II, 29
Alexander III, 29
Alexander A. (student), 111–12,
    127–28, 164–66
Alexei G. (surgeon/poet), 125,
    216–22, 258–59, 295
Alla G. (teacher/stewardess),
    45, 133–34, 161–64, 231
All-Union Institute of Geology,
    196
Alma-Ata, 97

America, *see* United States
American Council for Emigrés
    in the Professions, 304
American Exhibition, Moscow
    (1958), 245
Americanization, 297–98, 300ff.
American Jewish Committee, 22
Anastasia N., 47, 72–73, 97, 159,
    246, 259–60, 265–66, 289
Andrei P., 107
Anna D. (psychiatrist), 13, 47,
    138, 139, 160–61, 211–15
anti-Semitism, official, 20–21,
    33ff.; postwar campaigns, 93–
    98, 165, *and see* Zionism,
    campaign against
Architecture Institute, Lenin-
    grad, 123
Architecture Institute, Odessa,
    188
Arkady Z., 99
Arkhipova Street synagogue,
    19–20, 53–54, 112, 254, 272
Armenia and Armenians, 51,
    190
art institutes, 230
Artistic Fund, 190–91
artists, 173, 174, 175, 188–95,
    273–74, 304
Artists' Union, 155, 189, 190,
    191, 195, 277
art museums, 237

Ashkenazy, Vladimir, 180
Auschwitz, 40

Babi Yar, 24, 45, 251
Babi Yar (Kuznetsov), 251
Baby and Child Care (Spock), 109
Balfour Declaration, 30
ballet dancers, 14, 240
Baptists, 269
BBC, 114, 220, 274, 281
Beatles, 257
Begin, Menachem, 324
Beiliss, Mendel, 59–60
Berezhkov (KGB officer), 197
Bergelson, David, 182
Beria, Lavrenty, 80, 92
Berta R., 79
Beyond the Ocean (Gordin), 183
Bible, reading of, 19, 159, 160
Birobidzhan, 80, 97, 179
birth control, 188, 227
black market, 67, 69, 236
Bogoraz, Larissa, 268
Bolsheviks, 31, 48, 61, 65, 94, 202
Bolshoi Theater, 98, 176, 266–67
Bonner, Elena, 259
Boris F. (engineer/computer analyst), 143, 170, 234, 308
Boston, Mass., 17, 290ff.; émigré community in, 322–24
Boston College Law School, 114
Botkin Clinic, Moscow, 126
Brandeis University, 309
Brezhnev, Leonid, 117, 141
Brodsky, Joseph, 192
Brünn (Brno), 60
Bryansk, 75, 82
Budapest, Communist International Meeting in, 270
Bukharin, Nikolai, 94, 106, 228
Bukovsky (poet), 205
Bulldozer Exhibition, 193
Bund, 30, 31, 62, 71
Butyrka Prison, 64, 74, 76
Byelorussia (White Russia), 30, 48, 84, 190; nationalists in, 82

Cadets, 64
camps, 259, 261, 268, 269
Caravella Club, 192
Carpathian Mountains, 41, 146
Catherine II, 27
Catholics, 269
Catholic University (U.S.), 289
Caucasus, 150, 186
censorship, 17, 21, 28, 185, 187–188, 253–54, 258
Cheka, 31, 69, 70, 79
Chelyabinsk, 169, 170, 279
Chelyabinsk, University of, 40
Chelyabinsk Polytechnical Institute, 278
Chernigov, 65, 67
childbirth, 226–27
Children's Theater, Moscow, 43, 251–52
China, 117, 176
Chop, 15, 286
Chopin Express, 294
Cilo (village), 161–63
Cincinnati, Ohio, 318
circumcision, 18, 109
Civil Engineering Institute, 208
civil rights, *see* dissidents; human-rights movement
Civil War, Russian, 61, 62, 65–67, 68
Cliburn, Van, 180
collective farms, see *kolkhoz*
common-law marriage, 146–47
communal apartments, 121, 126–131 *passim*, 272, 273
Communist Party, 33; Central Committee, 102, 105, 159, 188, 270; Jewish department, 182; membership in, 163, 199–201; Regional, Leningrad, 255; 20th Congress, 199, 267
composers, 174, 176
conductors, 14, 177
conscription, 28–29, 31, 62, 155, 280
conservatories, 93, 155, 176–77, 178
Constitution of 1936, 82

Consultation Center of Lawyers, 208
cooperative apartments, 128, 131, 185
Cossacks, 88
Crimea, 150, 151, 186, 269, 270
cultural-exchange programs, 252, 255
Culture, Ministry of, 177, 180, 181, 183, 185, 188, 189, 266–67
Czechoslovakia: invasion of, 105–6, 117, 192, 250, 254, 263, 271–72; travel to, 186

Daniel, Yuri, 200, 205, 267–68, 270
Danielle I., 142, 145–46
Denikinites, 65, 88
Deremus publishing house, 107
De-Stalinization Congress, 100
détente, 303
Detroit, Mich., 310
Dickens, Charles, 157
directors, theater, 181–85
dissidents, 15, 17, 54, 197, 203, 230, 249, 267–71; in camps, 259, 268–69; denial of exit visas to, 106fn., 271, 280; and mental hospitals, 15, 274; and Soviet law, 201; trials of, 205, 207, 208, 268, 269. See also human-rights movement
divorce, 146
Dmitri T., 159, 174
Dobrushin, 182
doctors, 15, 33, 175, 209–27. See also Doctors' Plot
Doctors' Plot arrests and trials, 21, 47, 96–97, 99, 106, 130, 145, 171, 211; effect on Jewish doctors, 214–15, 219; and Israel, 284
Dombas, 212
Dora M. (teacher), 85, 97–98, 99–100, 141–42, 148, 149; in U.S., 296–97, 304, 310
Doroganova, 83
Dreiser, Theodore, 157, 302
drug use, 23, 273, 312

Dubnow, Simon, 247
Dubossary, Moldavia, 88, 155
Dylan, Bob, 257

education, 21, 58, 118–20, 121, 155–72, 173, 233, 234–35; under Bolsheviks, 70–71; ideological aspect, 227–29; in music, 174, 175–77, 180; physical, 229; restrictions against Jews in, 29, 37–38, 49, 59, 168–72
Education, Ministry of, 189
education tax, 16, 280
Edward K., 170
Efim S. (law student), 46, 114, 119–20, 130, 286, 303; in U.S., 319–20
Efros, Anatoly, 181, 184
Eleanora S. (critic/museum worker), 113–14, 138, 143, 230, 238, 241; in U.S., 310, 316
Elizavetgrad (Kirovograd), 58–60
Ella B., 180, 296
Emanuel D., 166–67, 175, 201
emigration, 13–24, 242–90; halting of, 242, 321, 325; red tape in, 16, 277–84. See also refusniks
Emil A., 233
Enchanted Tailor (Sholom Aleichem), 183
Engels, Friedrich, 176
engineers, 14, 170–72
Esther S., 316
Estonia, 190, 213
Eugenia S. (teacher), 38, 128–130, 158, 244

famine, 68, 156, 209
Faulkner, William, 302
Fefer, 182
Feldman, Professor, 219
Felix B. (conductor), 43, 140, 178–80, 251–52
Feuchtwanger, Lion, 94
films, 181, 185, 303
First Guild Merchants, 27

First Moscow Medical School, 223

Florina R. (lawyer), 175, 206–8

Fonda, Jane, 255

Foreign Office, Soviet, 31

freedom, adjusting to, 307, 309–310, 312–14

Frieda K. (teacher), 31–33, 79, 93, 96, 124–25, 155–56; in wartime, 81, 86–92

Frontline: "The Russians Are Here" (TV program), 323

Gagarin, Prince, 69

Galina K. (teacher), 49, 126, 167–68, 276, 288, 316–17

Galinskov, Yuri, 205

Galkin, 182

Galsworthy, John, 157

Gaza Palace of Culture, 192

Gennady P. (journalist/dissident), 131, 245, 253–54

geologists, 195–98, 229–30

Georgia, 33, 110, 190, 235

Georgi S. (philosopher/art critic/dissident), 157–58, 199–200, 267–72, 289, 294, 306–7

German occupation, 20–21, 81–84, 86, 88–90

ghettos, 27, 84–85, 247

Gilels, Emil, 93

Ginzburg, Aleksander, 205, 270

Gnesen Music School, 176

Gogol, Nikolai, 125, 156, 157

Gomel, 65, 66–67, 279

Gordin, Jacob, 183

Gorki, 125

grandmothers, 34, 136–38, 139

Greens, 66

Gulag Archipelago, The (Solzhenitsyn), 259

Harvard University, 302

Hasidic Jews, 312, 320, 321; "secret," 109

Health Ministry, 217, 223, 224

Hebrew College, Boston, 17, 290ff.

Hemingway, Ernest, 302

Hermitage, 237

HIAS (Hebrew Immigrant Aid Society), 288, 294, 295

hijackers case, 106, 196

hippies, Russian Jewish, 312

Hitler, Adolf, annihilation of Jews by, 250–51

hockey players, 255

hospitals, 186, 217, 220, 221–22, 223, 226–27

House of Journalists, 186

housing, 72, 120–34, 135, 148, 174, 185, 204

human-rights movement, 19, 192, 200, 269, 270–71. *See also* dissidents

Hungarian revolt, 105, 198, 261

identity cards, *see* passports, internal

"ideological workers," 175ff.

Igor G. (student), 78, 100–101, 109–11, 137, 235, 320–21

Ilya K. (engineer), 38, 170–71, 201, 317–18

Impressionists, 159, 189, 191, 237

Industrial Arts Institute, 199

Inna F. (artist/dissident), 272–275, 314–15

Institute for Advanced Training of Physicians, 218

Institute of Art History, 199, 267, 269, 270

Institute of Automobile Engineering, Kiev, 251

Institute of Chemical Technology, Moscow, 71, 80

Institute of Cinematography, 231

Institute of Higher Molecular Structure, 191

Institute of International Relations, Moscow, 111, 164, 165, 202, 208

Institute of Legality, 203

Institute of Optics, Leningrad, 169–70

Institute of Oriental Studies, 119, 236

Institute of World History, 278
institutes (technical schools),
    118, 119, 166, 168, 169–70, 174,
    228. *See also specific institutes
    by name*
intermarriage, 56, 144–47, 238
International Children's Day,
    281, 312
Irene A. (actress), 127–28, 147–
    148, 264, 310, 318
Irina G. (teacher), 140, 160, 295,
    300
Irkutsk, 127, 166
Irma Z. (chemist), 45, 228
Isaac V. (geologist/poet), 191–
    194, 195–99, 269
Israel, 93; emigration to, 13, 40,
    48, 167, 242–43, 284–88 *passim;*
    1973 war, 249–50, 259; 1967
    war, *see* Six-Day War;
    U.S.S.R. and, 19, 248, 252,
    262, 264, 272, 284. *See also*
    Israelis, contacts with
Israel, Chief Rabbi of, 242
Israelis, contacts with, 252–53,
    254, 263
Istkov R. (Orientalist), 116, 135,
    144, 246, 277, 314
Izabella K. (doctor), 280, 281,
    283–84
Izrael K., 58–61, 75–77, 103–4
Izvestia, 186

Jabotinsky, Vladimir, 247
Javits, Jacob, 281
Jewish Agency, 13–14, 287, 289,
    295
Jewish culture, suppression of,
    28, 31–34, 37–45, 51–55, 108–9,
    156, 243, 322
Jewish Encyclopedia, 53
Jewish identity, 34–57, 145, 262–
    263, 308–9, 316–24
Jews in the Soviet Union
    (magazine), 284
Joint Distribution Committee,
    13, 288
Jordanville monastery, 238

Joseph O. (music critic), 248,
    305
journalists, 21, 185–88, 253–54
"Judaism Without Embellish-
    ment" (pamphlet), 264
Julia V. (physicist), 126, 278,
    289–90
Juridical Institute, Moscow, 78
Juridical Institute, Ukraine,
    203–4

Kalinin, Mikhail, 70
Kalkas, 85–86
Kamchatka, 219
Kamenev, Lev, 31
Katya Z. (editor/translator), 54,
    114–15, 131–32, 139, 149, 240
Kavgary, 82
Kazakhstan, 95, 195–96, 251
KGB, 31, 62, 76, 92, 196–98, 259,
    260; and artists, 192–93; and
    Chief Rabbi, 239, 242, 254;
    and dissidents, 197, 274, 267–
    68; and Doctors' Plot, 219;
    and education, 165; in Estonia,
    213; and *refusniks,* 281–84;
    and synagogues, 38, 41; and
    travel, 151
Kharkov, 43, 61, 81
Kharkov, University of, 203
Khmelnik, 78
Khrushchev, Nikita, 40, 48, 117,
    167; speech against Stalin,
    100–101, 142
Khust, 40–41
Kiev, 27; anti-Semitism in, 32,
    49, 96, 258, 262; art shows in,
    189; bombing of, 81, 87;
    housing in, 127
Kiev, University of, 44, 146
kindergartens, 18, 137, 138–39
Kira G., 46–47, 151
Kirghiz, 86, 97
Kishinev, 87, 183
Kogan, Leonid, 176, 178
kolkhoz (collective farm), 90,
    152, 158fn., 162, 253, 299
Kolyma, 260–62, 276
Komsomol, 18, 70, 71, 165, 185,

Komsomol, *continued*
    241, 261; expulsions from, 80,
    97, 105; and "ideological
    workers," 190, 192, 199
Komsomolskaya, 253
Konstantin S. (journalist), 47,
    97, 117, 131, 150, 185–88, 248;
    identity problem, 106–7, 321;
    in U.S., 304, 313, 321
Kosygin, Alexei, 14
Krokodil, 253
Kultur, 120
Kuznetsov, 251
Kvitko, Lev, 107

Labor Zionists, 65
Larisa P. (engineer), 79, 98, 100,
    155, 233, 260–63, 265
Lasar R. (economist/dissident),
    74, 247, 249, 302–3, 311
Latvia, 70, 190, 269
lawyers, 175, 201–9, 313
Lazer A. (engineer), 260, 264,
    278, 286
Learned Council, 218
Lena B., 32, 61–62, 136
Lenin, Vladimir, 30, 31, 60–61,
    70, 176
Leningrad, 35, 235–36; arts in,
    183, 191–92; housing, 106, 130,
    132–33; schools, 167–70; siege
    of, 81–82, 85, 86. *See also*
    Petersburg; St. Petersburg
Leningrad, University of, 116,
    168, 195
Leningrad Mining Institute, 195,
    198
Leningradskaya Pravda, 257
Leningrad Union of Writers,
    198
Leningrad Worker, The, 255
Leonid K. (mathematician/dis-
    sident), 55, 105–6, 228, 234,
    241; emigration problems of,
    278, 280, 295; in U.S., 293, 297,
    302, 306, 307
Leo S. (engineer), 127, 144, 251
Lermontov, Mikhail, 156, 183
Lev S. (student), 312

Leya Y. (engineer), 85–86, 99,
    132–33, 151, 277–78
Leyb L. (student), 41–42
Lia K. (lawyer), 39, 73, 78–79,
    203–9, 271–72, 311
Literary Institute, 299
Literaturnaya Gazeta, 187, 253
Lithuania, 30, 241, 272
Litvinov, Maxim, 31
London, Jack, 157
Lubyanka Prison, 76, 157, 299
Luga, 92
Lumber Trade Management
    Company, 75
Lyosha D. (engineer/dissident),
    54, 240, 245
Lysenko, Trofim, 210
Lyubimov, Yuri, 184

Magnitogorsk, 45, 133, 159, 161,
    163, 183
Magnitogorsk, University of,
    161, 166
Maksimov, 303
Mandelstam, Osip, 160
Marc T. (student), 109, 272
Maria P. (translator), 139,
    232–33
Mark D. (researcher), 287, 312
Markish, Peretz, 182
marriage, 144–49, 323–24
Marsha L. (teacher/musician),
    98, 144–45, 160, 180, 227–28,
    308
Marton T. (student), 233, 234,
    280, 284
Marx, Karl, 176
Masha B. (art historian), 131
Massachusetts Institute of Tech-
    nology (M.I.T.), 281
Maxim K., 223–26, 245, 275
Maya G. (singer/actress), 62–
    63, 184, 305, 315, 318
Mayakovsky, Vladimir, 160
Mazerov (partisan), 48
Mendel, Gregor, 220
Mendeleev Institute, 166
Mensheviks, 64

mental hospitals, *see* psychiatric hospitals

Meshkovskiy, 88–91

Michael F. (film director), 101, 231, 275, 303

Mikhael M. (engineer), 42–43, 51, 142, 171–72, 243

Mikhoels, Solomon, 181–82, 184

Millerovo, 88

Minna M. (music teacher), 33, 114, 141

Minsk ghetto massacre, 84–85

Misha H. (musician/conductor), 49–50, 98, 119, 176, 266–67

Mogilev, 32, 62–63

Moishe S. (painter), 48, 71–72, 96–97, 101, 188–91, 236–37; emigration problems of, 277, 286–87; in U.S., 293, 302

Molecule Club, 191

Molotov, Vyacheslav, 87

Mordovia, 268, 269

Morozov, Pavel, 140, 158

Moscow, 27, 235–36; art shows, 189, 193–94; bombing of, 80, 81, 85; housing, 123–30, 148, 185; schools, 159, 164–65; synagogue, 19–20, 53–54, 112, 254, 272; theaters, 181–84, 251–52

Moscow, Chief Rabbi of, 239, 242, 254

Moscow, University of, 71, 105, 106, 159, 211; Juridical Faculty purge, 202; Mathematics Department, 228, 234; restrictions against Jews, 116, 165, 169, 206, 258

Moscow Art Theater, 184

Moscow Collegium of Lawyers, 205, 206, 209, 271

Moscow Conservatory, 176, 177

Moscow in 1937 (Feuchtwanger), 94

Moscow Philharmonic, 121, 127, 177

Moscow Special School Number Two, 164–65

Moscow Symphony, 174, 298

Moysei F., 40–41

Mukachevo, 41

Munich terrorist attack, 248

museum workers, 191, 230

musicians, 15, 173, 174–81, 240, 304

Music Institute, Lvov, 296

Music School for Gifted Children, 178

Nadya K. (science editor), 113, 115–16, 119, 133, 139

Nasha Strand, 288

Natasha U. (translator), 50

nationalities, 18, 33, 119

Naum L., 146

Nelly B. (engineer), 118

New Economic Policy, 69, 72

New York, 304

New York Association for New Americans (NYANA), 288, 296

New York University, 309

Nicholas I, 28

Nicholas II, 62

Nikolay S. (teacher), 202–3, 204, 208

Nina S. (Orientalist/dissident), 119, 142, 173–74, 236, 244–45, 247–48, 249, 305–6

Nineteen Eighty-four (Orwell), 247

Nixon, Richard M., 141, 184

NKVD, 107, 125, 157

Novosibirsk, 127, 166, 167

Nudel, Ida, 283–84

nursery schools, 138–39, 160

Obshehestvo Rasiya, 185

Odessa, 124–25; art in, 188, 190; and Jews, 39, 42, 46, 49, 51, 72, 93, 96, 211; in Revolution, 64–65; in World War II, 81, 86–87, 91–92, 125, 209–10

Odessa, University of, 171

Oistrakh, David, 93, 100, 176

old-age homes, 179

Oleg S. (editor/journalist), 264

Olga D. (nurse), 108–9, 137, 239
Orlov, Yuri, 274, 284
Orwell, George, 247
Ovir, 274–75

Pale of Settlement, 27, 29, 30,
    31, 62
Palestine, 30. *See also* Israel
parents and children, 15, 135–44,
    313
partisans, 24, 39, 48, 84, 90, 91,
    106
passports, internal (identity
    cards), 14, 18, 33, 72–73, 123,
    184
Pasternak, Boris, 160, 247
Pedagogical Institute, Odessa,
    156
"Pedology," 159
People's Court, 201
Petersburg (Petrograd), 58–61,
    63, 64. *See also* Leningrad;
    St. Petersburg
Peter V. (actor/director), 181
Petrograd, *see* Petersburg
Petrograd University, 64
Petrozavodsk, 126, 220
"Pink Ghetto," 185
Playboy, 247
Plekhanov Institute, 282
Pochep, 83
poets, 185, 192, 250, 299–300
pogroms, 20
Poland, Jews of, 27, 28, 30, 83
Polina N. (physicist), 40, 169–
    170, 173, 174, 258, 278–79,
    295–96
Polytechnical University,
    Odessa, 171–72
Polytechnic Institute, Moscow,
    164
Potsmy, 276
Pravda, 176, 186, 253
professional life, 173–241
prostitutes, 273
psychiatric hospitals, 62, 139,
    160–61, 214–15; dissidents in,
    15, 274, 312

purges (1930s), 20, 33, 70–80, 83,
    92, 182
Pushkin, Alexander, 125, 156

Queens College, New York, 304
quotas, 38, 59, 168, 170

Radek, Karl, 31
Rashel C. (student), 52
Rashel M. (teacher), 98, 102–3,
    237
Raya B. (doctor), 64–65, 73–74,
    136, 209–11
Red Army, 43, 50–51, 65–66, 82,
    90
refusniks, 16, 17, 230, 242, 263,
    279–84, 321–22, 324; demon-
    strations by, 275, 281–84
rehabilitation, 101–4, 111–12, 147
religion, 18, 237–39; and émigrés
    in U.S., 300, 316–21, 323–24.
    See also Jewish culture,
    suppression of
Research Institute of Electrical
    Machinery, Leningrad, 192
Reveka K. (actress), 182–84,
    318
Rhinoceros (Maksimov), 303
Rhya K. (teacher), 53–54, 55,
    94–96, 152–54, 159–60, 232,
    248; emigration of, 259, 287–
    288, 292, 307, 315, 317
Ribicoff, Abraham, 281
Richter, Sviatoslav, 93, 177
Riga, 27, 39–40, 278–79
Rima M. (dentist), 175
Rita S. (artist), 98, 160, 194–95,
    245–46, 275, 285–86; in U.S.,
    292–93, 310, 313
"ritual murder" charge, 59–60fn.
Rome, 287, 288, 289, 294–95, 317
Rosa G., 49
Royal Polytechnic Institute,
    Brünn, 60
Russian army, tsarist, 28–29
Russian nationalists, 82
Russian Orthodox Church, 18,
    237–39, 300, 318

Russian Revolution, 20, 30–33, 60–65, 155, 258
Russo-Turkish War, 58, 221

St. Petersburg, 27. *See also* Leningrad; Petersburg
Sakhalin, 219
Sakharov, Andrei, 240, 259, 274
samizdat, 131, 142, 198, 246–47, 259, 270–71
Samuelson, Paul, 281
Sarra S. (violinist), 78, 93–94, 96
Sasha M., 99–100
"Save Soviet Jewry" campaign, 17, 19
Schonau, 13–16, 19, 294
schools, 157–65, 168; Jewish, 18, 28, 31–32, 40, 58, 59, 155–56: special, 158, 159–60, 161, 164–165, 167–68, 235, 272; technical, *see* institutes. *See also* kindergartens; nursery schools; universities
"scientific communism," 228–29
secret language, 117
Security Committee, 150
Semyon R., 37
Serbsky Psychiatric Institute, 214
serfs, liberation of, 29
Sergei S. (engineer), 115, 122–123, 151–52, 295
Shakespeare, William, 168
Shaw, Bernard, 168
Shcharansky, Anatoly, 205, 284
Shipbuilding Institute, Leningrad, 170
Shostakovich, Dmitri, 257, 267
Shtern Publishing House, 96
Simon and Garfunkel, 257
Sinclair, Upton, 302
Sinyavsky, Andrei, 200, 205, 267–68, 270
Six-Day War (1967), 21, 52, 55–56, 105, 110, 112, 117–18, 247
Slepak, Vladimir, 284
Smirsh, 165
socialist realism, 189

Socialist Revolutionaries, 64
Solzhenitsyn, Alexander, 303
Sophie M. (lawyer), 32, 63–64, 72, 74, 77–79, 123–24
Soviet Sport, 255
Soyez Lift, 171
Spaniards, The (Lermontov), 183
Spock, Benjamin, 109
Stalin, Joseph, 20, 62, 82, 106, 180; death of, 98–100, 172; and Doctors' Plot, 47; toast to "Russian people," 48, 94; worship of, 98, 99, 100–101, 117, 140
Stalingrad, 88, 89–90
Stalin Prizes, 182
State Security Department, 255
State University of New York at Albany, 252
status levels, 113–16, 118–22, 124, 174–75, 201, 239–40
Supreme Court, Soviet, 67, 70, 205, 270, 284
Supreme Military Consulate, 76
Supreme Soviet, 268
Surgery Institute, Moscow, 218
Sverdlovsk, 81

Tairov (director), 183
Tamara S. (geologist), 148, 150–51, 229–30
Tashkent, 42, 182
Tashkent Canal, 205
Tashkent Collegium of Lawyers, 204
Tatars, 45, 92, 116, 161–63, 269, 270
Tbilisi, 52, 54, 78, 109–11, 159, 174, 235
Tbilisi, University of, 110
television, 200, 254–58
Temple Mishkan Tefilah, Boston, 323–24
Tevye the Milkman (Sholom Aleichem), 183
thaw, 101–4, 117, 142, 254–55
theater, 117, 181–85, 251–52
Tolstoy, Alexis, 86

Tolstoy, Lev, 129, 157
Tomachova, 92
Torgoble Central, 167
Trade Union Office, 255–56
travel, 150, 151–54, 186, 218;
  musicians and, 174, 176, 178–
  179; restrictions, 177, 180
Tribuna, 288
Trotsky, Leon, 31, 60, 70, 94,
  228
Tsibulovo, 58

Uganda, hostages in, 248
Ukrainian nationalists, 82
United States: cultural-exchange
  program, 252, 255; Jewish
  emigration to, 13, 17–25, 29,
  242–43, 285ff.; Soviet attitude
  toward, 23, 117, 118, 176, 303
universities, 227, 228; anti-
  Jewish restrictions in, 38, 49,
  51, 165–66, 168–72, 234, 265–
  266, 322
Urals, University of the, 170,
  258
U.S.S.R. Correspondence Polytechnic Institute, 112

vacations, 150–54, 174, 186
Victor C. (hockey player),
  137–38, 229
Victoria L. (pianist), 98, 175–
  176, 177, 180
Vienna, 13, 287–89, 293–94, 295
Vietnam War, 255, 302
Vilna, 62–63, 66, 201, 278–79
Vinnitsa, 65
Vladimir B., 301–2
Vofsi, Professor, 219
Voice of America, 143, 220, 248,
  256
Vologda, 152
Vorkuta, 76, 103–4

War and Peace (Tolstoy), 129
Warsaw: ghetto uprising, 247;
  music competition, 180
White Guards, 61, 65, 67
White Russia, *see* Byelorussia

Wiener Oral History Library,
  22–25
Wiesel, Elie, 19
Wilde, Oscar, 168
women's liberation, 313–14
World War I, 29–30, 60, 82
World War II, 24, 39, 42, 46–47,
  50–51, 80–92, 209–10, 212–13;
  suppression of records of,
  250–51
World Youth Festival, 252–53
writers, 175; censorship of,
  187–88; privileges of, 131,
  150, 173, 174, 185–86
Writers' Union, 131, 155, 185–
  186, 192, 198, 218, 270

Yakutsk, 219
Yefremov, 184
Yelena K., 47
Yerevan, 51
Yezhov, Nikolai, 159
Young Guard, 185
Young Pioneers, 18, 70, 101
Yuli F. (musicologist), 75, 81,
  82–85, 140–41, 256–58, 319
Yunost, 185, 251
Yuri B. (economist), 44, 102
Yuriev University, 129
Yuri K. (doctor), 223

Zakary K. (actor/director),
  117, 181–82
Zakharov, 184
Zarisa Y., 74
Zhitomir, 183–84
Zinaida T. (art historian), 44,
  52, 53, 230, 248–49
Zina K. (textile engineer), 72,
  81, 92–93, 102, 104–5, 147–49;
  emigration of, 276, 285, 313–14
Zinoviev, Grigori, 31, 94, 157
Zionism, 243; campaign against
  (1970s), 167, 243, 248, 264,
  265; and purges (1930s), 33,
  78; and Revolution, 30, 31
Zurich, 62
Zuskin (director), 182